A JESUIT CHALLENGE

A Jesuit Challenge

EDMUND CAMPION'S DEBATES AT THE TOWER OF LONDON IN 1581

by

JAMES V. HOLLERAN

Fordham University Press
New York
1999

[redacted]

LC
ISBN 0-8232-1887-2

Library of Congress Cataloging-in-Publication Data

Campion, Edmund, Saint, 1540–1581.
A Jesuit challenge : Edmund Campion's debates at the Tower of London in 1581 / [edited] by James V. Holleran.
p. cm.
Includes bibliographical references and index.
ISBN 0-8232-1887-2
1. Catholic Church—Doctrines Early works to 1800. I. Holleran, James V. II. Title.
BX1750.C265 1999
272′.7—dc21 99-23671
CIP

Printed in the United States of America

To
M. M.

CONTENTS

PREFACE

In preparing this edition of Edmund Campion's four disputations at the Tower of London in 1581, I faced a number of difficult editorial choices. A few deserve brief comment. First, practical considerations about potential readers were among the most troublesome. For example, should an edition of these previously unpublished Catholic manuscripts of the debates be prepared and organized primarily to meet the expectations of academic specialists in the field? Or should they be designed somewhat differently to accommodate the practical needs and probable interests of a broader audience of readers? One's decision on this crucial matter radically alters the kind of text and the amount of information to be provided. The specialist, already familiar with the historical circumstances in England that led to the debates in 1581, needs little contextual information about the issues or the disputants. The non-specialist, however, may be unnecessarily confused by the debates if relevant historical background information is not provided.

Second, other considerations posed additional problems. What kind of text should be presented? And how much textual commentary is sufficient for readers to appreciate the significance of the debates? For example, the specialist expects to be provided with a critical text that remains as close as possible to the original manuscripts. Ideally, such a critical text would consist of photocopies of the manuscripts, together with detailed analytical commentary. However, if such a text and commentary were offered, the non-specialist, who is unfamiliar with Elizabethan handwriting, spelling, abbreviations, interpolations, and foreign languages, would be virtually denied access to the debates.

Third, the realities of publication costs also create problems and impose limitations. Obviously, an editor may not include everything that bears on the debates and that may satisfy fully the expectations and interests of either scholar or non-scholar. One is forced to be selective.

Confronted with such difficult editorial choices and such practical constraints, I have attempted to strike a proper balance. In the spirit of the debates themselves, which took place before a mixed Elizabethan audience that included theologians and non-theologians, dignitaries as well as "many common persons," I have prepared a text from the extant manuscripts and included relevant commentary that, I hope, will be acceptable both to the expert in the field and to the general reader. To that end, with the expert in mind, I have prepared appendices that include: (1) an additional, partial manuscript (Scudamore MS. Add. 11055), (2) Campion's "Challenge," (3) a report of his trial, (4) supplementary accounts of the debates by Continental historians, and (5) a detailed survey of the texts of the manuscripts. For the non-expert, I have provided: (1) a broad historical introduction, (2) a full set of notes that are intended to clarify significant events and notable personages, and, within the text itself, and (3) translations of foreign languages [in brackets]. I have also expanded abbreviations, modernized spelling, and regularized inconsistent scribal punctuation. In short, without distorting or misrepresenting the texts of the debates, I have attempted to include a sufficient amount of textual and historical information to satisfy the anticipated needs and interests of both specialist and non-specialist.

In addition to the many editorial problems that arose in preparing an easily readable text and a helpful commentary, the relevance of these debates for the modern reader also became an overriding concern. In addressing this matter, I considered certain basic and practical questions. Why should one invite others to read a Catholic version of four daylong debates about religious issues at the Tower of London in 1581? Are not the place and time too remote? Are not the issues dated? And, historically speaking, are not most of the participants non-celebrities? In short, what benefits justify a reader's time and attention?

A few good reasons came to mind. First, I would argue that the debates are of special interest because Edmund Campion was involved in them. Although they deal with only four days in his public life, these days were among the most crucial for him personally and for the eventual fate of the Catholic Counter Reformation in sixteenth-century England. The debates allow us to witness Campion defending his beliefs and arguing for his life. In such circumstances, we learn as much about his personality in these few days as we do from any others in his recorded life. As is well known, Campion did much good for many during his short lifetime, but at the debates we observe him at his best. Unfortunately for his Catholic cause, however, the debates marked the end of religious freedom for Catholics in England for centuries to come.

Second, by reading the debates we discover that many of the issues addressed are still with us. What books belong in the canon of the Bible? How should key passages in the Bible be understood? How valid and authorative are papal bulls, the opinions of Church Councils and the Fathers, the decrees of monarchs, and parliamentary laws? Should the exercise of an individual's reason and conscience be the ultimate judge about both religious and national issues? What are the legitimate provinces of Church and of State? Whose claims should prevail? When and under what circumstances? Is religious freedom possible and/or compatible with ecclesiastical regulations and with the laws of nations?

Third, as historical documents, these Catholic accounts of the debates allow us to revisit our past and to decide for ourselves whether or not official documents, endorsed and published by the government, are entirely trustworthy. These previously unpublished Catholic accounts, for example, supply us with information that was deliberately deleted from the government account of the same debates.[1] That is, for over four centuries the debates with Campion

---

[1] Although the official government account of the debates was bound in a single volume, it contains two title pages: one for the first day's debate, and a second inserted for the following three debates. The two parts were joined for publication by John Field, the editor. The lengthy title pages read as follows:

A true report of the Disputation or rather private Conference had in the Tower of London, with Ed. Campion Iesuite, the last of August, 1581. Set downe by the Reverend learned men them selves that dealt therein. Whereunto is ioyned also a true report of the other three dayes conferences had there with the same Iesuite. Which nowe are thought meete to be published in print by authoritie. 1583 [O.S.]. [STC 18744].

The three last dayes conferences had in the Tower with Edmund Campion Iesuite, the 18: 23: and 27. of September, 1581, collected and faithfully set downe by M. Iohn Feilde student in Divinitie. Nowe perused by the learned men themselves, and thought meete to be published. 1583 [O.S.]. [STC 18744].

Future references to this work will be cited as *A true report*. Also, for insightful commentary on *A true report*, see Peter Milward, *Religious Controversies of the Elizabethan Age: A Survey of Printed Sources* (Lincoln and London: University of Nebraska Press, 1977), p. 60. Future references to this valuable study will be cited as Milward, *Religious Controversies of the Elizabethan Age*.

were officially reported one way. Now, for the first time, we discover that there were reports by the other side which had been confiscated and suppressed by the government. How reliable are official reports and how reliable are private reports? How should we deal with the personal and historical biases of conflicting contemporaneous accounts?

Fourth, in a legal sense, the debates invite us to take a position on their basic fairness. Was Campion treated justly in accord with any reasonable code of acceptable procedures? Were the disputations conducted as formal academic debates? veiled depositions? religious conferences? quasi-criminal trials? political inquisitions? ad hoc interrogations? Was Campion permitted to defend his positions? Was he given time and means? How fair and effective are any official debates, public hearings, or state trials when the proceedings deal with highly controversial issues in a controlled setting, and when the vested interests of those in positions of authority are at stake? Has our system of legal justice improved over the centuries since the days of Edmund Campion?

Fifth, read as historical drama, the debates are fascinating theater. They remind us of similar highly dramatic encounters in which celebrated non-conformists, such as Socrates and Thomas More, defended themselves and their unpopular opinions against their self-assured interrogators, who had already decided upon the outcome before hearing the testimony and weighing the evidence. When we come upon an intellectually gifted person who hazards his life by defending a worthy cause and by challenging the power of the establishment, we find ourselves dealing with some of the most basic and noble elements of human conduct.

Finally, no matter which side one takes in the controversy, each page of the debates invites our intellectual engagement in the proceedings. We may decide for ourselves whether Campion's or his opponents' arguments are reasonable and persuasive. We may judge, too, whether Campion was a traitor to his country or a saint in the making. Once into the debates, we find many tense and exciting moments in all the sparkling exchanges.

According to the authorized published account by the English government, Campion lost the debates. Soon after the final one, he was tried as a traitor, summarily convicted, and brutally executed. According to these Catholic accounts, however, Campion won. The

Catholic accounts allow us to see why in his own day he was venerated as a courageous martyr, and why today he is formally recognized and honored as a saint.

I wish to express my appreciation to all those who offered help and encouragement. Among the most generous have been: David M. Rogers, M. Bonner Mitchell, Rev. Francis Edwards, S.J., Patrick Barry, Rev. Fred Tollini, S.J., Rev. B. Winterborn, S.J., Rev. J. Robert Barth, S.J., Ken Brasier, Jennifer Good, Haskell Hinnant, Robert Smarr, Win and Isabel Burggraaff, Jill Raitt, Nancy Pollard Brown, Jack Roberts, Tom Tentler, D. C. and Maren Coleman, Allen and Tamara Oestreich, T. Tarkow, L. D. Clark, M. M. Schouman, M. Camargo, and A. F. Yanders. My largest debt is to the members of my family, to Ann, Erin, Brigid, and Meghan.

I wish also to thank the administrative and staff members at the following libraries for their generous assistance: Bodleian, British, Jesuit Archives (London), Campion Hall and St. John's College (Oxford), Stonyhurst, Library of Congress, Folger, Notre Dame, Michigan, Illinois, Chicago, Boston College, Detroit-Mercy, St. Louis, and Missouri-Columbia.

Introduction

Foreign Problems and Domestic Achievements

When Edmund Campion landed at Dover in the early morning of June 25, 1580, to launch what soon after became known as the Jesuit Counter Reformation in England, Queen Elizabeth was in the twenty-second year of her forty-five–year reign (1558–1603).[1] By 1580 she had effectively demonstrated her mastery of the art of political survival and had already emerged as one of England's most effective rulers. By fair means and foul, she had managed to achieve her main political objectives: (1) ensure a balance of power on the Continent, (2) keep England out of a costly foreign war, (3) promote her nation's prosperity, and (4) preserve her own security. These objectives were not easily gained or maintained at a time when wars, riots, and poverty were commonplace throughout Europe. Elizabeth, however, by the exercise of tact and shrewdness, avoided most of the pitfalls that plagued her rival continental monarchs and won for herself the appreciation of most of her subjects.[2]

Although usually successful, her political strategies were rarely either consistent or swift. She had learned well the lesson that today's allies may be tomorrow's enemies, and she acted accordingly. Delays, negotiations, and compromises became the guiding principles of her foreign and domestic policy and left both friends and foes alike at a loss to predict how she might finally act on any issue.

Her dealings with the major foreign powers illustrate her wide-

---

[1] Still one of the best biographies of Elizabeth is that by J. E. Neale, *Queen Elizabeth* (London: Jonathan Cape, 1934). For a more recent biography, see Carolly Erickson, *The First Elizabeth* (New York: Summit, 1983).

[2] A few of the many historical surveys of sixteenth-century England are: Stanley T. Bindoff, *Tudor England* (1950; Baltimore: Penguin, 1964); John B. Black, *The Reign of Elizabeth, 1558–1603* (1936; Oxford: Oxford University Press, 1959); Geoffrey R. Elton, *England Under the Tudors* (1955; London: Cox & Wyman, 1974); and Albert F. Pollard, *The History of England from the Accession of Edward VI to the Death of Elizabeth, 1547–1603* (London: Longmans, 1910).

ranging political maneuvering. At the start of her reign in 1559, she reluctantly ceded Calais to France in order to withdraw from a war that England could ill afford. A year later, however, she employed English land and sea forces to drive French troops out of Scotland in order to ensure England's northern border and her own safety. Her timely support of the French Huguenots against the French Catholics prolonged a civil war that virtually neutralized France as a dangerous rival.[3] And when all else failed, she was not above dangling the prospect of marriage to gain her ends. In 1581, for example, while Catholic priests, including Edmund Campion, were being hunted down, imprisoned, tortured, and executed in England, Elizabeth herself was in the process of conducting lengthy marriage negotiations with Alençon, the fourth son of Henry II of France and a Catholic heir to the throne of France.

Her dealings with Spain, England's chief rival, were no less politically unpredictable. In 1558 Philip II proposed marriage to Elizabeth. Although she politely declined his offer, determined to avoid Mary Stuart's mistake, she willingly accepted his advice and protection in the uncertain early years of her reign. By 1588, however, relations between the two countries had so deteriorated that Philip attempted an invasion of England with his mighty Spanish Armada. In the thirty years intervening between a marriage proposal and a military invasion, Elizabeth's occasional financial and military support to the Low Countries forced Philip to maintain a large and costly army there while English sea captains, such as John Hawkins and Francis Drake, raided the Spanish Main and brought home fortunes in booty.[4]

Closer to home, in her dealings with Scotland, Elizabeth faced a series of political dilemmas that haunted her almost to the end of her reign. Most of these difficulties revolved around Mary Stuart, a queen who matched Elizabeth in ambitiousness and intrigue if not in tact.[5] Mary Stuart, the daughter of James V of Scotland and Mary

---

[3] For a brief account of the religious wars in France, see J. E. Neale, *The Age of Catherine de Medici* (1913; New York: Harper & Row, 1962).

[4] For an account of the attempted Spanish invasion, see Garrett Mattingly, *The Armada* (Boston: Houghton Mifflin, 1959); for the English raids on the Spanish Main, see James A. Williamson, *The Age of Drake* (Cleveland: World, 1965).

[5] A highly regarded biography of Mary is T. F. Henderson's *Mary Queen of Scots* (London: Scribner's, 1905). For a more recent study, see Antonia Fraser, *Mary Queen of Scots* (1969; New York: Dell, 1972).

of Lorraine, a member of the powerful French Guise family, became queen of Scotland soon after her birth in 1542. In 1558 she married the dauphin of France, who ascended the throne in 1559 but died the following year. After the death of her mother, who had been serving as regent in Scotland, Mary returned to Scotland in 1561 as queen. Religious conflicts and domestic affairs occupied Mary's attention for the next few years until her marriage to Henry Stewart, Lord Darnley, in 1565 aroused smouldering Protestant feelings against her in both Scotland and England.[6] Darnley's ambition led to a series of plots and scandals that resulted in the murder of Mary's secretary, David Rizzio, in 1566 and to the sensational murder of Darnley himself the following year. Mary's subsequent marriage to her husband's alleged murderer, the Earl of Bothwell, provoked a national uprising. On June 15, 1567, her forces were defeated at Carberry Hill, and she surrendered herself to the Scottish lords, who forced her abdication in favor of her infant son, James VI. In 1568 Mary raised another army, which was defeated by the Earl of Moray at Langside, near Glasgow. Seeking the protection of Elizabeth, Mary fled to England, where she was detained as a prisoner of state for the remaining nineteen years of her life.

Virtually all Mary's adventures and misadventures, her triumphs and her defeats, had a direct bearing on the national security of England as well as on the personal safety of Elizabeth. Through her father's mother, the eldest sister of Henry VIII, Mary had a legitimate claim to the English throne, which she expressed publicly on the death of Mary Tudor by quartering the English arms on her shield. Her claim was a continual source of unrest in England until her execution in 1587. In addition to her claim to the throne, Mary's ties with France allied her with a powerful enemy of England, and as queen of Scotland she threatened England's northern border. Finally, as a Catholic, Mary was associated with England's archenemy, the Church of Rome, and she was looked upon by many English Catholics as their potential liberator. The English Parliament trembled at the prospect that a successful assassination plot against Elizabeth might make Mary Stuart their queen and that she, like Mary Tudor before her, would restore the old religion and make England a papal pawn in European power struggles.

---

[6] See Jenny Wormald, *Court, Kirk, and Community: Scotland, 1470–1625* (London: Edward Arnold, 1981).

Happily for Parliament, Mary's indiscretions delivered her into Elizabeth's hands. But even as a prisoner in England, Mary remained troublesome, for Elizabeth could not decide how to deal with her. If Mary were returned to Scotland, she would undoubtedly have been put to death. To exile her elsewhere would be to lose control of a dangerous rival. To execute her for her witting or unwitting associations with assassination plots was an option that Elizabeth resisted for years because of the precedent it established for dealing with a rightful queen. Finally, however, it was the course that Elizabeth took after the Babington plot (1586).

Ireland completed the agenda of Elizabeth's most pressing foreign problems.[7] In spite of her determined efforts, Elizabeth never fully succeeded in bringing the rebellious Irish into submission to her rule. Both her major strategies, the use of military force and the establishment of English settlements, led initially to minor victories and success. Ultimately, however, her troops had to put down still another rebellion, and many of her English colonists were absorbed by the Irish culture that they had been sent to change. Early in her reign she had been forced to deal with a national rebellion led by Shane O'Neill (1559–66); later, two more led by Fitzmaurice and Desmond (1569–72 and 1579–83); and, finally, one led by Tyrone (1594–1603). In addition to national rebellions, she had also to be on guard against the possibility of foreign invasions through Ireland, such as the papal force that Lord Deputy Grey annihilated at Smerwick in 1580. Large-scale efforts by such worthies as Walter Devereux and Walter Raleigh to colonize the island with English plantations failed. Few English nobles, including the dashing Essex, escaped from Ireland with their reputations intact. Enlightened efforts by an occasional Englishman, such as Sir Henry Sidney, to educate the Irish rather than exterminate them, as Edmund Spenser had recommended, were too advanced for the time. Because Ireland was Catholic, the Irish were treated not as British subjects but as the enemy, the religious allies of Rome and Spain.

Elizabeth's domestic policies were more consistently successful than her political stalemates abroad. The conditions of the poor were

[7] For historical surveys of Ireland in the sixteenth century, see Richard Bagwell, *Ireland Under the Tudors*, 2 vols. (London, 1885–90); Cyril Falls, *Elizabeth's Irish Wars* (London: Methuen, 1950); and T. W. Moody, F. X. Martin, and F. J. Byrne, eds., *A New History of Ireland*. III. *Early Modern Ireland, 1534–1691* (Oxford: Clarendon Press, 1976).

gradually improved throughout her reign by laws directing that indigents be cared for at the local level. There were clear signs of growth in wealth and industry. Improvements in agricultural methods resulted in a higher rate of production. Woolen products continued as a source of wealth, and new markets were found before the decline of Antwerp. Mining and manufacturing, primarily in the South and West, produced tin, iron, and copper. Fishing fleets, supported by laws encouraging the sale of fish, roamed the seas as far as Newfoundland. Trade either flourished or developed with Ireland, Scandinavia, the Continent, Russia, Africa, Guinea, and the New World. London became an important European marketplace.[8]

Thanks in part to Sir Thomas Gresham, the national debt was reduced, and there was a gradual growth in prosperity, as evidenced by new homes, new clothes, and a new patronage of literature.[9] Prosperous commoners built brick and stone farmhouses in which were to be found chimneys, pewter, and carpets. The wealthy, much interested in refinement and elegance, designed their new residences for comfort and beauty rather than defense. Italian gardens, terraces, and fountains began to be regular features outside new manor houses. Inside, tapestries and art decorated walls. Beautifully carved furniture became more commonplace, and glass windows were both plentiful and artful. English dress became colorfully elaborate. A new interest in learning, inspired by classical and continental works, soon produced a new and exciting body of English literature in poetry, prose, and, especially, drama. The queen and her subjects were acquainted with William Shakespeare, Philip Sidney, and Edmund Spenser. In short, during Elizabeth's long reign England was active and prosperous in virtually every field of human endeavor. It is not without reason that her name has been stamped on the age.

Religious Problems in England

If the queen's foreign policies succeeded in keeping her enemies at bay, and if her domestic policies created a new prosperity in Eng-

[8] Two standard works on sixteenth-century English economy are John H. Clapham's *A Concise Economic History of Britain from the Earliest Times to 1750* (Cambridge: Cambridge University Press, 1949); and R. H. Tawney's *Religion and the Rise of Capitalism* (1926; New York: Harcourt, 1952).

[9] See M. St. Clare Byrne, *Elizabethan Life in Town and Country* (New York: Barnes & Noble, 1961).

land, Elizabeth was not without serious problems. The most enduring one she faced throughout her long reign was that of religion, a problem she shared with other rulers of the day and one that would also haunt her Stuart successors. In England, Scotland, France, Germany, and the Netherlands, national impulses, coupled with long-standing religious abuses, had led to the establishment of national churches that eventually came into direct conflict with Roman Catholicism.[10] The basic thrust of these new national churches aimed at the reformation of religious abuses which, many reformers charged, had been introduced by the popes. Reformers, like Luther, Calvin, and Knox, were bent on returning to what they saw as the simple purities of the early primitive church, the church that Christ founded, the apostles propagated, and the early Church Fathers defined. They viewed the popes after the sixth century as a series of Antichrists who, through such unauthorized practices as marketing indulgences, selling relics, and promoting pilgrimages, had enriched themselves personally while contaminating the pure streams of Christian dogma.[11] The power of corrupt Rome, the reformers insisted, must be broken. The primitive church must be refounded.

Although the new reformers were all loosely allied in their opposition to papal authority and in their intention to return to the practices of early Christianity, they were not in agreement on either the dogma or the ritual of the early church. Calvinists, for example, practiced one brand of Christianity; Lutherans, another. The political situation in a country also exercised a powerful influence on the shape that a new national church would take. In Geneva, for example, Calvin was a virtual king; in France a series of weak kings failed to prevent civil strife between Catholics and Huguenots; and in Spain the Church adopted severe measures to reform itself.

In England the religious problem that Elizabeth inherited had originated with her father's (that is, Henry VIII's) decision in 1534 to reject papal authority and assume the title of Supreme Head of the national church himself.[12] Although Henry initiated the Refor-

[10] A highly regarded general survey is A. G. Dickens's *The Counter Reformation* (Norwich: Jarrold and Sons, 1969).

[11] Peter Lake, "The Significance of the Elizabethan Identification of the Pope as Antichrist," *Journal of Ecclesiastical History* 31 (1980): 161–78.

[12] For a survey of the English Reformation leading to the Catholic Counter Reformation, see A. G. Dickens, *The English Reformation* (London: B. T. Batsford, 1965). For a fuller account of the English Reformation by a Catholic historian, see Philip

mation in England, he did so gradually and thus met with little resistance in his own country. Thomas More and John Fisher were notable exceptions. Henry's success was in large measure due to the fact that he rejected extreme forms of continental Protestantism and retained most of the theology and ceremonial practices of the Church of Rome. Even in his dissolution of the monasteries, he was shrewd enough to make some of the rich spoils available to his favored subjects and thus ensured their support for his program of reform. After his death, however, in the reign of his son, Edward VI (1547–53), under the Protectors Somerset and Northumberland, the English Church moved further away from Rome. The English Prayer Book was introduced in 1549, and an Act was passed permitting the clergy to marry. Leading continental reformers, like Peter Martyr Vermigli and Martin Bucer, accepted positions at Oxford and Cambridge. The traditional seven sacraments were reduced to two (baptism and communion). Chantries were dissolved. The lands of the secular clergy were confiscated; bishops were displaced and concessions extorted from their successors.

But all these changes came to an abrupt halt with the accession in 1553 of Mary Tudor, who reversed many of the religious innovations introduced by her father and her half-brother over a twenty-year period. Once again, she reconciled the English Church with the Church of Rome.[13] By the time of Mary's death in 1558, England had in the course of a few decades under three monarchs passed from Roman Catholicism through various forms of Protestantism and back to Roman Catholicism. The dangers involved in these radical shifts from one set of religious beliefs to another were frightfully obvious not only in Mary's cruel treatment of English heretics but also in an even more terrifying way on the Continent, where in France, for example, religious differences led an entire nation into civil war. Thus, when Elizabeth succeeded her half-sister Mary as queen of England in 1558, she faced a problem that troubled almost all Europe and that really had no generally acceptable solution.[14]

Hughes, *The Reformation in England*, 5th ed., 3 vols. in 1 (1950; New York: Macmillan, 1963).

[13] Two biographies of Mary Tudor are: H. F. M. Prescott's *Spanish Tudor* (1940); rev. ed. *Mary Tudor* (New York: Macmillan, 1953); and Carolly Erickson's *Bloody Mary* (Garden City, N.Y.: Doubleday, 1978).

[14] Although most historical accounts about religion in sixteenth-century England have their doctrinal biases and must be read with caution, a few studies deserve

While the majority of her subjects, having already shifted three times from one religion to another, appear to have been relatively indifferent about the particular kind of Christianity they practiced, there were at one end of the religious spectrum large numbers of fiercely loyal Roman Catholics and at the other end a growing number of equally zealous Puritans. Some members of both groups were quite willing to suffer and, if necessary, die for their religious beliefs. Like most of her subjects, Elizabeth herself appears to have been a moderate in religious matters, a queen interested more in keeping her throne, maintaining the peace, and promoting the nation's prosperity than in advancing a particular religious dogma. She had been an Anglo-Catholic under Henry, a Protestant under Edward, and a Catholic under Mary. But the times would not allow for moderation or toleration in a nation's religion, and she was forced to take a position. The one she chose, of course, eventually became known as Anglicanism, a form of English Christianity established as a compromise between traditional Roman Catholicism and the new reformed Protestantism.

The nation's new church was more easily established than maintained. In her first Parliament (1559), by the Acts of Supremacy and Uniformity, Elizabeth refounded the national church and was acknowledged its Supreme Governor.[15] The Articles of Edward's reign were reinstituted in revised form, and all the Catholic bishops of Mary's reign, except Kitchin of Llandaff, were replaced. At first, it appears, Elizabeth must have thought that the religious changes she had made would please the majority and be accepted, or at least tolerated, by Catholics and Puritans alike. For her Catholic subjects,

---

mention. For example, among the many writings of John Strype (1643–1737), I shall refer to his *Annals of the Reformation under Elizabeth*, 4 vols. in 7 (Oxford, 1824), *Historical Collections of the Life and Acts of John Aylmer* (Oxford, 1821), *The Life and Acts of Matthew Parker*, 3 vols. (Oxford, 1821), and *The Life and Acts of John Whitgift*, 3 vols. (Oxford, 1822). Future references to these works will be cited as: *Annals*, *Aylmer*, *Parker*, and *Whitgift*. For another work, pro-Protestant in sympathy, see W. H. Frere, *The English Church in the Reigns of Elizabeth and James I, 1558–1625* (London: Macmillan, 1904); and for a work pro-Catholic in sympathy, see Hughes's *Reformation in England*. One of the most objective historical accounts remains Arnold Oskar Meyer's *England and the Catholic Church Under Queen Elizabeth*, trans. J. R. McKee (1916; London: Routledge & Kegan Paul; New York: Barnes & Noble, 1967).

[15] An authorative study of Elizabeth's parliaments is J. E. Neale's *Elizabeth I and Her Parliaments, 1559–1601*, 2 vols. (1953; London: Jonathan Cape, 1957). Neale traces the development of anti-Catholic laws.

she had retained some Roman dogma, some sacraments, some ceremony, and a version of their episcopal hierarchy. The Puritans should have been pleased by her break with Rome and her establishment of a revised version of the new Protestant dogma and ritual. But Elizabeth was only partly right. The majority of her people did indeed submit, but neither Catholics nor Puritans were appeased. The Puritans insisted that her reforms had not gone far enough. In Parliament and at the universities, they denounced loudly everything that smacked of popery. The new ecclesiastical hierarchy as well as the old Romish vestments, images, and altars came under their general attack. They wrote treatises and preached sermons condemning Rome and chastising the Archbishop of Canterbury. As a result, they became a constant source of annoyance to Elizabeth and were often imprisoned and punished for expressing their views. But there was no systematic nationwide persecution against them as a sect during her reign. If Elizabeth hated Puritan arrogance and intolerance, she apparently recognized that they were a religious minority within her own national church and that they were not allied and supported by dangerous foreign powers.[16] Elizabeth dealt differently with the Catholics.[17]

[16] The term "Puritanism" has been redefined by many scholars. Reevaluations show that, like Catholics, not all Puritans in the sixteenth century thought alike or held the same religious views. See, for example, Patrick Collinson, *The Elizabethan Puritan Movement* (London: Jonathan Cape, 1967), and Elton, *England Under the Tudors*, pp. 489–90. An account of the alternatives available to "moderate" Catholics and "moderate" Puritans appears in *Cases of Conscience* by Elliot Rose (Cambridge: Cambridge University Press, 1975). See also Patrick McGrath, *Papists and Puritans Under Elizabeth I* (London: Blandford Press; New York: Walker, 1967); M. M. Knappen, *Tudor Puritanism* (1939; Chicago: The University of Chicago Press, 1970), esp. pp. 494–518, for an historical survey of studies about Puritanism; Mark H. Curtis, *Oxford and Cambridge in Transition, 1558–1642* (Oxford: Clarendon Press, 1959); and V. H. H. Green, *Religion at Oxford and Cambridge* (London: SCM Press, 1964).

[17] A large number of historical studies reveal a renewed interest in the religious problems of Elizabeth's reign. A recent collection of essays, for example, commemorating the first centenary of Campion Hall, Oxford, which supplies valuable background information is: Thomas M. McCoog, S.J., ed., *The Reconed Expense: Edmund Campion and the Early English Jesuits* (Woodbridge, Suffolk: Boydell Press, 1996). Essays of special interest in this collection for my edition of Campion's debates are: James McConica, "The Catholic Experience in Tudor Oxford," pp. 39–63; Thomas M. McCoog, S.J., " 'Playing the Champion': The Role of Disputation in the Jesuit Mission," pp. 119–39; and John J. LaRocca, S.J., "Popery and Pounds: The Effect of the Jesuit Mission on Penal Legislation," pp. 249–63. In addition, many less recent regional studies also indicate that a better understanding of the degree of

Queen Elizabeth and English Catholics

Until Elizabeth was excommunicated by Pope Pius V in 1570, many English Catholics continued to practice their religion. To be sure, she had available both the laws and the authority to suppress them

---

Catholic conformity or non-conformity is slowly emerging. R. B. Manning argues in *Religion and Society in Elizabethan Sussex* (Leicester: Leicester University Press, 1969) that it took two decades for Elizabeth's Acts to be effectively enforced in Sussex. In *Catholic Recusancy in the City of York, 1558–1791* (St. Albans, Hertfordshire: Catholic Record Society, 1970) J. C. H. Aveling acknowledges that his research on the topic is "no more than a preliminary study" (p. vi), and that his use of the records is not complete; however, some tentative conclusions seem evident: no papist community existed in York before 1572, but by 1576 a small group of recusants had sprung up among the middle classes; between 1578 and 1582 the first priest arrived, and the community was "being decimated by heavy persecution" (p. 159). Another study of regional Catholicism is *Reformation and Resistance in Tudor Lancashire* by Christopher Haigh (Cambridge: Cambridge University Press, 1976). Haigh demonstrates that the Catholics in Lancashire endured persecutions but remained loosely united because the laws bearing on religion were subverted by the gentry. Another important regional study is K. R. Works's *Elizabethan Recusancy in Cheshire and Manchester* (N.p.: Printed for the Chetham Society, 1971).

More comprehensive studies of the subject indicate that the actual number of Catholics in England during Elizabeth's reign is uncertain. Although Robert Persons, Campion's companion, reported that there were a great many and that they could be relied upon to overthrow the government, the government documents themselves contradict his claims. It appears more likely that most Marian Catholics, when required, subscribed to the new state religion under Elizabeth but continued secretly to practice the old religion. Until additional regional studies have been completed, it will be difficult to determine accurately the actual number of Elizabethan Catholics. Because of the complicating factor of faulty or lost records, the truth may not soon emerge. The largest number of Catholics appears to have been at the level of the educated gentry and their households. The lower classes were apparently occupied with the realities of making a living. On this subject the reader may wish to see Alison Plowden's *Danger to Elizabeth: The Catholics Under Elizabeth I* (New York: Stein and Day, 1973). In *The English Catholic Community, 1570–1850* (New York: Oxford University Press, 1976), John Bossy, a leading authority, argues that after 1570 Catholicism in England took a new form. Pre-Reformation Catholicism was characterized by such figures as Henry VIII, More, Fisher, and Pole (p. 4). The new Catholicism, however, became less clerically dominated and involved more of the laity in active roles. In *The Handle and the Axe: The Catholic Recusants in England from Reformation to Emancipation* (London: Blond and Briggs, 1976), J. C. H. Aveling agrees that a new Catholicism appeared. He discusses the still-unresolved number of Catholics (pp. 9–73) and modifies some traditional views in maintaining that most Catholics conformed to Elizabeth's laws. In contrast with views held by Bossy and Aveling, Christopher Haigh ("The Continuity of Catholicism in the English Reformation," *Past and Present* 93 [1981]: 37–69) argues in favor of the continuity of English Catholicism. The missionaries, Haigh says, came not to convert Protestants but to minister to Catholics; and although priests were essential for the con-

or to force them into conformity, but Elizabeth refrained from imposing severe measures. If the clerical hierarchy were forced to conform or be dismissed and imprisoned, the Catholic laity, especially in the North, suffered little for their religious beliefs. Elizabeth claimed that she did not wish to look into the minds of her subjects as long as they did not represent a threat to her person and to the peace of her nation. Her hope was that time would quiet their objections to the new national church. Aging Catholic bishops, she calculated, would soon die off; the lower secular clergy would gradually be won over; and the wealthy Catholic laity would be fined into at least outward conformity. In the main, her strategy seemed effective. The bishops did indeed die off, and many of the secular clergy, together with their congregations, accepted the new state religion. In all probability Elizabeth's plan would have succeeded without persecution and bloodshed if it had not been for William Allen.

William Allen (1532–94), perhaps the most influential of all Elizabethan religious exiles, devoted most of his adult life to the reconversion of England to Roman Catholicism.[18] He became the moving

---

tinuance of Catholicism, they did not create a new church. Haigh's documentation is especially helpful in summarizing the scholarship on the fate of the Catholics during Elizabeth's reign. Other sources include an important early work on the subject, *Catholicism in England: The Portrait of a Minority: Its Culture and Tradition* by David Mathew (1936; London: Eyre & Spottiswoode, 1955); and M. D. R. Leys's *Catholics in England, 1559–1829: A Social History* (London: Longmans, 1961).

It should also be noted, as Arnold Pritchard shows (*Catholic Loyalism in Elizabethan England* [Chapel Hill: University of North Carolina Press, 1979]), that various kinds of "Roman Catholic" beliefs were held by Catholics in England and by Englishmen on the Continent. Because of the differences among English Catholics, Pritchard argues, Catholicism in England survived. After Campion's time, serious disagreements developed between the regular and the secular clergy which led eventually to open dispute, especially at Wisbech Castle (see Bossy, *English Catholic Community*, pp. 11–48).

For an account of English Catholic education during the Reformation, see A. C. F. Beales's *Education under Penalty: English Catholic Education from the Reformation to the Fall of James II, 1547–1689* (London: Athlone Press, 1963). For a survey of the treatment of the English Catholic laity primarily as reported in the Calendars of State Papers, see William Raleigh Trimble's *The English Laity in Elizabethan England* (Cambridge, Mass.: Harvard University Press, 1964). Another important study is Adrian Morey's *The Catholic Subjects of Elizabeth I* (London: George Allen & Unwin; Totowa, N.J.: Rowman and Littlefield, 1978). Renewed historical interest in the religious problems of Elizabeth's reign suggests that a new religious history of sixteenth-century England may soon be written.

[18] For accounts of Allen's life, see *The First and Second Diaries of the English College, Douay, and an Appendix of Unpublished Documents*, edited by Fathers of the Congrega-

spirit behind the English Counter Reformation. Born in traditionally Catholic Lancashire, Allen studied at Oriel College, Oxford, where he received his M.A. in 1553 and became principal at St. Mary's Hall. Refusing to conform to the Acts of Supremacy and Uniformity of 1559, he fled to Louvain, where he studied theology and was ordained a priest at Mechlin in 1567. For the remaining twenty-six years of his life, he labored tirelessly for his religion. Although his controversial writings alone would have earned for him a creditable reputation as the defender of the Catholic position, he is remembered chiefly for having founded the English College at Douai for the education of young exiles, many of whom were the sons of wealthy English families. With financial support from a host of benefactors, Allen established a seminary within the college for training priests who after ordination would be sent to England as missionaries. He recognized the fact that if replacements were not trained for the dwindling number of loyal Catholic priests in England, the country would surely be lost. From its modest beginning in 1568, the seminary grew quickly in size and influence under Allen's able leadership until by the end of Elizabeth's reign it had produced well over four hundred priests. Their training, directed by some of the leading Catholic scholars of the day, many of whom were graduates of Oxford and Cambridge whom Allen had attracted to his college, included intensive study in the scriptures and theology, with special emphasis on preaching and disputing.[19]

The first of these young seminary priests, as they were called, arrived in England as early as 1574, and others continued to come in increasing numbers. Between 1574 and 1578, fifty-two of the seventy-four priests ordained were sent, and in the next seven years (1579–85) additional priests followed. For his work, Allen was called to Rome by Pope Gregory XIII in 1585 and raised to the rank of cardinal. He remained there for the rest of his life, but his college continued his missionary program. From 1585 until Elizabeth's

---

tion of the London Oratory, with an historical introduction by T. F. Knox, D.D. (London, 1878); *The Letters and Memorials of William Cardinal Allen*, edited by Fathers of the Congregation of the London Oratory, with an historical introduction by T. F. Knox, D.D. (London, 1882); and Martin Haile, *An Elizabethan Cardinal, William Allen* (London and New York: Pitman, 1914).

[19] For a brief account of the English academic exiles, see Morey, *Catholic Subjects of Elizabeth I*, pp. 96–116.

death in 1603, 167 more priests were sent, which brought the total number to about 438.[20]

Allen's young missionaries returned to England in small groups and became part of a Catholic underground network that extended throughout the country. In the main, these seminary priests were not politically motivated. Their charge was to administer the sacraments, preach, and say Mass. They recognized Elizabeth as the rightful queen, but they spoke privately against her supreme authority in religious matters. In sermons they instructed their congregations not to attend Protestant services. By the example they set, they inspired many Catholics to acts of extraordinary courage.

To judge from the increasing number of sterner laws enacted against Catholics, the young missionaries, together with the assistance of some of the native secular clergy who had remained in England, were successfully launching a Counter Reformation. Fines against Catholics were increased and led to imprisonments, which, in turn, led to torture and executions. By the end of her reign, Elizabeth had given the Catholics approximately the same number of martyrs as Mary had given the Protestants in hers, although, it should be remembered, Elizabeth's reign lasted forty-five years, Mary's only five.[21]

Law and Religion

Many historical accounts of the period that attempt to explain the Elizabethan persecution of Catholics do so on the grounds of law rather than religion. The distinction generally made is that Mary persecuted heretics and Elizabeth executed traitors. No less an au-

---

[20] Because many of the missionaries used aliases, the exact number of seminary priests sent to England is uncertain. The *Douai Diaries*, for example, list 452 missionaries. See also Godfrey Anstruther, O.P., *The Seminary Priests: A Dictionary of the Secular Clergy of England and Wales, 1558–1850*, 4 vols. (Great Wakening: Mayhew-McCrimmon, 1975–77).

[21] It is difficult to determine the number of Catholics who died for their religion during Elizabeth's reign, for not all records are complete, nor have all been studied. Also, many Catholics died while imprisoned and many others soon after their release. For accounts about these Catholics, see P. Caraman and J. Walsh, *The Catholic Martyrs of England and Wales, 1535–1680: A Chronological List* (London: Catholic Truth Society, 1979); Philip Caraman, *The Other Face: Catholic Life Under Elizabeth I* (London: Longmans, 1960).

thority than Lord Burghley, Elizabeth's chief minister, felt obliged to explain this distinction to the world in his *Execution of Justice in England* in 1583, and William Allen replied for the Catholics with his *Defence of English Catholics* in 1584.[22] Although such a nice distinction as Burghley's may have provided intellectual comfort to some, the Catholic victims in Elizabeth's reign were just as dead as the Protestant victims in Mary's.

It is perhaps more meaningful to trace the development of events that produced laws against the English Catholics than to decide whether these laws were just. Elizabeth's first Parliament in 1559 undid most of Mary's religious legislation.[23] The Act of Supremacy, recognizing Elizabeth as Supreme Governor in both spiritual and temporal matters, required that an oath be sworn to the queen by all the clergy and officials under the crown. Recognition of a foreign prince or prelate was punishable by fine, imprisonment, and death. The Act of Uniformity reestablished in slightly revised form the 1552 Prayer Book and ordered its use. Clergy refusing to comply were to be imprisoned; laymen who failed to attend services were subject to a fine of one shilling for each offense. Thus, papal authority was rejected in favor of the queen's, and a Protestant ritual was restored.

By the time of her second Parliament in 1563, Elizabeth was more secure on the throne, and Parliament was able to take a firmer position on religious matters. Accordingly, the provisions of the Act of Supremacy were extended and its penalties made more exacting. Additional classes of people, including members of the House of Commons, were required to take the oath, and a second refusal was punishable as high treason. Also, the Thirty-Nine Articles regulating religious matters were adopted.

---

[22] Robert M. Kingdon, ed., *The Execution of Justice in England, by William Cecil, and A True, Sincere, and Modest Defence of English Catholics*, by William Allen (Ithaca, N.Y.: Cornell University Press/Folger Shakespeare Library, 1965). See also Thomas H. Clancy, S.J., *Papist Pamphleteers:, The Allen-Persons Party and the Political Thought of the Counter-Reformation in England, 1572–1615* (Chicago: Loyola University Press, 1964).

Whether or not the Catholics who were put to death during Elizabeth's reign were martyrs for their religion or traitors to their country is an issue beyond the scope of this study. Burghley and Allen show that both sides have strong arguments. This issue, however, has allowed many historians to air their biases.

[23] See Neale, *Elizabeth I.*

From 1568 through 1571 a series of events heightened parliamentary concern about the religious problem, especially as it related to the personal safety of Elizabeth. The presence of Mary, Queen of Scots, in England (1567–87), the Rebellion of the Northern Earls (1569), the Ridolfi plot (1571), and Pope Pius V's bull of excommunication (*Regnans in excelsis*) in 1570 aroused Parliament to retaliate.[24] In Elizabeth's fourth Parliament of 1571, two important Acts were passed. The first confirmed the queen's title and imposed the penalty of high treason on anyone attempting to deprive her of it. The second, with similar penalties, forbade the introduction into the country of papal bulls and the absolution of the queen's subjects from their allegiance to her. The following year Norfolk and Northumberland were tried and executed. Two additional Acts in Elizabeth's fifth Parliament of 1572 extended the penalty of treason to anyone who conspired to seize the queen's property or to set free political prisoners. All these laws awaited Allen's seminary priests, and the first to feel their sting was Cuthbert Mayne, who was captured, tried, and hanged in 1578.[25] Two more priests were executed the next year, and in the following two decades their number reached almost one hundred.

The arrival in 1580 of two Jesuits, Edmund Campion and Robert Persons, aroused Parliament to pass in 1581 even sterner laws against Catholics.[26] The mere attempt to convert a subject of the

---

[24] The Northern Earls, Northumberland and Westmorland, conspired in 1569 to free Mary Stuart and restore Roman Catholicism in England. Elizabeth put down their uprising and punished the rebels (see Neale, *Elizabeth I*, pp. 183–90). Roberto Ridolfi, a Florentine banker, plotted (1570–71) with Spanish and papal support to place Mary Stuart and Norfolk on the throne. And not only did Pius V's bull excommunicate Elizabeth, but it also directed her Catholic subjects to withdraw their allegiance to her.

[25] A biography of Mayne (and other English martyrs, including Campion) may be found in the official presentation of documents and cult: *ARCHDIOCESE OF WESTMINSTER. Cause of the Canonization of Blessed Martyrs John Houghton, Robert Lawrence, Augustine Webster, Richard Reynolds, John Stone, Cuthbert Mayne, John Paine, Edmund Campion, Alexander Briant, Ralph Sherwin and Luke Kirby, Put to Death in England in Defence of the Catholic Faith (1533–1582)*. Sacred Congregation of Rites, Historical Section 148 (Vatican City: Vatican Polyglot Press, 1968), pp. 107–76. This work will be referred to hereafter as *Cause of the Canonization*. For a brief account of Mayne and Francis Tregian, his host, see, E. E. Reynolds, *The Roman Catholic Church in England and Wales* (Wheathampstead, Hertfordshire: Anthony Clarke, 1973), pp. 229–34.

[26] For these new laws and proclamations, see Paul L. Hughes and James F. Larkin, C.S.V., eds., *Tudor Royal Proclamations*, 3 vols. (New Haven, Conn.: Yale Univer-

queen to Catholicism was made a treasonable offense; saying or hearing Mass was forbidden under rigid penalties; and a fine of twenty pounds a month was imposed on recusants. Another Act, with punishments ranging from a fine to the death penalty, was passed against the uttering of seditious words, prophesying the queen's death, publishing a seditious book, or forecasting the queen's successor. Even though sterner laws against Catholics would be passed in the future, a sufficient number had already been enacted by 1581 to ensure that if Catholics in England did not accept the dogma and abide by the regulations of the national church, they risked the loss of their lives and possessions. For the remaining twenty-two years of Elizabeth's reign, hundreds of Catholics, especially priests, were executed, and many hundreds more were fined and imprisoned.[27]

Campion's Background

Perhaps the most famous victim of Elizabeth's persecution of Catholics was Edmund Campion, a young scholar from Oxford.[28] Campion

---

sity Press, 1969), esp. 2:481–91; and Frederick A. Youngs, Jr., *The Proclamations of Tudor Queens* (Cambridge: Cambridge University Press, 1976). For an account of the Campion–Persons mission, see E. E. Reynolds, *Campion and Persons: The Jesuit Mission* (London: Sheed and Ward, 1980).

[27] It is not uncommon for modern historians to view a priest's willingness to risk death for his religious beliefs as a form of neurotic behavior. Joel Hurstfield, for example, observes that the historian "falters in trying to analyze the outlook of these priests. He feels it needs other disciplines, perhaps of the psychologist and the anthropologist, to explain the passion for martyrdom, the death-wish . . ." (*Elizabeth I and the Unity of England* [1960; New York: Harper & Row, 1969], pp. 110–11).

Prison conditions were indeed grim. See, for example, Sidney and Beatrice Webb, *English Prisons Under Local Government* (London: Longmans, Green, 1922).

[28] Of the many biographies of Campion, the following deserve special mention. Robert Persons's account, *Of the Life and Martyrdom of Edmund Campion*, was written in 1594, and a transcription of it by C. Grene, S.J. (1629–97) may be found in the Archives of Stonyhurst College, England. Grene's *Collectanea P*, vol. I, has been printed in *Letters and Notices*, 11 (1877): 219–42, 308–39; 12 (1879): 1–68, but the account is incomplete and at times faulty on dates. Yet we must keep in mind that Persons was Campion's close friend and fellow missionary. Paolo Bombino wrote the earliest detailed biography, *Vita et martyrum Edmundi Campiani* (Antwerp, 1618), and apparently consulted with Persons about it, but the work is apologetic. The most complete biography of Campion is Richard Simpson's *Life of Edmund Campion* (1866; London: John Hodges, 1896), but the author's pro-Catholic and pro-papist

(1540–81) was born in London and attended grammar school there. We know little about his family other than that he had two brothers and a sister and that his father was a bookseller.[29] It is reported that he was a gifted student and won many prizes in grammar school competitions, one of which may have been the honor of welcoming Queen Mary into London (August 3, 1553) on the occasion of her accession to the throne.[30]

After completing his grammar school education, Campion, supported by one of the London companies, entered the newly founded St. John's College at Oxford in 1557 and remained there until he fled to Ireland in 1570.[31] During his years at Oxford he gained an excellent academic reputation and was greatly admired by his fellow students for his brilliance and personal charm. His studies, as he himself tells us, included seven years of philosophy and six years of theology.[32] An especially gifted speaker, he was selected to deliver

---

views often intrude. Evelyn Waugh's *Edmund Campion, Jesuit and Martyr* (1935; London: Longmans, 1961), written in elegant prose to commemorate the founding of Campion Hall at Oxford, is based almost entirely on Simpson.

No modern complete edition of Campion's works has been published. An older incomplete edition is P. Silvester's *Edmundi Campiani, Angli e Soc. Iesu, Decem Rationes propositae in causae fidei, et opuscula eius selecta* (Antwerp: Balthasar Moretus, 1631); also, Robert Turner has published a series of editions, such as *Edmundi Campiani, Societatis Iesu, martyris in Anglia, Orationes, epistolae, tractatus de imitatione rhetorica* (Ingolstadt). For a detailed list of Turner's editions, see A. F. Allison and D. M. Rogers, eds., *The Contemporary Printed Literature of the English Counter-Reformation Between 1558 and 1640: An Annotated Catalogue*, 2 vols. (Aldershot, Hant. and Brookfield, Vt. : Scolar Press; 1989, 1994), 1:167–68. Campion's "Challenge" has often been reprinted, and his *Rationes Decem* often translated, but many of his other Latin writings (for example, poems, orations, letters) have not been translated.

[29] For a study of Campion's "possible" family background see Leslie Campion, *The Family of Edmund Campion* (London: The Research Publishing Co., 1975); and Carl I. Hammer, "Robert Campion: Edmund Campion's Brother?" *Recusant History* 6 (1980): 153.

[30] See John Gough Nichols, ed., *The Chronicle of Queen Jane and of Two Years of Queen Mary* (N.p.: Camden Society, 1850): "The queenes grace stayed at Allgate-streete before the stage wheare the poore children stood, and hard an oration that one of them made, but she sayd nothinge to them" (p. 15). The child orator may have been Campion.

[31] W. H. Stevenson and H. E. Salter's *The Early History of St. John's College, Oxford* (Oxford: Oxford Historical Society, 1939), corrects information about Campion contained in William Holden Hutton's *St. John Baptist College* (London: F. E. Robinson, 1898), and in Simpson's *Life of Edmund Campion*.

[32] Simpson, *Life of Edmund Campion*, p. 6.

the eulogy at the funeral of Sir Thomas White, the founder of St. John's College, and he also disputed before Queen Elizabeth when she visited Oxford in 1566.[33] His eloquence so impressed the queen that she recommended him to Leicester and Burghley, at that time the two most influential men in the kingdom.[34] His love of learning and the recognition he was receiving from both his peers and his superiors were apparently heady enough stimulants to turn Campion away from Catholicism. He took the oath in 1564 and was later ordained deacon in the English Church. His subsequent readings in the Church Fathers, however, seem to have led him back to Catholicism; and when his Catholic views were reported, the Grocer's Company, his London sponsors, sought demonstration of his religious conformity by inviting him to preach at St. Paul's Cross in London, a pulpit in the churchyard of St. Paul's Cathedral that had been filled by many distinguished Protestant clergy.[35] Because of his own religious uncertainties, Campion requested postponements. Eventually, however, because he was unwilling to preach at St. Paul's Cross and because religious conformity at Oxford was being more rigorously enforced, he felt obliged to leave St. John's and England in 1570.[36]

Campion's flight to Ireland rather than to the Continent, where most Catholic exiles went, suggests that he had not yet formally returned to the Catholic Church. In Ireland he found generous patrons in James Stanyhurst, the father of one of his Oxford students and then a member of the Irish Parliament, and Sir Henry Sidney, the father of Sir Philip Sidney and then Lord Deputy of Ireland.[37]

---

[33] Charles Plummer's *Elizabethan Oxford* (Oxford, 1887) contains a collection of rare texts, including a brief description of college rules and educational practices by Nicholas Fitzherbert (pp. 15–19), and John Bereblock's summary account of Campion's participation in a disputation on Tuesday, September 3, 1566, before Queen Elizabeth (pp. 131–33). Campion's speech appears in Silvester, *Edmundi Campiani . . . Decem Rationes*, pp. 330–40.

[34] See Derek Wilson's *Sweet Robin: A Biography of Robert Dudley, Earl of Leicester, 1533–1588* (London: Hamish Hamilton, 1981). For Burghley, see Conyers Read's *Mr. Secretary Cecil and Queen Elizabeth* (London: Jonathan Cape, 1955), and his *Lord Burghley and Queen Elizabeth* (London: Jonathan Cape, 1960).

[35] See Millard MacLure, *The Paul's Cross Sermons, 1534–1642* (Toronto: University of Toronto Press, 1958).

[36] See Curtis, *Oxford and Cambridge in Transition, 1558–1642*.

[37] For an account of Richard Stanihurst's and Campion's stay in Ireland, see Colm Lennon, *Richard Stanihurst, the Dubliner, 1547–1618: A Biography, with a Stanihurst Text, On Ireland's Past* (Blackrock, County Dublin: Irish Academic Press, 1981).

Because both these influential men were at that time attempting to persuade the Irish Parliament to establish a university in Dublin, some speculate that they may have considered Campion a potential member of its faculty. During this waiting period, he occupied himself with writing a brief *History of Ireland*, which eventually found its way into Holinshed's *Chronicles*.[38] His dedication of this work to Leicester argues not only that he was still interested in maintaining his connections with the mighty, but also, in view of Leicester's well-known Protestant sympathies, that Campion himself had not yet formally gone over to Rome.[39] However, Campion's presence in Dublin attracted the attention of the anti-Catholic authorities. He went into hiding for a brief period but, unwilling to embarrass or endanger his protectors, fled from Dublin in disguise and returned to England in May 1572. At the beginning of June 1572, he left England again, this time to attend Allen's recently founded English College at Douai.[40]

Campion spent more than a year at Douai, where he completed his studies in theology, earned his degree of Bachelor of Divinity, and received minor orders and the subdiaconate. We also know that he was employed as a teacher at the college, for he speaks of Cuthbert Mayne as having been his pupil at Douai. Also, one of his orations and part of another that he delivered there have been preserved.

From Douai Campion went on to Rome in the spring of 1573, where he was accepted into the Society of Jesus in April and assigned to the province of Austria.[41] By August he had arrived in

[38] For a description of Campion's *History of Ireland*, see Southern, *Elizabethan Recusant Prose*, pp. 283–97; for a facsimile edition of it, see Rudolf B. Gottfried, ed., *A History of Ireland (1571) by Edmund Campion* (New York: Scholars' Facsimiles and Reprints, 1940); and see also A. F. Vossen, *Two Bokes of the Histories of Ireland* (Assen, The Netherlands: Van Gorcum, 1963). Vossen maintains that Campion did not go to Ireland to accept a university post (pp. 1–25).

[39] For an excellent account of Leicester's patronage of Campion, and Campion's *Historie of Ireland*, see Eleanor Rosenberg, *Leicester, Patron of Letters* (New York: Columbia University Press, 1955), pp. 80–94.

[40] John Morris, S.J., "Blessed Edmund Campion at Douay," pamphlet, London, 1887, pp. 1–17.

[41] The Society of Jesus, founded by Ignatius of Loyola in 1540, became one of the most influential and controversial religious orders in the Roman Catholic Church. The Society attracted a large number of gifted men who were especially noted as missionaries and educators. Protestants, however, looked upon the Jesuits as religious and political intriguers.

Prague, and in October moved on to Brunn, Moravia, where he served his year's probation in the Society.[42] In October 1574, he was reassigned to Prague and spent the next five and a half years there teaching, preaching, and catechizing. In 1578 he was ordained deacon and later priest by the archbishop of Prague.

Campion's duties at Prague were numerous and wide ranging. As professor of rhetoric, he trained his young students to speak and write in the style of Cicero.[43] Later he was appointed professor of philosophy. In addition to his teaching duties, he worked in the kitchen and was charged with ringing the bell for rising and retiring, for prayers and meditation. He headed a confraternity, a religious society established at all Jesuit colleges, intended for the careful supervision of the best young scholars. He composed and delivered occasional Latin orations and wrote Latin plays for his students.[44] He preached, heard confessions, visited prisons and hospitals. During this time he also corresponded with such old and new friends as Gregory Martin, Robert Persons, and his own students. He was visited by Sir Philip Sidney and preached before the emperor, Rudolf

---

For general histories of the Society, see William V. Bangert, S.J., *A History of the Society of Jesus* (St. Louis: Institute of Jesuit Sources, 1972), and Bernard Basset, S.J., *The English Jesuits, From Campion to Martindale* (London: Burns & Oates, 1967). One of the main sources for Jesuit activities in sixteenth-century England is H. Foley, S.J.'s *Records of the English Province of the Society of Jesus*, 7 vols. (London: Burns & Oates, 1877–83).

Campion's reasons for leaving Allen's seminary at Douai and going on to Rome where he entered the Society of Jesus are unknown. He must have recognized, however, that remaining at Douai would almost certainly result in his being sent back to England as a missionary priest, whereas joining the Society, which had no mission in England at that time, would ensure an assignment elsewhere. If this consideration was part of Campion's motivation, it underscores the truth of his later statements that his mission to England was not political; and it also suggests that, for whatever good reason, he may have deliberately attempted to avoid taking part in the English mission.

[42] For accounts of Campion's activities at Brunn and Prague, see Bohuslao Balbino's *Miscellanea, Historica regni Bohemiae Decadisti* (Prague, 1682), Book IV, pp. 189–96; and Joannes Schmidl's *Historiae Societatis Jesu Provinciae Bohemiae*, 4 parts (Prague 1747–59). The first part deals with the years 1555–92 and contains an account of Campion's life at Prague, together with some of his letters not found elsewhere.

[43] Miguel A. Barnad, S.J., "The 'Treatise on Imitation' of Blessed Edmund Campion," *Folia* 6 (1952): 100–14, and 7 (1953): 20–29.

[44] See, for example, Joseph Simons, ed. and trans., *Ambrosia: A Neo-Latin Drama by Edmund Campion, S.J.* (Assen, The Netherlands: Van Gorcum, 1970).

II, and the archbishop of Prague.[45] Caught up in a swirl of religious and academic activities, Campion probably enjoyed the happiest years of his life at Prague. He told a friend that he was too busy to get sick. His active routine soon changed.

Catholic Mission to England

In a letter during the winter of 1579, William Allen, head of the English College at Rheims, informed Campion that he would soon be recalled from Prague to Rome by his superior and sent to England as a missionary. In March 1580, the official notice arrived. Campion left Prague on March 25, 1580, and arrived in Rome on April 5.

William Allen had preceded Campion to Rome in the autumn of 1579 in order to resolve a dispute that had arisen at the English College there and to enlist Jesuit involvement in the English mission.[46] His two objectives were related. A number of the students at the English College charged that the president of the college, Maurice Clennock, had shown partiality toward his Welsh countrymen. The appointment of two Jesuits to the college did not resolve the problem, for it served only to arouse the Welsh students, who accused the Jesuits of attempting to gain possession of the college.[47] Allen's plan was to unite all factions in the common cause of the English mission. Appealing to Everard Mercurian, the General of the Society, and Pope Gregory XIII, he argued that a combined missionary effort of Jesuits, English secular clergy, and laymen would hearten the English Catholics, especially if the effort involved a new

[45] For accounts of Campion's meeting with Sir Philip Sidney in Prague in 1577, see Roger Howell, *Sir Philip Sidney: The Shepherd Knight* (London: Hutchinson, 1968), pp. 37–39; and James M. Osborn, *Young Philip Sidney, 1572–1577* (New Haven, Conn.: Yale University Press, 1972), pp. 281–82. Osborn also suggests (pp. 466–68) that Sidney may have met briefly with Campion on the occasion of his earlier visit to Prague in 1575. Both Howell and Osborn include Campion's optimistic letter to Dr. John Bavand about the meeting.

[46] An account of the circumstances leading to the formation of the Catholic mission to England and Campion's part in it may be found in Ludwig Freiherr von Pastor's *The History of the Popes*, ed. Ralph Francis Kerr, 35 vols. (London: Kegan Paul, 1930), 13: 376–403.

[47] For an account of the college, see Michael Williams, *The Venerable English College, Rome: A History* (London: Associated Catholic Publications, 1979).

religious order (the Society of Jesus) that had no claim to confiscated church property in England. Also, because there were more Englishmen in the Society than in all the other religious orders, the Jesuits could not stand by as educators while their non-Jesuit students were sent to endure the hardships and dangers of missionary work. England, he urged, had greater claim for spiritual aid than did India or the Orient, for missionaries must preserve the faith in countries they had already won before setting out to establish it in new ones.

Mercurian, recognizing the extreme dangers of the English mission, delayed giving his approval. He knew that his Jesuits would be treated as traitors by the government. They would be isolated from one another, hunted down by informers, imprisoned, tortured, and killed.

In spite of the risks involved, Allen's arguments eventually prevailed, and Pope Gregory XIII appointed the aged Dr. Goldwell, bishop of St. Asaph in Mary's reign, to serve as Ordinary for all England and charged him with leading the new English mission. To that end, instructions were carefully prepared for the band of missionaries. The Jesuits, for example, were to observe the rules of the Society as conditions permitted. They were advised to be wary of those with whom they associated, and to keep in touch with one another. Above all, the missionaries were ordered neither to involve themselves in political matters nor to speak against the queen. Detailed recommendations were prepared to cover almost all the circumstances in which they were likely to find themselves, including even the danger of familiar conversations with women and boys. But elaborate instructions and detailed advice could not alter the fact that Pope Pius V had excommunicated Elizabeth and all who obeyed her laws. The missionaries themselves knew well that this was the petard on which they would be hoisted. A mitigating proviso had been attached to the bull of excommunication declaring that even though the bull should always bind Elizabeth and heretics, it should not bind Catholics while things remained as they were (*rebus sic stantibus*). In other words, Catholics would be bound by the bull only when it could be publicly executed. Although this proviso was intended by authorities in Rome as a way of ensuring a greater degree of safety for the missionaries and English Catholics, it was understood quite differently by the government in England. There the proviso was interpreted by the authorities as further evidence that Catholics could not be trusted.

Disguised as a servant, Campion left Rome on foot for England on April 18, 1580, with a group of a dozen missionaries, including Robert Persons, his immediate superior, Brother Ralph Emerson, and two secular priests, Ralph Sherwin and Alexander Briant.[48] They stayed briefly with Cardinal Paleotto at Bologna and with Cardinal Borromeo at Milan before passing on to Turin. Encountering Spanish soldiers in Savoy and at Aiguebelle, they decided to proceed by way of Geneva, where they engaged in a brief disputation with Beza, the noted Calvinist, before passing on to Rheims. The journey from Rome to Rheims took nearly six weeks.

Campion and his missionary colleagues were welcomed at Rheims by Allen and their old friends, and they learned there for the first time of the ill-fated papal military expedition into Ireland in 1580, which resulted in the annihilation of the Catholic forces, including the brilliant Nicholas Sanders, at Smerwick.[49] They also learned that English seaport authorities had been alerted to their coming and would be waiting for them. In view of these dramatically changed circumstances, Campion consulted with Allen about the advisability of canceling their mission to England. He felt that he could do more good in Prague, but Allen disagreed, and Campion did not protest.

In order to avoid capture by the English port authorities, the mis-

---

[48] For a detailed account of the journey, see John H. Pollen, *The Journey of Bd. Edmund Campion from Rome to England, March–June, 1580, with an Unpublished Letter of St. Charles Borromeo and of Bd. Ralph Sherwin*, reprinted, with additions, from *The Month* for September, 1897 (Roehampton, S.W.: Manresa Press, n.d,), pp. 1–29.

Robert Persons (1546–1610) was perhaps the most able Jesuit administrator and apologist of his day. Educated at Oxford, he entered the Society of Jesus soon after Campion and was appointed the superior of this first Jesuit mission to England in 1580, which he managed with extraordinary skill. After Campion's capture, Persons returned to the Continent where he spent the remainder of his busy life writing defenses of Roman Catholic positions and founding schools and seminaries. His activities earned him the respect of both pope and princes. In England, he was condemned by the government as a notorious traitor.

For biographies of the missionaries and their co-workers in England, see the following: *Concertatio ecclesiae Catholicae in Anglia adversus Calvinopapistas et Puritanos*, with an introduction by D. M. Rogers (1588; Westmead, England: Gregg International Publishers, 1970); Foley, *Records*; Joseph Gillow, *Bibliographical Dictionary of the English Catholics*, 5 vols. (London, 1885); and Reynolds, *Campion and Persons*.

[49] Thomas McNevin Veech, *Dr. Nicolas Sanders and the English Reformation, 1530–1581* (Louvain: Bureaux du Recueil, Bibliothèque de l'Université, 1935).

sionaries divided themselves into small groups and set out for England from the French ports of Boulogne, Dunkirk, Dieppe, and Calais. Campion, Persons, and Brother Ralph Emerson, traveling as one group, left Rheims on June 6 for St. Omer, where they were received by priests at the college who advised them against going to England. Their mission and their identities, they learned, were known to Queen Elizabeth and her Council. Despite the warnings, Campion and Persons made plans to go forward. Persons, disguised as a soldier returning from war in the Low Countries, went from Calais to Dover and, according to their plan, established contacts with English Catholics in London before sending for Campion. Campion, pretending to be a jewel merchant, sailed from Calais with Brother Ralph on the evening of June 24 and arrived at Dover the following morning. On entry, there were a few tense moments when Campion was seized and sent to the mayor of Dover for questioning, but for some unknown reason he was soon released and allowed to travel on to London, where he was met by Thomas Jay and taken to a house in Chancery Lane. Persons, having prepared the way, had left word that Campion should remain in London to await his return from the country.

While waiting for Persons, Campion preached a sermon to a great number of Catholics at Paget House on the feast of Sts. Peter and Paul. His sermon so impressed his listeners that his name spread quickly about London, and his presence became known to the Council. Informers sought him out, and plans were made to trap him. Having been warned about them, Campion limited his activities to private conferences in the homes of trusted friends until Persons returned.

Persons and Campion, realizing that they could not remain in London without being captured themselves and endangering their friends, made arrangements for their departure. Before leaving, however, they scheduled a meeting to explain their mission. They gathered in conference a small group of Catholic priests and laymen at a home in Southwark to discuss the most important ecclesiastical problems facing them. First, they assured those assembled that their return to England was not part of a political conspiracy to overthrow Elizabeth, in spite of the bull of excommunication and its recently attached *rebus sic stantibus* proviso. They were, they insisted, in England to deal only with religious matters. Second, on the matter of church attendance, they bore the unwelcome Roman directive that English Catholics were not to attend Protestant religious services.[50] Third, with regard to fasting, they reported that the different fasting practices that existed in the different regions of the country should be preserved. Fourth, they agreed to divide the kingdom into three ecclesiastical districts: Wales, Lancashire and the North, and Cambridgeshire. Campion and Persons were to have free range over the entire country.

Campion's "Challenge"

After the conference, Campion and Persons left London in the company of George Gilbert and Gervase Pierrepoint, two trusted Catholic laymen, and rode on to Hogsdon, where they were unexpectedly joined by Thomas Pounde, who had secured a temporary release from prison.[51] Pounde, an ardently devout but rather eccentric Catholic layman who had spent most of his life in prison for his religion, warned that if the two missionaries were captured the Council would surely attempt to discredit them publicly by charging that they had come into England for political purposes. He advised, therefore, that both should write a brief declaration explaining their mission in England and leave a copy of it with a trusted friend who would make it public in the event of their capture. Campion, according to Persons, seated himself at the end of the table and in less than half an hour wrote his famous "Challenge" (or "Brag") to Elizabeth's Council.[52]

In his hastily written "Challenge," Campion acknowledged that he was a Jesuit priest who had been ordered by his superior to go to England on a religious mission, not a political one. He volunteered to appear before Elizabeth and her Council to explain his purposes

[50] Conflicting opinions among Catholics about whether or not they could attend Protestant religious services were still being debated in the 1580s. Apparently, many Catholics gave themselves the benefit of the doubt and attended Protestant services to avoid fines and imprisonment. See, for example, Geoffrey de C. Parmiter, *Elizabethan Popish Recusancy in the Inns of Court*, Bulletin of the Institute of Historical Research, Special Supplement No. 11, November 1976.

[51] For Campion's association with Pierrepoint and an account of Gilbert's life, see Foley, *Records*, 3:658–704; for Pounde's life, see 3:567–657.

[52] *Letters and Notices* 12 (1878): 46. See Appendix B.

and to discuss religious matters with them. Perhaps most important, as future events would prove, he also offered to meet in public debate about religious issues with "the Doctors and Masters and chosen men of both Universities" as well as with "the lawyers, spiritual and temporal."

Campion gave a copy of his declaration to Pounde, who read it after returning to prison at Marshalsea in Southwark. Pounde was so impressed with Campion's statement that it inspired him to write his own "Challenge," modeled on Campion's, and he sent petitions for public conferences to the Council and to the bishop of London. Pounde's "Challenge" resulted in his being transferred to another prison and placed in solitary confinement. Before he was moved, however, Pounde passed Campion's "Challenge" on to a fellow prisoner, who, in turn, passed it on to others. In due course it fell into the hands of the authorities and soon after became widely known throughout England.[53]

Campion's "Challenge," or "Brag" as it is sometimes called, is a very interesting document, not only because it leads directly to his famous published defense of the Roman Catholic Church, *Rationes Decem*, and later to his disputations at the Tower of London, but also because of the insights it provides into his personality. For example, it shows him to be direct, articulate, truthful, obedient, respectful, but politically naïve. He explains clearly what his charge allows him to do as well as what it prohibits. He recognizes that he will probably be captured, and he is willing "to carry the cross" for his religion and, if necessary, "to die upon your pikes." Many of his fellow priests shared these same attitudes and suffered the frightening consequences, but Campion goes beyond his colleagues in what might be described as his academic cast of mind. That is, when asked to respond quickly in a crisis, his mind turned immediately to propose an academic solution: let all differences be disputed publicly. This method was, of course, the traditional practice at the universities, where disputations were a time-honored part of the educational system.[54] Young scholars studied rhetoric and learned the strategies of

---

[53] For more detailed commentary, see Peter Milward, *Religious Controversies of the Elizabethan Age: A Survey of the Printed Sources* (Lincoln: University of Nebraska Press, 1977), pp. 54–56; Southern, *Elizabethan Recusant Prose*, pp. 148–60; and J. H. Pollen, S.J., "Blessed Edmund Campion's 'Challenge,'" *The Month* 115 (1910): 50–65.

[54] For example, A. L. Rowse comments: "The method of disputation still pre-

argumentation and persuasion. They attended disputations regularly and gradually came to take part in them. The Elizabethan Statutes of 1564–65, for example, redefined rules for them, and in 1574 Leicester, then chancellor at Oxford, reminded the Masters of their importance. Although the rules for disputations were modified over the years, it was customary for a respondent to defend his thesis in a half-hour presentation before being questioned by one or more opponents. To be sure, colorful rhetoric and youthful enthusiasm often substituted for profound thought in these academic exercises, but the disputations allowed the young scholars to show their intellectual wares in a public forum where even the losers came away better prepared for the next encounter. In time, of course, the young scholars grew into confident, articulate graduates, fully prepared to defend their views in the pulpits and at the courts of law as well as in Parliament. So intricately were disputations a part of formal university training that they were included among the entertainments provided for Elizabeth when she visited her two universities, and by them Campion himself had first come to her attention. On the occasion of her visit to Oxford in 1566 he was respondent to the topics of whether the tides are caused by the moon's motion and of whether lower bodies of the universe are regulated by the higher.

Indeed, with regard to disputations, the academic way at this time was also the way of the world. Martin Luther and John Eck, for example, had debated about papal authority for weeks at Leipzig in 1519.[55] In England, the Westminster Disputations of 1559 between English Catholics and Protestants, dealing with ceremonies and the Mass, were allowed by Queen Elizabeth and her Council.[56] And in the same year John Jewel, bishop of Salisbury, issued his famous challenge to the Catholics to disprove his objections to Roman Catholicism from the early Fathers, church councils, scriptures, and the practices of the primitive church during the first six centuries. In 1566, when Campion was disputing in public before Elizabeth at

---

vailed and was the royal road to success—sometimes proved to be so in the presence of the Queen . . ." (*The England of Elizabeth: The Structure of Society* [New York: Macmillan, 1957], p. 521).

[55] Donald J. Ziegler, ed., *Great Debates of the Reformation* (New York: Random House, 1969), pp. 3–31.

[56] See, for example, W. H. Frere, *The English Church in the Reigns of Elizabeth and James I (1558–1625)* (London: Macmillan, 1904), pp. 23–25.

Oxford, Jewel was still engaged in his long-term written disputations with Thomas Harding. The Jewel–Harding controversy continued for years and drew in others on both sides, including Alexander Nowell, who later disputed with Campion at the Tower.[57]

Thus, Campion's challenge for public disputations was not new; nor was the forum of a public debate looked upon as a radical or unacceptable procedure for addressing problems and resolving differences. However, because of his political naïveté, or perhaps because of his natural openness of mind, Campion either did not realize or was unwilling to admit that the time for debate about religious matters in England had long passed; but he would soon learn that if there were to be any disputations, they would be carefully controlled and the outcome predetermined.

The government's initial reaction to his proposal was not long delayed. Thinking that Campion's "Challenge" was part of a larger and more dangerous Catholic conspiracy, the authorities adopted new repressive measures against the recusants. Catholics were watched with greater care, and many were imprisoned at their own expense in newly designated castle-prisons throughout the country.[58] The most influential were confined in Wisbech Castle, where they were forced to join in common prayer each day, attend sermons twice a week, and confer twice a week with Protestant divines. Prisoners were permitted to speak with one another only at meals, and reading materials were carefully restricted to the Bible, the Fathers, and those works approved by the Protestants. Offenders were fined and placed under stricter watch. In addition to these repressive measures aimed mainly at the influential clergy, many of the nobility, the heads of old Catholic families, were summoned to London for questioning, and an intensive search was begun for priests, especially Campion.

Catholic Missionary Activity

While the authorities filled English prisons with Catholics, Campion and Persons traveled separately throughout most of the country for

[57] For an account of the Jewel–Harding controversy and others drawn into it, see Milward, *Religious Controversies of the Elizabethan Age*, pp. 1–24.

[58] For accounts of Catholic prisoners and prison conditions, see John Morris, S.J., *The Troubles of Our Catholic Forefathers Related by Themselves*, 3 vols. (London: Burns &

a few months, preaching, saying Mass, administering the sacraments, counseling the laity, and winning converts. Of course, precautions were necessary. Each was usually accompanied by a young man from the district they visited who assisted them in gaining entrance to a gentleman's home. Because of the large number of government informers, the Jesuits would usually stay only overnight at each house before moving on early the next morning. Both Campion and Persons report the courtesy and courage of their many hosts and the success of their missionary efforts.

By October 1580, both young Jesuits were back in London to confer once again and exchange the results of their missionary activities. Because the government's search for Campion had grown more intense, they moved outside the city to a home near Uxbridge. Campion reported on his travels in Berkshire, Oxfordshire, and Northhampton. Persons recounted his in Gloucestershire, Herefordshire, Worcestershire, and Derbyshire.

Encouraged by their success, the two made plans for their next mission. Because Catholics in Lancashire had requested that Campion visit them, it was decided that he should go there. The area, far from London, was strong in Catholic sympathies; and it was a place where books would be available for him to prepare a reply to the Protestant attacks on his "Challenge" which, they expected, would certainly be forthcoming. He was also urged to write something to the universities. Both these intentions—that is, to answer anticipated attacks on his "Challenge" and to write something more scholarly to the universities—Campion eventually fulfilled in his book *Rationes Decem*. Persons, it was agreed, could best carry on their work in the London area. Other priests in the group were sent to the universities and to Scotland.

While Campion went off to the North, Persons established ties with Catholics in London, including Mendoza, the Spanish ambassador. In October and November the Council issued new proclamations that intensified the search for the Jesuits and forced Persons to move frequently from house to house in order to avoid capture. Some of his fellow priests were taken. In the course of the next few months, Ralph Sherwin, Thomas Cottam, and Luke Kirby joined

Oates, 1872–77); and E. D. Pendry, *Elizabethan Prisons and Prison Scenes*, 2 vols. (Salzburg, Austria: Institut für Englische Sprache und Literatur, Universität Salzburg, 1974).

James Bosgrave and John Hart in prison.[59] Persons, however, escaped the traps of his pursuers and set up a printing press outside London, which he and Campion had decided they would need if they were to publish answers to the written attacks of their Protestant opponents.[60] Persons had not long to wait. Two books, one by William Charke and another by Meredith Hanmer, soon appeared and, in Campion's absence, were answered by Persons in his *Brief Censure*.[61] Soon after, Persons published a second book defending the practices at the English seminaries at Rome and Rheims against the charges brought against them by John Nichols, who claimed to have been a former scholar of the pope's.[62]

While Persons supervised the Jesuit mission in the London area, Campion made his way successfully through a network of government informers to Lancashire. Accompanied by Gervase Pierrepoint, he visited the house of his guide's brother around Christmas before moving on to the house of Henry Sacheverell and to houses in Derbyshire. Then with a new guide, Mr. Tempest, he continued through Yorkshire in January and February. Campion's longest stay at any of these houses appears to have been for about two weeks at the house of Mr. William Harrington of Mount St. John, where he probably wrote most of *Rationes Decem*, a short scholarly book in which he presents ten general reasons in defense of the truths of the Roman

---

[59] For biographies of Sherwin and Kirby, see *Cause of the Canonization*, pp. xxxviii–xli, and 233–365. For biographies of Cottam, Bosgrave, and Hart, see Foley, *Records*, 2:145–77.

[60] Censorship laws, which were strictly enforced in sixteenth-century England, made the publication, importation, and distribution of Catholic books extremely difficult and very dangerous. Catholics, however, found ways to skirt the laws and, on occasions, to escape the dangers. On this matter, see Southern, *Elizabethan Recusant Prose*, pp. 30–43, and 338–63. For a listing of Catholic publications, see A. F. Allison and D. M. Rogers, *A Catalogue of Catholic Books in English Printed Abroad or Secretly in England, 1558–1640* (Bognor Regis: The Arundel Press, 1956); and both volumes of their *Contemporary Printed Literature of the English Counter-Reformation Between 1558 and 1640*.

[61] See *An answere to a seditious pamphlet lately cast abroade by a Iesuite, with a discoverie of that blasphemous sect, By William Charke.* 1580 [STC 5005]; and *The great bragge and challenge of M. Champion a Jesuite, commonlye called Edmunde Campion, latelye arriued in Englande, contayninge nyne articles here severallye laide downe, directed by him to the Lordes of the Counsail, confuted & answered by Meredith Hanmer, M of Art, and Student in Divinitie.* 1581 [STC 12745].

[62] For accounts of works by Charke, Hanmer, Persons, and Nichols, see Milward, *Religious Controversies of the Elizabethan Age*, pp. 51–56.

Catholic Church.[63] With Mr. More, a former Oxford student, and his wife, Campion passed on into Lancashire, where he visited the houses of a number of prominent Catholics. He preached to large congregations, held private conferences, and revised his book.

When Campion finished his book around Easter (March 26, 1580), he sent it to Persons in London so that his numerous marginal references could be checked for accuracy. Persons delegated the task to Thomas Fitzherbert, who had free access to London libraries, and requested Campion to return to London to oversee the printing of his book.[64] About mid-May Campion left Lancashire for London. In the meantime Alexander Briant, a close friend of Persons's, had been captured in London and imprisoned at Marshalsea, where, deprived of food and water, he was questioned about Persons. When Briant remained silent, he was transferred to the Tower and racked so mercilessly that he became insensitive to pain.[65]

Campion's *Rationes Decem*

Informed of Briant's arrest and also of the capture of one of his workmen, Persons transferred his press to a lodge in Dame Cecilia Stonor's Park near Henley, where Campion's *Rationes Decem* was finally printed in time for distribution by William Hartley at commencement exercises at Oxford, June 27, 1581.[66] There, copies of the slim volume were secretly placed on the benches at St. Mary's Church for the students.

While commencement was in progress, the students read Campion's book. They read his account of how he had challenged his opponents to dispute their differences publicly. Instead of accepting his challenge, Campion maintained, his opponents pretended to answer it by personal attack, by calling him arrogant, a Jesuit, and a traitor.

[63] Foley (*Records*, 3: 670) identifies Tempest as the brother-in-law of William Harrington of Mount St. John.

[64] See ibid., 2: 198–230, for a brief account of Fitzherbert's life.

[65] See ibid., 4: 343–67. for a brief account of Briant's life.

[66] The fullest account of the Stonor family, including its involvement in the printing of Campion's *Rationes Decem*, is Robert Julian Stonor's *Stonor: A Catholic Sanctuary in the Chilterns from the Fifth Century Till To-day*, 2nd ed. (Newport, Mon.: R. H. Johns, 1952).

Thus, he explained, it became necessary for him to express his arguments in writing when denied the opportunity to deliver them openly in public debate. His ten reasons follow.

Campion's ten reasons or arguments are intended to prove the falseness of Protestantism and the truth of the Roman Catholic Church. His first argument deals with the scriptures. He charges that, like the old heretics, the new Lutherans, Calvinists, and Protestants omit those parts of the scriptures that do not comport with their doctrinal positions. In the second he asserts that Protestants distort the meanings of scriptural texts in order to fit their purposes. In the third, dealing with the nature of the church, Campion states that Protestants pretend to accept the authority of the church but define "church" in such a way that it loses all rational meaning. In the fourth, he charges that if Protestants accept the teachings of four church councils, they must accept the authority of the pope, the Mass, the invocation of saints, and clerical celibacy. He points out in the fifth that the teachings of the Fathers do not support Protestantism. In the sixth, he demonstrates how Protestants reject the scriptural commentaries of the Fathers that do not conform with their interpretations. In the seventh he shows how the history of the church will not support the doctrines espoused by Protestants. The eighth reason consists of a collection of offensive Protestant sayings, such as, God is the author of sin; Christ despaired; and good works are mortal sins in God's sight. The ninth reason deals with the alleged general weakness of Protestant arguments, as, for example, the use of the text "marriage is honorable" to reject celibacy. In his tenth and final reason, Campion maintains that virtually everything Christian argues in support of and makes plain the truth of the Roman Catholic Church: heaven, hell, apostolic succession, episcopal succession, doctors and pastors, princes and kings. He calls upon Elizabeth to join with her royal ancestors and with the past great monarchs of the world in supporting the Roman Catholic Church. Historical evidence of Catholicism, he claims, is everywhere evident: at the universities, the signs of houses and the gates of towns, coronation rituals, vestments and church windows, and the lives of their ancestors. He concludes by urging his readers to accept the truth of the Roman Catholic Church and to reject gold, glory, and pleasure.[67]

[67] For an account of *Rationes Decem* and contemporaneous publications associated

Although *Rationes Decem* is perhaps as much the work of a rhetorician as a biblical scholar, and was obviously intended for a broader audience than university theologians, it apparently succeeded in providing English Catholics with a public explanation and defense of their religious beliefs. At the same time, it forced a response from the government. For quite different reasons, it also made Campion the most celebrated and sought-after Jesuit in England by both Catholics and Protestants alike.[68]

Campion Captured, Imprisoned, Tortured, and Accused of Exposing Benefactors

During the actual printing of *Rationes Decem* and for about a week after its distribution at Oxford, Campion made occasional visits to Catholic houses near Stonor Park until July 11, 1581, when he and Persons parted for what would prove to be the last time. Persons had decided to return again to London. Campion and Brother Ralph Emerson planned to return to Lancashire to collect books and papers before proceeding to Norfolk. Almost as an afterthought, Campion asked Persons's permission to visit the house of Mr. Yate at Lyford, near Oxford. Yate, in prison at the time, had requested that Campion visit his family. Because Yate's house was well known to the authorities as a gathering place for Catholics, Persons was reluctant at first to grant permission but eventually relented when Campion agreed to stay at Lyford only one day. Fearing that Campion might be persuaded to remain longer, Persons made Brother Ralph his superior.

At Lyford, Campion was graciously received as an honored guest by Mrs. Yate and by the two priests and eight Brigittine nuns who lived with her. After holding conferences, hearing confessions, saying Mass, and preaching a sermon, Campion, with Brother Ralph, set out on July 12 for Lancashire. The two had traveled only as far as an inn near Oxford when they were overtaken by a group of Catholics who had arrived at Lyford after his departure and were disappointed to learn that they had missed him. They urged Campion to return

with it, see Milward, *Religious Controversies of the Elizabethan Age*, pp. 56–59; and for an excellent translation, see Joseph Rickaby, trans., *Campion's Ten Reasons*, with an introduction by J. H. Pollen (London: Manresa Press, 1914).

[68] See, for example, Strype, *Aylmer*, pp. 31–36.

to Lyford for a few days. Campion refused at first, explaining that he must obey his superiors, Persons and Brother Ralph. The group immediately turned on Ralph and eventually persuaded him to allow Campion to return to Lyford while Ralph went on to gather the books in Lancashire.

Campion was back at Lyford the next day, July 14, 1581, where a group of Catholics had assembled to receive him. On Sunday, July 16, he preached a sermon to a large congregation that included Oxford students. Also among those present was George Eliot, a former Catholic who had turned informer. Eliot had been on Campion's trail for some time and carried a warrant for his arrest. Having gained admission to the house through one of the servants who had known him when he was a Catholic, Eliot attended Campion's Mass and sermon, waiting his chance. After the service, he left the house immediately and returned soon after with a company of deputies. They surrounded the house, cutting off all ways of escape. Campion and his two fellow priests, Thomas Ford and John Collington, were hastily hidden in a secret priest-hole in a wall over the gateway while Eliot and his men searched the house for the rest of the day, sounding the walls and floors but finding nothing.[69] During the night, when it seemed certain that the searchers would give up and leave the next day, Campion and the two priests were moved to another hiding place just off Mrs. Yate's bedroom. But the move proved to be a mistake, for the next morning when the searchers were at the point of leaving, Eliot broke into a wall over the stairs and found their hiding place. Inside the tiny priest-hole were Campion, Ford, and Collington.[70]

Campion was detained for three days at Lyford while his captors awaited orders from the Council. Finally, instructions arrived advising them to bring him and the other prisoners under strong guard to London. After stops at Abington and Henley, the company was further ordered to stay the night of Friday, July 21, at Colebrook, ten

[69] Many homes of Catholic aristocrats had priest-holes. Nicholas Owen (see Foley, *Records*, 2:245–67) built many of them but was eventually captured and so cruelly tortured that he died. For an account of these hiding places for priests, see the series of articles by Michael Hodgetts, "Elizabethan Priest-Holes," *Recusant History* 1 (1972): 279–98; 2 (1973): 99–119; 3 (1974): 171–97; 4 (1975): 18–55; and 5 (1976): 254–79.

[70] For written accounts of Campion's capture and subsequent fate, see Milward, *Religious Controversies of the Elizabethan Age*, pp. 61–63.

miles from London, so that they could enter London on Saturday, a market day, and the prisoners could be paraded before throngs of people. Accordingly, the next day Campion, a paper stuck in his cap on which was written "Campion the Seditious Jesuit," was escorted through the city streets of London to the Tower, where he was turned over to the custody of Sir Owen Hopton, Lieutenant of the Tower.[71]

Campion spent his first four days at the Tower in a tiny 4′ x 4′ cell named "Little-ease," a cubical so small that a man could neither stand nor lie at length. In the evening of the fourth day, July 25, he was released from Little-ease and taken secretly by boat to Leicester's house, where he was met by Leicester, the Earl of Bedford, two secretaries, and Queen Elizabeth herself.[72] To their questions about his mission in England, he answered that his only purpose was the salvation of souls. Elizabeth offered him liberty and preferment if he would recant, but Campion refused.

When he was returned to the Tower after his interview with Elizabeth, Campion was at first treated more kindly by Owen Hopton, who apparently hoped to advance himself by converting such a famous Jesuit. With premature confidence and perhaps with intent to dishearten the Catholics, Hopton allowed reports to circulate about London that Campion was on the point of rejecting Catholicism and would soon preach a sermon favoring Protestantism at St. Paul's Cross. Within a few days, however, Hopton learned that his arguments and promises of rewards had no effect on his prisoner. When persuasion failed, the Council turned to force. On July 30 an order was sent to Hopton that Campion and certain of his fellows were to be interrogated. The order included a set of specific questions dealing with his allegiance to the queen, as well as a complete list of

[71] The numerous references to Owen Hopton in *Acts of the Privy Council* (vols. 7–23) reveal his various duties as Lieutenant of the Tower. See especially 13: 144–45, and passim, for his dealings with Campion. The fullest biographical account of Hopton and his family may be found in an unpublished, eight-volume typescript entitled *Yoxford Yesterday* by Robert Parr at the Suffolk Record Office, Ipswich, Suffolk. See 2:1–39.

[72] Campion himself alludes to his interview with Elizabeth at his trial. See *A Complete Collection of State Trials and Proceedings for High Treason and Other Crimes and Misdemeanors from the Earliest Period to the Year 1783, with Notes and Other Illustrations*, compiled by T. B. Howell, 21 vols. (London, 1816–1828), 1:1052. Future references to this work will be cited as Howell, *State Trials*.

questions about his friends, hosts, and activities in England. If Campion refused to answer, he was to be racked. The rack, a wooden bed-like frame on which a prisoner was tied by the ankles and wrists and then stretched, was one of the most painful and frequently used torture devices in the Tower. Campion must have refused to answer their questions, for, soon after the order, he was racked, either at the end of July or at the beginning of August.

Campion's Alleged Confession

What Campion confessed or did not confess on the rack has remained a mystery.[73] The authorities, anxious to discredit him, reported that he had confessed all, and they made efforts to substantiate their claim publicly by ordering a series of arrests of those Catholics who, they charged, had dealings with him or had received him into their homes. Some information that the Council had gathered about his travels and activities, including names and dates, seemed accurate. As a result of these arrests, which included such dignitaries as Lord Vaux, Sir Thomas Tresham, and Sir William Catesby, Campion's reputation as the public spokesman for English Catholics was seriously damaged.[74] In the course of two weeks after his first racking, from August 4 to August 18, scores of Catholics were arrested and questioned by the authorities about their associations with Campion and about other matters. At the time, many Catholics must have believed that their Jesuit hero had betrayed them, and the government did much to encourage this belief.

---

[73] The most complete source of official information about Campion's treatment at the Tower and about orders for the arrest and questioning of Catholics, especially during the month of August 1581, may be found in *Acts of the Privy Council*, 13:144ff. The *Calendar of State Papers, Domestic, Elizabeth, 1581–1590* also contains reports about Campion and the Catholics associated with him as late as 1587, six years after his death.

Strype lists Campion's hosts in two places: *Parker*, 2:166–67, and *Annals*, 2.2. 358–60. For Simpson's account, see *Life of Edmund Campion*, pp. 264ff. Many regional histories, such as Haigh, *Reformation and Resistance in Tudor Lancashire*, pp. 9, 251 and passim, contain information about Campion's hosts. Also, most of Campion's Lancashire hosts are identified in "Lord Burghley's Map of Lancashire, 1590," *C.R.S., Miscellanea*, IV: 162–222.

[74] For an account of the trial of Vaux, Tresham, and Catesby as well as Campion's alleged confessions and Catholic reactions, see Godfrey Anstruther, *Vaux of Harrowden* (Newport, Mon.: R. H. Johns, 1953), pp. 115–40.

The matter is not at all clear, however. It must be kept in mind that virtually all the information we have about Campion after he was imprisoned in the Tower on July 22 until he appeared in public at the first disputation on August 31 was provided by the authorities, and the completeness of their reports must be suspect. Because Campion was a prize catch, it would be naïve to assume that once the authorities had tried and failed to win him over to their side they would subsequently report anything favorable about him, and the surest way to do the most damage to the Catholic cause would be to portray him as an informer.

Still, one must account for the fact that so many Catholics were arrested immediately after Campion was racked. Although no conclusive evidence has as yet appeared to resolve this issue, certain arguments in defense of Campion's integrity seem evident. First, we must not lose sight of the fact that long before Campion's capture the names of prominent Catholics had already been made known to the authorities by church officials and by government spies; but the government, unwilling to stir up more religious turmoil than was necessary, and hopeful that the Catholics would eventually conform, had refrained from imposing the harshest penalties.[75] Campion's arrival on the scene, however, forced a change in their strategy. Second, Campion was not the only Catholic prisoner interrogated. Many other Catholics had also been questioned, and it is entirely possible that other prisoners may have provided some of the information that the government had attributed to Campion.[76] Indeed, some of those questioned who had firsthand knowledge about Campion's activities recanted and were released. Third, by the time of Campion's capture, the authorities had developed rather sophisticated methods of interrogation. For example, because prisoners were isolated from one another and questioned privately, the authorities were at liberty to deceive one prisoner into believing that another had already given the pertinent facts and that they sought only corroboration. Thus, a

---

[75] See, for example, Conyers Read's account of the government's plan to deal with Catholics in 1577 in *Mr. Secretary Walsingham and the Policy of Queen Elizabeth*, 3 vols. (Oxford: Clarendon Press, 1925), 2:280ff. Also, note that ecclesiastical commissions had been established to ensure that laws regarding religion were followed. See Henry N. Birt, *The Elizabethan Religious Settlement* (London: G. Bell, 1907), pp. 209ff.

[76] Both Gervase and Henry Pierrepoint, for example, were questioned and apparently confessed. See Strype, *Annals*, 2.2.358.

prisoner, stretched on the rack or pressed into a ball with a torture device called the "Scavenger's Daughter" and confronted with accurate details about himself and events that he knew had already been fully or partially reported, could hardly be expected to deny them, especially when assured that no harm would come to anyone as a result of his testimony. Indeed, the methods of interrogation that invited Campion to confirm or to deny the confessions of his fellow Catholic prisoners would have forced him into the dilemma of revealing either one group of his friends or another. Furthermore, it is quite possible that the confessions of other Catholics that he had been asked to corroborate may have been only partial ones which, if he denied, would have led to reexaminations of his fellow prisoners and would have resulted in even further disclosures. Finally, in addition to the terrors of the rack and the tricks of the interrogators, the dehumanizing effects that prolonged periods of isolation produce on prisoners are well enough known.[77] Campion may indeed have confessed all, as the government claimed. But if he had, why was it necessary to rack him twice more after his alleged full confession? And why were his confessions not produced or published? Although all these possible circumstances may neither prove nor disprove that Campion gave all or some of the information that the authorities claimed, they establish an element of serious doubt about the fullness and accuracy of the government reports.

Other evidence, events, and circumstances provide additional reasons for doubt. For example, on August 6, four days after the authorities received information about Campion's missionary itinerary and two days after the first arrests were ordered, Burghley wrote two pertinent letters.[78] In the first, to Lord Shrewsbury, he states that though Campion was apprehended, "He denieth to any question of moment. . . ." In the second, to Walsingham in Paris, he reports that "a number of choice" Catholics had been arrested, but he does not say that Campion had betrayed them. A second point worth noting is that the authorities would not allow Campion to be questioned

[77] Campion's treatment at the Tower, one may assume, was not entirely unlike that of John Gerard. See his *The Autobiography of an Elizabethan*, trans. by Philip Caraman, with an introduction by Graham Greene (London: Longmans, Green, 1951).

[78] For an account of these two letters, see Simpson, *Life of Edmund Campion*, pp. 345–46.

publicly about his alleged confessions. Sir Thomas Tresham, when ordered to swear that Campion had not been at his house, asked to see Campion and to hear him speak before taking any oath. His request was denied. Again, according to the Protestant version of the first debate at the Tower (*A true report*), Campion was asked if while on the rack he had been questioned "upon any point of religion." He answered that he had been urged "to confess in what places he had been conversant since his repair into the realm." Beale, a clerk of the Council who had asked the question and who had also been one of his examiners at the Tower, explained that the question had been posed because many priests "had reconciled divers of her Highness' subjects to the Romish Church." Campion's reply to Beale was that, like the Christians of old who refused to give over their religious books to their persecutors, "he might not betray his Catholic brethren, which were (as he said) the Temples of the Holy Ghost."[79] If Campion had, in fact, betrayed his "brethren," this occasion would have been an ideal time for his opponents to confront him publicly with his alleged past disclosures, for those who were present at the racking and who had been commended by the Council for supposedly having extracted a confession from him (Beale, Hammond, Hopton, and Norton) were also present at this disputation.[80] Their silence is conspicuous, and Campion's own failure to elaborate on this point suggests further that at this time he may not have been fully aware that government reports charging him with betraying his friends had seriously damaged his reputation. It should be further noted that the Council's list of places where Campion stayed is surprisingly incomplete. For example, the places he visited with Gervase Pierrepoint, who was also examined, are specified, but the Council could discover no more about his travels with Mr. Tempest than that they had visited inns. One naturally wonders why the confessions of a man who had, reportedly, told all are not more consistent.

---

[79] See *A true report*, C2. A few pages later (C4) when Nowell and Day offer to send to Oxford for his books, assuring him that the person who had them would not be endangered, Campion refused the offer. The reader will note that in the Catholic (Tresham) version of the first debate Campion also vigorously denies that he has betrayed "the places and persons with whom he had conversed with as concerning the Catholic cause. . . . I ought to suffer anything rather than to betray the bodies of those that ministered necessaries to supply my lack."

[80] For brief biographies of Beale, Hammond, and Norton, see *DNB*.

At his public trial on November 20, 1581, the topic of his confessions was briefly considered. The following excerpt from a letter that he is reported to have written to Thomas Pounde in the Tower was read into evidence by the clerk: "It grieveth me much to have offended the Catholic cause so highly as to confess the names of some gentlemen and friends in whose houses I had been entertained; yet in this I greatly cherish and comfort myself that I never discovered any secrets there declared, and that I will not, come rack, come rope."[81]

The prosecution introduced this excerpt in order to prove that the "secrets" Campion had refused to reveal must have been plots against the state and, therefore, treasonable offenses. Campion, however, answered that the "secrets" had been simply the private confessions of Catholics, which by priestly vow he was forbidden to reveal. For our current purposes, the point of this excerpt from the no-longer-extant letter is that Campion did not deny having revealed "some" of his benefactors when publicly charged with it. Richard Simpson's explanation, although plausible, is not entirely convincing. He believes that if Campion had denied revealing his benefactors at his trial, the government would have begun a new search and "would have subjected the whole Catholic society to endless annoyance."[82]

The final words on the issue of whether or not Campion betrayed his friends may be Campion's own. An anonymous account of his execution, probably written by Thomas Alfield, a seminary priest, reports that when Campion was about to die on the scaffold at Tyburn, he requested forgiveness from those whose names he had given to the authorities.[83] Assuming that this account is accurate, there seems little doubt that Campion provided some information which, at least by hindsight, he himself viewed as improper. Yet the question remains whether it was a full disclosure, as the authorities claimed, no disclosure at all, as Simpson argues, or a partial disclosure, perhaps within one or more of the various contexts described above. Although obviously incomplete and somewhat contradictory, the available evidence seems to suggest a very limited and highly

[81] Howell, *State Trials*, 1:1060.

[82] Simpson, *Life of Edmund Campion*, p. 442.

[83] For an account of Alfield, see, "Life and Martyrdom of Thomas Alfield," *Rambler*, N.S., 7 (1857): 420–31.

qualified disclosure. Whatever the truth may be, this still unresolved matter remains the only shortcoming with which Campion has ever been seriously charged.

Debates at the Tower of London

Campion's first public appearance after his imprisonment on July 22 occurred more than a month later when, on August 31, he appeared in the Tower church (or chapel) before a crowd of spectators to debate with two distinguished Protestant divines.[84] When he saw the large gathering, Campion must have thought that his challenge to meet with learned doctors in public debate had finally been accepted by the authorities; but he would soon discover that extraordinary restrictions had been attached, restrictions which he could not have anticipated. In effect, he would find that the public debate he had requested would prove to be less a public debate than a carefully controlled semi-private interrogation.

In all, there were a total of four debates and, focusing as they do on some of the central doctrinal issues that divided the Roman Catholic and Protestant churches, they drew widespread attention not only in England but also on the Continent. Word-of-mouth reports and written pamphlet accounts of each circulated immediately in England and shortly thereafter on the Continent. That these accounts of the debates continued to attract attention long after the debates had ended is attested to by the fact that the government authorities felt obliged to direct the publication of an official version of them, entitled *A true report*, as late as three years after Campion's execution.[85] The publication of all Catholic accounts was, of course, prohibited in England, but manuscript copies of them had circulated at least as far as Rome.[86] Both William Allen and Paolo Bombino, for

[84] There is some uncertainty about the actual site of the first debate, because two chapels/churches are located at the Tower. St. John's, the rather small royal chapel, is located in the White Tower; and St. Peter ad Vincula, the larger parish church (or chapel), is across the Tower courtyard from White Tower. The manuscripts refer to the site of the first debate as both chapel and parish church. The large number of people present, however, suggests that the first debate was held in St. Peter's.

[85] For the full title of *A true report*, see above, p. xi, n. 1.

[86] For detailed accounts of the manuscript copies, see Appendix E.

example, stated an intent to publish accounts but neither did, although Bombino and other Catholic writers included excerpts from them in their writings. Thus, the authorized Protestant edition, *A true report*, now a rare book, remains the only published version of the debates.

For the first time on August 31 and again on September 18, 23, and 27, these day-long debates between Campion and three different pairs of Protestant clergymen were held at the Tower of London.[87] Before the debates were scheduled, Campion's Protestant opponents had met privately in conference to plan their strategy and prepare their arguments.[88] Each debate, it was determined, would last approximately six hours, from 8 to 11 A.M., and from 2 to 5 P.M. The general format decided upon by the Protestants and imposed upon Campion was that he would be examined on statements he had made in his *Rationes Decem*. On each of the four days he faced two opponents who posed questions for him to answer. The format further stipulated that Campion would not be permitted to ask questions or to introduce any topics himself; nor would be given access to or allowed the use of books to prepare his answers. In fact, as events proved, he was given little or no advance notice about the number of debates, about when or where a debate might be scheduled or held, about what the topics for questioning might be, or about the opponents he would face. Government notaries, sitting between Campion and his opponents, would be appointed to record all statements.

Of course, as Campion reminded his adversaries on several later occasions, such arrangements for debates were grossly unfair to him and were certainly not the kind he had requested in his "Challenge." He had asked to meet his adversaries in open debate at Cambridge or Oxford. In spite of his repeated objections, however, as a prisoner in the Tower, he was in no position to protest, to negotiate, or to expect fair treatment. The religious issues at stake for the English clergy and their political consequences for the English government were too important to be left to chance remarks at an open debate.

---

[87] For Simpson's account of the debates, see *Life of Edmund Campion*, pp. 363–79.

[88] For Bishop Aylmer's involvement, see Strype, *Aylmer*, pp. 31–36. In *Whitgift* (pp. 195–96) Strype also includes a statement, signed by a number of prominent clergymen, about recommended procedures on how best to deal with Campion.

First Debate

The first disputation, on Thursday, August 31, 1581, differs significantly from the following three in ways that deserve our attention. First, because the first debate was held in the chapel at the Tower, a sizable and diverse audience could be accommodated, one that would surely include Catholic sympathizers. The selection of the chapel also suggests that Campion's first opponents, Alexander Nowell and William Day, were rather confident about the outcome. A large audience, they must have calculated, would allow reports of their victory to spread quickly. Second, at this disputation a number of Campion's fellow Catholic prisoners were allowed to be present with him. Their presence testifies further to Protestant confidence, and it also created the appearance of generosity. That is, Campion's Protestant opponents would appear to allow him whatever assistance he could get from a group of his fellow Catholics. Finally, the published version of the first debate was prepared by Nowell and Day themselves, who state that they reconstructed their summary account both from notes and memory and also from conferences with others. They make no mention of consulting the official transcripts of the notary.

Many of these features of the first disputation were changed at the following three meetings in September. The location was shifted from the chapel to the much smaller private quarters of the Lieutenant of the Tower, Owen Hopton, presumably to ensure greater control over the size and composition of the audience. Many reports about Nowell and Day at the first disputation had not been favorable. Indeed, the pamphlets claimed that Campion had won. Also, because Campion's fellow prisoners had been much more argumentatively aggressive than Nowell and Day had anticipated, they were excluded from the three subsequent meetings. At these, Campion sat alone and answered all questions himself from four new opponents: William Fulke and Roger Goade at the second and third meetings, and John Walker and William Charke at the fourth meeting. Finally, the authorized published accounts of the second, third, and fourth disputations were later gathered and edited (with separate title page) by John Field, a Cambridge divinity student, from the notary transcripts after the transcripts had first been reviewed, modified, and approved by the Protestant disputants. Thus, the published accounts of the second, third, and fourth days give the appearance of being verbatim accounts; but, as we know, they were not. Field admits to having cut Campion's answers.

While such manipulative tactics by the Protestants to gain every advantage must have offended the objective observer's sense of fairness, the arrangements for the debates seem not to have unduly troubled Campion's opponents; and, to compound the unfairness, Campion himself could do nothing to change them. However, in dealing directly with his adversaries, who sat across the table from him, and in responding to their questions he did exercise at least some degree of control. Indeed, given all the circumstances that worked against him, and given the impressive scholarly credentials of his opponents, Campion's performance at the first debate is remarkable.

Alexander Nowell and William Day were rather formidable adversaries for Campion and his fellow Catholic prisoners to meet at the first disputation. Nowell (1507?–1602), born in Lancashire and educated at Oxford (B.A. in 1526, M.A. in 1540), was highly respected by the leading church and state officials of his day as a theologian, scholar, preacher, and disputant. Burghley, the queen's chief adviser, had placed his name on a list of eminent divines worthy of preferment after Nowell returned from self-imposed exile at Frankfort on the accession of Elizabeth. As a consequence, Nowell served on many ecclesiastical commissions and held a number of ecclesiastical appointments, such as archdeacon at Canterbury and Westminster, before being appointed Dean of St. Paul's in London. He preached often at St. Paul's as well as before the queen, and he had earned a reputation for winning converts from Roman Catholicism. As a disputant he engaged in a written controversy with Thomas Dorman, who had attacked Jewel's *Apology*. As a theologian he produced well-known catechisms which in question-and-answer form explained the tenets of Protestant doctrine. These catechisms were widely used as texts for religious instruction in English schools and were translated and reprinted well into the nineteenth century. Although Nowell had been nominated to write a formal answer to Campion's *Rationes Decem*, the work was eventually written by his able nephew, William Whitaker, then Regius Professor of Divinity at Cambridge, who also served as a notary at the first disputation.[89]

---

[89] William Whitaker (1548–95) was the first to answer Campion's *Rationes Decem* in 1581 while Campion was still alive. His refutation is titled: *Ad Rationes Decem Edmundi Campiani Iesuitae, quibus fretus certamen Anglicanae ecclesiae ministris obtulit in*

William Day (1529–96), Campion's other opponent on the first day, was born in Shropshire and educated at Eton and at King's College, Cambridge, where he received his B.A. in 1549 and M.A. in 1553. He remained at Cambridge during Mary's reign, but after the accession of Elizabeth he was ordained deacon by Grindal in 1559 and priest the following year. Preferments soon followed, such as his appointment first as fellow and later (1562) as provost at Eton, where he had all traces of Roman Catholicism (for example, images, tabernacle, and rood screen) removed. He was an active participant on the side of the ultra-Protestants at Elizabeth's first convocation in 1563, and in the same year he was appointed canon at Windsor, where he preached before the queen. Later he received additional preferments, including appointment as Dean of Windsor in 1572. Although Day had actually written little, his academic appointments and his active participation in convocations earned him a reputation as a scholar and an able controversialist.

For purposes of comparison with the Catholic reports, the Nowell-Day version of what took place at the first debate is worth our review. In addition to their summary account of the argumentative exchanges, as published in *A true report*, Nowell and Day also provide some interesting supplementary information about the debate in the form of attached commentaries. One consists of introductory remarks addressed "To the Reader"; the other is an appendix that focuses mainly on refuting Catholic pamphlet accounts of the first debate.

In their introductory remarks, "To the Reader," in *A true report* (A2), Nowell and Day explain the circumstances that led to the publication of their version of the first disputation. They state that initially they had seen no reason to publish an account of it because at the meeting with Campion they had dealt with only a few points contained in his *Rationes Decem*, and since that meeting his book had

---

causa fidei Responsio Guilielmi Whitakeri Theologiae in Academia Cantabrigiensi professoris regii. 1581. At Burghley's urging, Bishop Aylmer had directed the Regius Professors of Divinity at Oxford (Laurence Humphrey) and Cambridge (Whitaker) to answer Campion. Humphrey published his elaborate answers in two parts (1582 and 1584) after Campion's death: *Iesuitismi pars prima: sive de Praxi Romanae Curiae contra respublicas et principes, et de nova legatione Iesuitarum in Angliam* . . . , 1582; and *Iesuitismi Pars Secunda: Puritanopapismi, seu doctrinae Iesuiticae aliquot Rationibus ab Ed. Campiano comprehensae* . . . , 1584. For full titles and brief commentaries, see Milward, *Religious Controversies of the Elizabethan Age*, pp. 56–59.

been fully answered by William Whitaker. Also, they felt that publication of their account could be viewed as unfair because Campion, having since died, would be unable to respond to it. However, as they explain further, because numerous Catholic reports of the disputation had falsely claimed that Campion had won, they were urged "by some of great authority" to publish an accurate account. Their summary account follows.

Although Nowell and Day insist that Catholic reports of the disputation were untrue and that Campion himself was such a weak opponent that they doubted he had actually written *Rationes Decem*, their own summary of the first debate in *A true report* is often surprisingly vague and conveniently selective, especially in view of all the documents available to them. For example, in addition to their own notes, which they report having recorded immediately after the disputation, they also had access to the transcript of the notary (Whitaker), to conferences with others who had been present, and to Whitaker's own elaborate refutation of *Rationes Decem*. They do, however, include accounts about the main points at issue.

As reported by Nowell and Day in *A true report* and confirmed in the Catholic manuscript version (Tresham MS), the first disputation dealt primarily with two topics that were of central importance during the Reformation both in England and on the Continent: (1) the canon of the Bible and (2) justification by faith alone. The morning session concentrated on the first; the afternoon, on the second. According to his own account, Nowell, who did most of the interrogating at the morning session, introduced the argument about the canon of the Bible by questioning Campion on his written statement in *Rationes Decem* that Martin Luther had rejected the Epistle of St. James. Nowell argued that no such statement could be found in editions of Luther's work, and he presented an edition for Campion to examine. After looking at it, Campion answered that it was a recent one, much revised by Luther's followers, and that he was willing to send to Germany for an earlier true edition of Luther in which the statement could be found. Although at that time Nowell and Day ridiculed Campion and charged him with lying, Whitaker later acknowledged that Campion had been correct.[90] The 1529 Jena edi-

[90] William Whitaker's reply to Campion's *Rationes Decem* was first translated by Richard Stocke (*An Answere to the Ten Reasons of Edmund Campian the Iesuit* . . .) in 1606 at the request of William Knowles. In this work Whitaker reluctantly admits

tion of Luther's works contained the words that Campion had quoted.[91] In their published account, Nowell and Day do not acknowledge their error.

Nowell's questioning of Campion about Luther's view of the Epistle of St. James was, however, only a small part of much larger problems. What books belonged in the canon of the Bible? What books were of doubtful authenticity and fell outside it? In both Protestant and Catholic versions, Campion argued that the Roman Catholic Church, acting through general councils, such as the Council of Trent, had the authority to establish the canon of the Bible. Nowell and Day disagreed and cited such authorities as Jerome, Eusebius, and Augustine to prove their position that certain books, including the Epistle of St. James, had been considered doubtful by some Doctors of the early church. They distinguished the books of the Bible in terms of their being canonical or apocryphal. Canonical books, the most authoritative, could be used to derive church doctrine. Those designated as apocryphal, or doubtful books, could be used only to establish manners. Both sides quoted numerous authorities to support their positions and disagreed, at times heatedly, on how the authorities—the Doctors, the church councils, and papal decrees—were to be understood.

As reported in both the Protestant and the Catholic versions, the afternoon session shifted the argument from the canon of the Bible to the topic of justification by "faith alone." The crux of this issue centered on whether or not a person could be justified by faith alone or by faith and other virtues (for example, charity). Nowell and Day argued for the former view; Campion and the Catholics, for the latter. Nowell and Day based their arguments on scriptural passages

in a marginal note (p. 29) that Luther had indeed called the Epistle of St. James "strawie" in the 1529 Jena edition. Stocke's translation of *Rationes Decem* is the first to appear in English, and it demonstrates that Campion's work was still controversial in 1606. It is also interesting to note that in the same year (1606) Thomas Dekker based one of his dramatic characters (Campiani) on Campion in his drama *The Whore of Babylon*.

[91] For a brief review of Luther's comments on the Epistle of St. James, see Martin Dibelius, *A Commentary on the Epistle of James*, rev. by Heinrich Greeven, trans. by Michael A. Williams (Philadelphia: Fortress Press, 1976), pp. 54–56. This issue about Luther's view of the Epistle of St. James must have been an embarrassment to Nowell and Day, for by raising it at the first debate they showed either that they had not carefully researched their argument or, worse yet, that they had deliberately suppressed factual information.

and on commentaries by the early Church Fathers that emphasized the efficacy of Christ's passion and the sinful nature of man. That is, because Christ's passion and death had been entirely sufficient to redeem us, Nowell and Day maintained that we did not earn our salvation. Christ had already earned it for us. Thus, justification was given to us as a free gift from a merciful God if we would but believe. The Catholics, often using the same passages from scripture and the same commentaries by the Fathers, answered that faith, although essential, must also be complemented by other virtues, such as hope and charity, in order for a person to be saved. While not denying the importance of faith, or the efficacy of Christ's sacrifice, or the mercy of God, the Catholics urged the special value of a person's good works. Nowell and Day, like Luther, relied heavily for proof on St. Paul's insistence on the importance of faith; Campion and the Catholics cited the Epistle of St. James, which emphasizes the importance of good works. The two sides, of course, not only referred to many other scriptural passages and to biblical commentators in support of their positions, but also interpreted the same passages in quite different ways. The reader may judge the merits of their respective arguments and interpretations in the Tresham account.

Attached to the end of the published authorized version of the first day's disputation is a nine-page appendix (F3–G3) with the heading: "A brief recital of certain untruths scattered in the pamphlets, and libels of the papists, concerning the former conferences: with a short answer unto the same."[92] This appendix by Nowell and Day is of special interest not only because it contains additional information about the first debate but also because in attempting to rebut the Catholic positions it includes excerpts from contemporaneous Catholic pamphlets that had been circulated at the time but are no longer extant. It also includes a number of revealing personal observations about the disputants themselves.

In the appendix Nowell and Day list what they believe to be the principal false observations made against them in the Catholic pamphlets, including remarks about Campion's racking, sickness, lack of either notebooks or library, and their "sudden coming upon him." They defend themselves on the grounds that Campion, not they,

[92] A manuscript account of "A brief recital . . ." together with the second and part of the third disputations may be found in Harl. 1732, ff. 32–78.

had issued the "Challenge," that his recently published book, *Rationes Decem*, must have been fresh in his mind, that they had questioned him on only a few points at the beginning of it, and that they had provided him with all the books he cited. Campion's loud speeches and bold behavior, they contend, argued against his illness. Nor, they claim, did Campion himself complain about the conditions of their meeting. They answer the pamphlet charge that they had been discourteous to the Catholics by making the countercharge that Campion was so outrageous in behavior and speech that they were forced to admonish him, tactfully in Latin. They claim that Campion's fellow Catholics had also been unruly. In addition to censuring Thomas Pounde, whose mocking and scornful looks were obviously intended to distract them, they were forced to reprimand others for their shouting, muttering, and scornful laughter. Nowell and Day defend themselves against the particular pamphlet allegation that they had silenced Sherwin for talking too much by reminding the reader that they had been charged to question only Campion. And about Campion, they insist that he had not been "modest in his answering," as the pamphlets state, any more than he had been modest in his "Challenge" or in his book.

On the much-discussed personal issue of Campion's ability or inability to read and understand Greek, they cite two Catholic pamphlet accounts that assert that Campion, after first refusing to read the Greek text of St. Paul, later skillfully read aloud and explained clearly a passage in Greek from Basil. According to the Catholic pamphlets, when asked why he had not read the first passage from St. Paul, Campion answered that the print was too small. Nowell and Day deny the truth of these accounts, explaining that when Campion finally agreed to read the Greek text, he read it very quietly, as though to himself; and Stollard, who stood next to Campion, reported that he did not read well. In fact, as Nowell and Day point out, Campion may simply have repeated some of the Greek words that the ministers themselves had just read a few times aloud.

Nowell and Day continue their attack on the Catholic pamphlets by denying the reported erudition of Campion and Sherwin. They confess that, in view of reports about Campion's learning and scholarship evidenced in his book, they had been fearful before the disputation that they may well have been overmatched. At the actual disputation, however, they soon satisfied themselves that he was not the learned scholar they had expected, and they also speculate that he had probably not written *Rationes Decem*. The book, they believe, had been written earlier by learned Jesuits on the Continent and given to Campion. In addition, they hold Sherwin, who also refused to read a passage from the Greek Testament, in equally low regard. Although the pamphlets claimed that Sherwin had feigned ignorance or that he had been ordered previously to remain silent, Nowell and Day believe that he could not read Greek, but they chose not to make an issue of his ignorance.

In making their final point in the appendix, Nowell and Day return to the central issue debated in the afternoon session, the issue of "faith alone." According to one pamphlet account, the Catholics cited Augustine's *De fide et operibus*, chapter 14, as evidence against the "faith alone" doctrine of the Protestants, a charge that in the confusion of a noisy debate Nowell and Day claim they had let pass. The pamphlets asserted that this passage was most damaging to the Protestant position, for in it Augustine said that the doctrine of justification by faith only was a heresy in the apostles' time and that John, Peter, Jude, and James had written against it, emphasizing the importance of good works. Nowell and Day assert, however, that Augustine actually wrote against those who mistook Paul's words on justification "by faith without works" to mean that one could "neglect to live well." Nowell and Day insist that the Catholics are wrong in thinking that Protestants exclude everything except faith, for Protestants do not make "faith the chief and only cause of our justification." Protestants maintain that the "grace and mercy of God by our savior Jesus Christ promised to the faithful in his holy word is the principal and original cause . . . of our justification." They believe that "God's promise of his mercy in Christ is the instrumental cause in us" of our justification, "without the merit of our works; and yet being justified, we are bound to walk in all good works, as much as it shall please God to give us grace thereunto." Protestants do not "exclude the doing, but the merits of our good works, which is no heresy," as the Catholics charge. In the Protestant view, it is the truth taught by the scriptures and the ancient Fathers.

Nowell and Day conclude their account by denying the claim in the pamphlets that the Catholics had won the debate and that the Protestants had brought it to a hasty conclusion to avoid further embarrassment. On the contrary, Nowell and Day maintain that the lengthy disputation had continued until the heat of the day became intolerable, and that Campion had been very close to agreement with them on the proper meaning of justification when Owen Hopton ended the proceedings.

Catholic Accounts of the First Debate. Unfortunately, the Catholic pamphlet accounts of the first disputation, against which Nowell and Day wrote, have not survived. The single extant manuscript account, found among the Tresham papers, was not discovered until 1828 and remained unpublished until it was transcribed by Mrs. Lomas and printed by the Historical Manuscript Commission in 1903–1904.[93] I have used the Tresham account as my text for the first debate. For additional Catholic accounts of the first day, one must turn to such secondary sources as contemporary or near-contemporary biographical and historical accounts written by authors who apparently had access to the pamphlets and to other sources. Of the many secondary sources dealing with Campion, the two fullest accounts of the disputations were written by Paolo Bombino and Daniello Bartoli. As supplements to the very brief Tresham account, I have included relevant excerpts from Bombino and Bartoli in Appendix C. Each of these three Catholic versions of the first debate (that is, Tresham, Bombino, and Bartoli) deserves brief consideration.

The Tresham account of the first day, which appears in this edition, seems to be the most objective of all the versions. Also, unlike the more detailed and defensively crafted Protestant account by Nowell and Day, the Tresham version appears to be the kind of general summary that a Catholic observer might have composed from hurriedly written notes actually taken at the disputation and then hastily expanded soon after for private circulation. It contains, for example, little direct discourse and includes few specific references to the many scholarly sources cited in the Nowell–Day published

[93] The account appears in *Various Collections*, vol. 3 (Historical Manuscript Commission, 1904), pp. 8–16. Information about Sir Thomas Tresham may be found in the following: J. Taylor, *A Calendar of Papers of the Tresham Family* (London, 1811); Morey, *Catholic Subjects of Elizabeth I*, pp. 162–67; and Eric St. John Brooks, *Sir Christopher Hatton: Queen Elizabeth's Favorite* (London: Jonathan Cape, 1947), pp. 210ff.

account. However, containing as it does another point of view, this brief Catholic account enlarges our understanding of the first disputation in a number of important ways. First, it corroborates some basic points: that the general topic of the morning session was the canon of the Bible, and that the afternoon session dealt mainly with the issue of whether one could be justified by faith alone. Second, it confirms in a general way both the order and the substance of the principal arguments each side presented in addressing the two major issues. In the morning session, for example, after describing a few sharp exchanges between the two sides, the Tresham account also reports how Nowell raised the issue of Luther's estimation of the Epistle of St. James, how he presented an edition of Luther for Campion to examine, and how Campion claimed that the edition had been revised by Luther's followers. Then, like the Nowell–Day authorized version, the Tresham account addresses the larger issue of which books properly belong in the canon of the Bible. Jerome, Augustine, and Eusebius are again cited as authorities. Thus, the Tresham account of the first disputation is not, in general outline, basically different from the Nowell–Day published account.

However, in almost all particular respects, some trivial and some substantial, the two versions differ dramatically. Among the trivial, for example, is the Tresham account of the curt and arrogant treatment of the Catholics by Nowell and Day, as opposed to the Nowell–Day version, which charges the Catholics with rudeness. Among the most substantial differences between the two accounts is the emphasis given to Campion's forceful denial in the Tresham version that he revealed the names of those Catholics who had aided him: "I ought to suffer anything rather than to betray the bodies of those that ministered necessaries to supply my lack." Another major difference between the two is the Nowell–Day assertion that they and Campion had been close to agreement on the issue of justification when Hopton ended the debate, as opposed to the Tresham account that reports how Campion explained to the Protestants how justification should be properly understood. The Tresham version also directly contradicts Nowell–Day regarding Campion's ability to read Greek. The Tresham version credits Campion with having read, understood, and translated Greek, much to the admiration of the Protestants.

A second Catholic account of the first day's disputation, written in Latin, is contained in Campion's first major biography, by Paolo Bombino, *Vita et martyrium Edmundi Campiani* (Antwerp, 1618).[94] Although Bombino's inflated prose and his overly pious intrusions detract from the objectivity of his work, his life of Campion remained the most authoritative until Richard Simpson's *Life of Edmund Campion: A Biography* (1866; London: John Hodges 1896). The special value of Bombino's comments on the debates is that he had access both to written accounts coming out of England about Campion and to personal interviews with individuals, notably Robert Persons, who had known Campion and been familiar with the Jesuit mission in England. In view of all the information that Bombino had apparently gathered about the disputations, his accounts of them in his biography are disappointingly brief. The reason for this brevity he himself explains: "Yet were it not I intend to set forth in a treatise by themselves Campion's disputations word for word, as I have rendered them by help of a friend out of English into Latin, I would not suffer so much as one word of those disputations to be wanting here in this present history" (see below, Appendix C). Unfortunately, Bombino never published the "treatise," but it is very likely that his written sources for the second, third, and fourth disputations were those that I have included in this present volume.

Bombino's account of the first day is worth reviewing briefly. Like the Tresham account, it begins with Nowell's bombastic attack on Campion for having vaingloriously challenged all the English divines to public disputation. Then Bombino takes us over familiar ground. Nowell set the limits of their debate to a few issues in Campion's book, insisted that Catholics fared better under Elizabeth than Protestants had under Mary, and charged Campion with lying in saying that Luther had rejected the Epistle of St. James. Campion defended himself against the charge of impudence, complained about the unequal conditions of the debate as well as the cruelty of Protestant torture. To Hopton's objection that his torture had not been extreme, Campion answered that a victim was better able to testify about the degree of suffering than an observer. Another nobleman,

[94] A revised and expanded edition was published at Mantua in 1620 and, according to Richand Simpson (*Life of Edmund Campion*, p. 500), the author's marginal notes in a copy of the second edition indicate that he had apparently planned to publish a revised third edition.

presumably Norton, insisted that Campion had been punished not for his religion but for treason. Campion answered that his religion was his only crime and that he had been tortured because he would not reveal the identities of his Catholic benefactors.

According to Bombino, the debate then turned to Campion's charge that Luther had rejected the Epistle of St. James. Nowell called Campion a liar and produced an edition of Luther in which the words Campion had quoted could not be found. Campion claimed that the edition was false and offered to send to Germany for a true one. His offer was rejected, and he was ridiculed. When Campion's fellow priests supported his claim, they too were ridiculed. Then the argument shifted to another of Luther's works, *The Babylonian Captivity*. Campion pointed to a passage in which Luther questioned the authenticity of St. James as being unworthy of an apostolic spirit. When Nowell answered that many ancient writers had doubted the authenticity of St. James, Campion demonstrated convincingly, according to Bombino, that all the ancient writers, except Cajetan, had supported the authenticity of the Epistle of St. James.

Bombino tells us that Nowell ended the morning session with a summary of the Protestant arguments; but when the Catholics asked permission to summarize their arguments, they were silenced. Some time after the debate, Bombino rightly points out, the earlier edition of Luther's works that Campion had cited was indeed found and the truth of Campion's statement was acknowledged even by the Protestants.

Bombino concentrates on two issues at the afternoon session: first, whether Campion could read Greek; and, second, whether Luther's advocacy of "faith alone" was true. Day, who had replaced Nowell as chief interrogator, presented to Campion a Greek text that bore upon the issue of justification. Campion, knowing the text to be corrupt, refused to read the passage and laid the book aside. The Protestants interpreted his refusal as an admission that he was unable to read Greek, and they ridiculed him for his ignorance. Then they continued to argue that, although the word "only" did not appear in scripture, the Fathers themselves had used it in interpreting the scriptures. To prove their point and to embarrass Campion further, they presented him with another Greek text, this one from Basil. Much to their surprise, Campion took the text, read it, and translated it correctly into English. With his fellow prisoners Campion then took the offensive and demonstrated the proper sense and meaning of the Fathers' use of "faith only" in their writings. Campion concluded with the following argument: If faith alone justifies, it justifies without charity, but without charity, if we believe St. Paul, it justifies not; therefore, faith alone justifies not. When the Protestants protested that the syllogism contained four terms but were unable to substantiate their objection, Sherwin pressed them with additional arguments until they silenced him. Soon after, Nowell interrupted Campion's masterful explanation of the proper meaning of justification and abruptly ended the disputation.

The third Catholic account of the first day's disputation, by Daniello Bartoli (*Dell' Istoria della Campagnia di Giesu: l'Inghilterra* [Rome, 1667]), goes over much of the same ground as the two other Catholic accounts (that is, Tresham's and Bombino's) and shows the same kind of partisan loyalty to Campion and to the Catholic cause as Bombino did. Campion is cast as a saintly hero and the Protestants, especially Nowell and Whitaker, as despicable heretics. Bartoli, however, makes no systematic attempt to follow the order of the arguments presented by each side. Instead, he seizes upon certain issues in the morning and afternoon sessions that best illustrate Campion's courage, intelligence, and modesty. Campion's torture, the unfair conditions set by the Protestants for the disputation, Nowell's arrogance, Hopton's minimization of the cruelty of English torture, and Campion's insistence that he was a prisoner only because of his religion are again rehearsed before the debate turns to the issue of Luther's comments on the Epistle of St. James. The afternoon session, as previously reported in all accounts, deals initially with the issue of faith alone; but Bartoli emphasizes the point that Campion did indeed know Greek, though at first he permitted his opponents to think otherwise.

In spite of both Catholic and Protestant biases in reporting, it is reassuring to find that these four summary (rather than verbatim) accounts of the first debate corroborate one another on the two main topics of the morning and afternoon sessions: (1) the canon of the Bible (espcially James's Epistle) and (2) the issue of justification by "faith alone." Equally reassuring, they also confirm one another regarding the order and substance of the main arguments advanced by each side. Thus, on many basic matters the different versions are in general agreement. On personal and tangential matters, however, significant differences become progressively more prominent. For example, Campion's objections to his racking and to the unfair conditions of the debate are minimized or rationalized by the Protestants but repeatedly emphasized by the Catholics. His accuracy in citing Luther's comments on St. James's Epistle is wrongly challenged by the Protestants but correctly maintained and documented by the Catholics. His ability to read and understand Greek is doubted by the Protestants but vouched for by the Catholics. His intelligence and conduct are condemned as shallow and unruly by the Protestants, but he is praised by the Catholics for his brilliance, modesty, and composure. In short, as we observe how the various accounts concur or differ in reporting the debate, we are made increasingly aware that the logic and weight of opposing arguments seem gradually to become less important than such other matters as the fair or unfair conditions attached to the debates, the heated personal conflicts among the disputants, and the subsequent true or false reports that circulated after the debate. As a result, an impartial reader's final verdict on the winner or loser of the first disputation is difficult and may well be influenced as much by personalities as by arguments.

Such a highly personalized response to the accounts seems to be almost inevitable when we reflect on the first debate within its own historical context. That is, when we consider the debate as a part of the momentous religious conflicts and controversies that occurred throughout Christendom during the Reformation and the Counter Reformation, we are reminded that the issues debated and the arguments advanced at the first debate were not new, even in their own day. They had all been aired many times, in many ways, and in many places before 1581 at the Tower of London. Nor did Campion and his opponents add much to them that was new—other than to provide a new public setting in England. Certainly, as the debate shows, Campion and his opponents knew all the basic arguments that could be brought for and against such issues as the canon of the Bible and justification by faith alone. Like many other scholars, they had studied the scriptures and had read the major commentaries. They were quite familiar with church history, with church councils, with the views of the Doctors, with canon laws, and with the decrees of the popes. Having already weighed the evidence and formed their opinions about the doctrinal issues raised, the debaters were not likely to change their own religious views about anything. At the same time, they must have considered how their arguments and their conduct might affect the views of a broader and less well-informed general audience. In speaking to this larger audience, the debaters must have seen their roles as public defenders of the true faith, chosen spokesmen for the word of God.

Of course, as readers we may see the disputants, the issues, and the arguments somewhat differently. Detached from the historical immediacy of the debate and separated from it by centuries filled with similar kinds of controversial religious encounters, we may be inclined to see the disputants (Campion, Nowell, and Day) with less doctrinal fervor than some of their own ardent supporters. Indeed, if our own religious views do not intrude, some of us may see the debaters as another group of very experienced and capable actors sincerely engaged in a not unfamiliar dramatic conflict about opposing creeds. Regarding the issues and the arguments, we are also aware by hindsight that the debate did not settle much. Even today we hear similar arguments, and we know that many of the same issues remain unresolved. Consequently, our range of options in choosing the winner of the first debate is wide. We may side with the Protestants, Nowell and Day, who claimed they won. Or we may side with the Catholic pamphlets who chose Campion. Or with the advantage of hindsight, we may set aside our personal religious preferences and choose the winner on the basis of effective dramatics rather than doctrinal distinctions. Or we may take another tack. We may shape our opinions, perhaps more objectively, by historical inference. That is, by considering the implications of the changes introduced by the authorities at the following debate, we may deduce how those in positions of power and influence at the time judged the first debate.

Second Debate

As noted above, the changes introduced at the second disputation suggest that the authorities, after having reviewed and weighed the results of the first debate, were not entirely satisfied with its outcome or with the performances of Nowell and Day. First, the surprisingly lengthy interval of seventeen days which separated the first (August 31, 1581) from the second debate (September 18, 1581) allowed plenty of time for the authorities to assess the situation. Second, Nowell and Day, the disputants of the first day, were replaced by William Fulke and Roger Goade. Third, the location of the debate was shifted from the Tower chapel to Owen Hopton's smaller private quarters.[95] Fourth, the size of the audience was reduced. And, fifth, Campion's fellow Catholic prisoners were excluded from the meeting. Although accounts of the subsequent debate provide no explanations for all these changes, it seems patently obvious that they were made in order to give the next two Protestant disputants, Fulke and Goade, additional advantages. It should also be noted that in its published form in *A true report* the second debate appears to be a verbatim account. That is, it appears to be objectively authentic; but, as we know, it is not verbatim. The editor, John Field, cut Campion's speeches. Finally, perhaps what is most curious, we shall see that at the fourth debate the issues of the first debate are redebated. The introduction of so many changes indicates clearly that the authorities did not share the Nowell–Day view that Campion had been soundly defeated. On the contrary, the authorities must have hoped that Fulke and Goade would see to it that the outcome of the second debate would be more favorable.

Like their two predecessors, both William Fulke and Roger Goade were highly qualified debaters. Fulke (1538–89) was born in London and educated at St. Paul's school where, according to tradition, he is reported to have lost a schoolboy competition to Campion. Fulke entered St. John's College, Cambridge, in 1555, earning a B.A. in 1558 and an M.A. in 1563. After reading law at Clifford's Inn for six years, he returned to Cambridge to study languages and theology. He held various academic posts at Cambridge and associated actively there with Thomas Cartwright, the controversial Puritan leader. His involvement in religious conflicts resulted in his expulsion, but the dismissal was brief. Readmitted in 1567, he was soon after elected Senior Fellow. Leicester, the queen's favorite at the time, appointed him to serve as his chaplain and secured for him additional sources

[95] In a letter to Burghley (September 29, 1581), Bishop Aylmer states that he had written to Owen Hopton expressing his disapproval that so many people had been admitted to the first debate. See Thomas Wright, ed., *Queen Elizabeth and Her Times*, 2 vols. (London: Henry Colburn, 1838), 2:155.

of income. With Leicester's support, he was granted a D.D. in 1572 by royal mandate. Fulke continued to associate with Cartwright, and on one occasion he visited Field and Wilcox, who had been imprisoned in London for their publication of "Admonition to Parliament." Field, it will be recalled, served as notary at the second and third disputations and was also editor of the authorized Protestant version of the debates, *A true report*. Again with Leicester's backing, Fulke was named Master of Pembroke Hall, Cambridge, a position that he held until his death.

Throughout his stormy career, which included marital problems as well as questionable administrative practices at Pembroke Hall, Fulke, a staunch Puritan, remained at or near the center of endless religious controversies. He was often appointed to hold conferences and to engage in disputations with imprisoned Catholics and priests; he was invited to preach sermons on the evils of Roman Catholicism; and he was involved in numerous written controversies with William Allen, Gregory Martin, Thomas Stapleton, Nicholas Sanders, and Richard Bristow.[96] A learned scholar and a fierce competitor, Fulke proved to be Campion's most able opponent.

Roger Goade (1538–1610), Campion's other adversary at the second disputation, was born at Horton, Buckinghamshire, and educated at Eton and at King's College, Cambridge, where he earned a B.A. in 1559, an M.A. in 1563, and a B.D. in 1569. He was a Master at a grammar school at Guildford until appointed provost at King's College, Cambridge, in 1570. He held a number of other appointments: Vice Chancellor of the University (1576, 1595, and 1607), Vice Chancellor of the Church of Wells, and chaplain to Ambrose Dudley, Earl of Warwick. Although recognized as a scholar and an ardent Protestant, Goade was better known as an academic administrator than as a religious controversialist.

As reported in both Protestant and Catholic accounts, the second disputation deals primarily with two principal topics and a number of highly controversial side-issues. The morning session centers on the topic of whether the "church militant" on earth is visible. Campion argues that it is visible; Fulke and Goade, that it has not always

[96] For Fulke's involvement in written religious controversies, see Milward, *Religious Controversies of the Elizabethan Age*, which itemizes and annotates Fulke's various publications.

been visible. The afternoon session addresses the topic of whether or not the true church may err in matters of faith. Campion argues that the church cannot err; Fulke and Goade, that it has erred.

These two new topics for debate were not considered to be minor religious concerns in sixteenth-century England. At the time, they highlighted major doctrinal differences between Catholics and Protestants. Roman Catholics, for example, claimed that the true church (the *Ecclesia* of the Bible) has always been visible. Uninterrupted continuity was one of its essential qualities. Protestants, such as Calvin, however, maintained that the true church, which had always been based on an individual's faith, was not always visible. According to Protestants, Rome could not assert the primacy of its religious authority on continuity and visibility. As we see in the course of the morning session, Campion and his opponents presented their arguments primarily within historical contexts. Historically, for example, Fulke and Goade cited individual figures, events, and passages taken from the Old and the New Testaments to demonstrate that the true church has not always been visible. And, with a single notable exception when he was allowed to advance his own argument, Campion rebutted their arguments mainly by reinterpreting their interpretations of the scriptures.

As was the case with the first debate, the Catholic and Protestant accounts of the second agree on the order and substance of the arguments presented. (Indeed, in both versions the arguments are numbered sequentially in the margins.) Also, once again, Campion chose to pray privately; and as before we find preliminary disagreement about the unequal conditions of their meeting.[97] In this instance, according to both Catholic and Protestant versions, Campion complained that this conference was not the sort of debate he had requested, and he charged that Fulke and Goade had been able to prepare for the meeting but that he had been "brought hither altogether unprovided." In addition, because he had heard that published accounts of the first disputation had belied him in print, Campion asked that he be allowed his own notary to record the

[97] It should be noted that Campion's refusals to join his opponents in prayer at the beginning of the debates were apparently intended to emphasize the Roman Catholic prohibition that advised Catholics against participating with Protestants in acts of religious worship. This papal prohibition caused a great deal of grief for many English Catholics.

debate properly. Finally, he requested being given advance notice of any forthcoming debates. In responding to Campion's objections, Fulke stated that, like Campion himself, they had no authority to determine the time, place, and format of the debates. They, too, were directed by others. He dismissed the published account as "indifferent." The notary was present, he said, simply to prevent false reports. Further, he pointed out that Campion, having selected the topic of their debate on the previous Saturday (September 16, 1581), had been given as much notice of their topics as had he and Goade. Campion replied pointedly that the pile of books on the table in front of Fulke and Goade argued the contrary.

Fulke then turned to the topic to be considered. But before presenting formal arguments about the visibility/non-visibility of the church, Campion and Fulke disagreed on the meaning of the term "church." Fulke claimed that it included the church triumphant in heaven, while Campion argued that he himself had meant only the church militant on earth.

After finally accepting Campion's limitation, Fulke advanced arguments from the Old Testament that (1) because Elias complained that there had been none of the faithful left but himself, and (2) because in ancient times the temple had been polluted, sacrifice had been omitted, and the high priest had committed idolatry, the church had not been visible (1 Kings 19:10–14). Campion answered that, even though Elias had known none of the faithful in Samaria where he had made the statement, he knew some elsewhere. And, he continued, if in ancient times the priest had committed open idolatry, it did not follow that one of the faithful had not known another.

The next argument, which began with philosophical distinctions about the meanings of the terms "note" and "accident," led to a difference of interpretation regarding Chrysostom's statement that the church is known only from the scriptures. Goade then presented arguments from the New Testament: because in Christ's time the scribes and Pharisees had ruled the church, the church was not visible. On the contrary, Campion answered: Christ preached openly and had visible followers. Goade went on to argue that later in times of persecution, when imprisoned Christians had no place of resort, the church was invisible. Campion replied that Christians had escaped from prisons. To prove that the faithless did not know the faithful, Goade quoted St. John, "The world doth not know us." Campion qualified the context of the passage to mean that the faithless did know the faithful, but not with regard to their salvation. This distinction led to the question of election, and Campion challenged Goade to name any one person who was elected. Goade and Campion then differed on the selection and meaning of the biblical text that a city may not be hidden on a mountaintop (Matt. 5:14), which Goade had intended to show was not a strong text to prove the Catholic position that the church had always been visible. Campion, however, claimed that the text was allegorical and stated that he knew a better one.

Whether the biblical passage about the city on the mountaintop applied only to the apostles or to the apostles and the church became a question. Goade asserted that Jerome and Chrysostom supported him; but when he was unable to find the source in his notes, he allowed Campion to present his "stronger" text (Matt. 18:15–17) which, in effect, directed Christians in difficulty to bring their problems to the church ("Dic Ecclesiae [tell it to the church]"). Campion maintained that if the scriptures tell us to bring our problems to the church, there must be a visible church. Goade replied that the order must be executed if and when possible, but that sometimes it was not possible, as in times of persecution. Citing the reign of Queen Mary as an analogy, Campion argued that people had always gone to other places when the church had not been available to them where they were.

Fulke offered the final argument of the morning session: since faith is invisible, the church is invisible. According to the Catholic account, Campion answered that Fulke's statement led logically to the conclusion "that Christ could not be seen when he was here on earth." He urged his opponents to reply. Again, according to the Catholic account, Fulke and Goade charged Campion with arrogance, and Campion answered that "he must not betray the truth by using too much humility." In the Protestant account, however, it is reported that Campion seemed to have been persuaded by Fulke's argument that because the true church is based on faith, and faith is not visible, then the church is not visible. Such discrepancies between the two versions are not unusual.

At the afternoon session, which dealt primarily with the topic of whether the church may err in matters of faith, a number of controversial side-issues arose, and both Fulke and Goade became more aggressive in their questioning. To support their thesis that the church had erred, they cited numerous instances of what they claimed were doctrinal errors. For example, they argued that since individuals within the church (for example, St. Peter and later popes) as well as church councils (for example, Nicaea and Constantinople about images) had erred, the church had erred. In responding, Campion's general strategy was either to qualify or to correct their statements. To their charge that individuals within the church and particular churches had erred, Campion argued that even if individuals and certain churches may have erred, it did not prove that the church as a whole had erred, for Christ had promised the protection of the Holy Ghost to the whole church. Regarding conflicting decrees by church councils, he pointed out that because Constantinople had not been a general council and Nicaea had, Nicaea must be followed.

Other sharp exchanges dealt with such related controversial topics as election (whether those in the church can leave it), baptism (whether it takes away original sin), temptations (whether they constitute sins), angels (whether they have bodies), and justification (whether we are justified by following God's commandments). In the Catholic version, Campion himself offers a partial summary of the issues addressed and of what he believed to be the patently false positions taken by Fulke and Goade at this session: "Here hath been many strange paradoxes granted this day. I would they were noted: That a thing may be a matter of faith, and no matter of salvation. That baptism taketh not away original sin. That if a man be once of the church, he shall never be out of the church, and so fall from the church. That every temptation is sin. That David in committing adultery and murder was not in that act the servant of sin." The Protestant version, as edited by Field, omits Campion's summary.

At least from the Protestant perspective, the second debate was more efficiently managed than the first. Fulke and Goade guided its direction more forcefully than had Nowell and Day, who at times had lost control of the first debate. No doubt, part of the success in improving its management may be accounted for by the fact that Campion's fellow prisoners, who had distracted and upset Nowell and Day, had been excluded. Also, the authorities must have discovered from the first debate that it was dangerously unwise to allow

Campion to speak unchecked. Thus, at the second debate Fulke and Goade ensured brief rather than discursive answers by insisting that the arguments and responses be presented in the form of syllogisms. Yet even with this new restriction, they found it necessary on many occasions to interrupt and to cut short some of Campion's explanations, and Field, who later edited the published version, deleted others by inserting an "etc." where he omitted Campion's "waste words." However, as both the Catholic and Protestant accounts reveal, Fulke and Goade did not limit their own responses to syllogisms. Nor did Field cut short many of their speeches with an "etc."

Seen as fair or unfair, the procedural changes introduced at the second debate produced a more rapid pace in questions and answers, and they also led to sharper exchanges between the disputants. The magisterial attitudes of Nowell and Day toward Campion at the first debate become intensely combative attitudes with Fulke and Goade. Campion, the Protestants seem to have learned from the first encounter, must not be allowed to speak at length, or to influence the direction of the arguments, or to introduce new ones. He must be restricted in his responses and prevented from seizing the offensive. Campion was there to answer questions, not to ask them. Repeatedly, in both Catholic and Protestant versions, Fulke and Goad dismissed Campion's answers as either mistaken or nonsense. For example, according to Fulke in the Protestant account, Campion misunderstood the meaning of "church," misrepresented Elias's situation, and failed to grasp the true meaning of Calvin's position on justification. In addition, Goade charged Campion with absurdities in maintaining that the commandments were intended to be kept, in maintaining that St. Peter did not seriously err in keeping company with the Jews, and in maintaining that Christ may be present in a sacrament and in heaven at the same time.

In short, the second debate seems to be more evenly contested than the first. The pace is faster, the issues more focused, the arguments more pointed, the exchanges less discursive. Whether Fulke and Goade actually persuaded their audience in the Tower that the true church was invisible and could err is perhaps less important than that they apparently convinced the authorities that they had held their own with Campion and deserved another chance to confront him on a new topic.

Third Debate

At the third disputation, which took place five days later, on September 23, 1581, again in Hopton's quarters, Campion faced Fulke and Goade for a second time. At this meeting, no mention is made in either the Catholic or the Protestant versions that Campion had been informed in advance about the new topics to be discussed. Nor, for the first time, does Campion himself object in an opening statement about the unequal conditions imposed upon him; but in the course of the disputation he continually objects to the "imperious" way his opponents treat him; and he asks again for writing materials and permission to pose questions to Fulke and Goade. His requests, however, lead only to a growing number of sharp exchanges, especially with Fulke.

The topics debated at morning and afternoon sessions are more closely related to each other than the topics are at the other debates. In fact, the two topics may be considered to be facets of the same topic. The morning session deals with whether Christ is really present in the sacrament of the Eucharist (that is, the Mass/the Lord's Supper), and the afternoon, with transubstantiation. At first, the issues at stake may appear to be philosophically simple, but in the course of the debate we soon discover that they become theologically complex. All the arguments lead to one of the most crucial doctrinal issues of the Reformation—the Roman Catholic Mass.[98] Because Roman Catholics have always regarded the Mass as being at the center of their theological beliefs, it seems logical, and also politic, that Fulke and Goade would attempt to disprove its doctrinal validity. Roman Catholics take the position that at the moment of consecration the priest's words (that is, "This is my body . . .") transform bread and wine into the true body and blood of Christ, and that Christ is really present in both forms. English Protestants claim that, although some mysterious change takes place, the bread and wine do not become the true body and blood of Christ. Rather, the bread and wine are sacramental symbols or tokens of Christ's body and blood. As Campion's opponents argue, Christ's body, having been resurrected, is in heaven.

---

[98] For a discussion of the Mass in England, see C. W. Dugmore, *The Mass and the English Reformers* (London: Macmillan; New York: St. Martin's Press, 1958); and George Every, *The Mass* (London: Gill and Macmillan, 1978).

The introduction of these new topics, real presence and transubstantiation, at the third debate represents a departure from the established procedure at the previous debates. At least some precedent seems to have been set aside. We recall that in their own account of the first debate Nowell and Day had insisted that they had questioned Campion on only a few points at the beginning of his book. Later, at the second debate, Fulke pointed out that he had requested Campion to select a topic from his book. Campion's answer was that because they had already debated parts of the first two reasons presented in his *Rationes Decem* at the first debate (the canon of the Bible and faith alone), he chose those parts immediately following (whether the church is visibile and can err). Thus, if the subsequent debates were to follow the established order of the first two and, as one might expect, to move on systematically through Campion's ten arguments or reasons, the next topic should have been the teachings of church councils and the Fathers rather than the real presence or transubstantiation. No reason is given in either version for the departure from precedent. Other than a few passing remarks in his first two "Reasons," Campion does not deal at any length in *Rationes Decem* with Christ's real presence in the Eucharist or with transubstantiation.

As was the case with the previous debate, the Catholic and Protestant versions of the third debate are very similar with regard to essential matters, that is, with regard to the order and the substance of the arguments. Also, we find again that the Protestant version is a fuller account, primarily because it includes lengthy passages from the scriptural commentators that are cited (usually in Latin and in English) and analyzed by the debaters, and because it reports more fully many of the exchanges between the debaters. At times, as reported in the Protestant version, the exchanges (questions and answers) appear, or purport, to be verbatim accounts of the proceedings. By way of contrast, the briefer Catholic version relies more often on summary and paraphrase. That is, the anonymous Catholic writer seems to have been primarily concerned with preserving a substantial record of each argumentative exchange rather than a verbatim record.

In addition to differences in length and detail, we find other notable differences between the two accounts. For example, a number of Campion's statements included in the briefer Catholic version do not appear in the more lengthy Protestant version. Conversely, many of the extended remarks by Fulke and Goade, including opening and closing prayers, are reduced to brief comments in the Catholic version. But, of all the differences, perhaps the most important are the subtle ways in which each version slants its coverage, by expansion, compression, or omission, to favor its own side. For example, in the Catholic version we read that Campion charges Fulke with having written in his book against Allen that the church erred in "teaching prayer for the dead and invocation of saints . . . saying that it is idolatry. And do you make it no matter of salvation to teach or not to teach idolatry? Then they fell to the questions of transubstantiation."

In the Protestant version we read:

> CAMPION. You make invocation of saints a matter of great weight.
>
> FULKE. The church did err in that point, but not as you Papists do err in it. There is a great difference between their error and yours. But let us turn to the appointed question . . . transubstantiation.

In these two equivalent passages we note that the Catholic version omits Fulke's answer and that the Protestant version evades Campion's question. Because of similar kinds of editorial license we are not surprised to find that in the Protestant version Fulke and Goade clearly win the debate, and in the Catholic version Campion prevails.

The third debate began rather politely on a diplomatic note. In response to Hopton's opening admonition that he should acknowledge the queen's mercy in allowing the debate, Campion willingly recognized her "benevolence" but not without reminding the audience that, like his opponents, he had come to debate "wholly resolved in matters of faith." And he asked that they view his intentions as good, as he viewed theirs.

Politeness and diplomacy, however, soon give way to combat. After Campion's refusal to join his opponents in prayer, Fulke first warned him that they would not tolerate his lengthy answers as they had previously. Then Fulke turned to some unfinished matters from the previous debate which, he claimed, were instances of errors made by the church. The issues had been discussed but not documented. First, he produced a decree of Pope Innocent III's which stated, according to the Catholic version, "that infants could not be saved without receiving the sacrament of the altar." Campion answered that it was merely "the practice of the church at that time." Second, Fulke cited a reference from the Second Council of Nicaea stating that angels have bodies. Campion replied that since angels had been reported to have assumed bodily forms when they appeared to humans, their bodies may be thus painted. Third, Fulke returned to his earlier charge that the prayer said at the end of council meetings asking forgiveness for error implied error, but Campion explained that the prayer's intent was to seek forgiveness for those who during debate had made "objections contrary to the truth established in that decree." In addition, Campion qualified the alleged Catholic belief that no one may reprehend the pope to mean that anyone may admonish him but not "judicially reprehend him."

Goade then took over the questioning and turned the argument back to their earlier discussion about the apparent contradiction between the decrees of the Councils of Nicaea and Constantinople about images. Campion again argued that because Constantinople was not a general council and Nicaea was, Nicaea must be followed. Goade went on to charge that the Council of Trent had erred in its statement that justification is in us. Campion explained that justification is "not of us, but in us, by the special mercy and gift of God." Finally, after these preliminaries, they turned to the main question of whether Christ is really present in the sacrament of the Eucharist.

In the course of the morning disputation, Fulke and Goade advanced a dozen arguments, usually in the form of syllogisms, to prove that Christ was not present in the sacrament. Citing passages from the New Testament as well as from such scriptural commentators as Augustine and Chrysostom, Fulke and Goade argued that Christ could not really be present. For example, if He were present, Goade argued that He would have to be on earth. But He was in heaven. Campion answered that we must see Christ on earth in many ways, as in purity of life and mortification. As Campion explained, Christ was miraculously present on earth in the sacrament and visibly present in heaven. Fulke argued that if Christ were really in the sacrament, then His body would be eaten by the wicked. Campion discounted the argument, stating that the wicked did indeed receive Christ's body, though not worthily and not in grace. The other arguments advanced by Fulke and Goade, and refuted by Campion, often turned on similar kinds of qualifications and distinctions.

Although the arguments at the morning session, largely because of their abstract nature, may appeal more to theologians than to nontheologians, there developed at this meeting an increasing number of personal conflicts between Campion and Fulke which frequently rose above the issues debated. Also, the reporting of these conflicts often reveals some of the typical differences between the Catholic and the Protestant accounts. For example, in the Catholic version Campion's explanation of Innocent's decree about infants' receiving the Eucharist is both brief and pointed (that is, the decree represented a practice of the church at that time). In the Protestant version, however, we read the following:

CAMPION. Mine answer was that it [that is, Innocent's decree] was never simply necessary, but necessary according to the practice of the church.

FULKE. What need these repetitions?

CAMPION. I must declare mine answer.

FULKE. We have it already.

CAMPION. You come to oppose me as if I were a scholar in the grammar school.

FULKE. You think by multitude of words to carry away the matter; but you shall have no such scope as you had the last day.

CAMPION. You are very imperious. I trust I answered you sufficiently the last day.

Throughout the session, as reported in both versions, Fulke pressed Campion to remain brief in answering, and he called some of Campion's responses foolish and absurd. Campion, in turn, often replied in kind. He feigned surprise, for example, that Fulke, one of the "doctors of Cambridge," would use four terms in a syllogism. To one of Campion's explanations, Fulke said, "Your answer is no answer. You know not what you say." Campion's sharp reply was: "There is no cause why I should forbear you. I am the Queen's prisoner and not yours. And if you use such words, I will return them." When Campion challenged Fulke and requested "books and things necessary" to prepare and to document his answers, Fulke refused his request: "There is no cause why I should be a means unto the Council for any such as you are." A little later Campion asked permission to present his own arguments from the Church Doctors. When Fulke answered that there were no Doctors to support him, Campion replied: "No, you cannot answer, and herein I challenge you for the credit of your cause and, if you distrust not in it, to procure me a day to dispute." Fulke's response was: "We will not make such suit for any such as you."

Like the morning session, the afternoon meeting returned to the issue of Christ's actual presence in the sacrament of the Eucharist, but the emphasis shifted slightly to focus specifically on transubstantiation. The arguments, twelve in number, often turned on abstract, semantical, philosophical, theological, and exegetical distinctions. Campion, of course, argued in favor of transubstantiation, and he based his position on the scriptural passage (Matt. 26 and 1 Cor. 11): "This is my body. . . ." He also cited Ambrose in support. However, when his request for permission to cite additional supporting authorities was denied, he was forced to spend most of the afternoon responding to and interpreting passages from the authorities that Fulke and Goade presented in support of their own positions. Fulke and Goade conceded that although something profitable and mysterious happened to the bread and wine at the Lord's Supper, they remained bread and wine, serving only as figures or signs of Christ's body and blood. The Fathers, such as Augustine and Chrysostom, whom they cited and interpreted to support their views, Campion reinterpreted as supporting his. And when they argued that Christ's "true" body could not be in heaven and on earth at the same time, or that the bread and wine appeared the same before and after consecration and, therefore, there could be no transubstantiation, Campion answered by qualifying abstract terms and by making philosophical and theological distinctions about such concepts as material, substance, accidents, matter, form, figure, sign, symbol, quality, quantity, species, and being. Of course, when pressed hardest, Campion also insisted that, because the sacrament was a miracle, it was exempt from physical laws and the rules of logic.

As in the morning session, Campion continued to engage in sharp personal exchanges with his two opponents, especially with Fulke. To one of Campion's answers, as reported in the Catholic version, Fulke stated sarcastically: "Natural philosophy and logic are beholding unto you." Later, Campion issued another challenge to Fulke: "I challenge you before this honorable company to answer my authorities. You cannot answer the doctors that I shall allege." The corresponding exchanges in the Protestant version are equally spirited.

In general, at both morning and afternoon sessions Fulke and Goade based their many (and often redundant) arguments on what they claimed was common sense or logical reasoning. To a large extent they relied on biblical exegesis, and on excerpts from the commentaries of the Fathers, especially Chrysostom and Augustine. They rejected Campion's claim that Christ is really present through a miracle. And they disallowed his repeated requests either to pose questions to them or to cite the views of those Fathers and commentators who, he claimed, supported his positions. Thus, instead of an open debate or an open discussion of the topic, we witness a relentless interrogation, one full of seemingly endless philosophical distinctions and contentious theological haggling.

One's final judgment about the winner or loser of the third debate may rest ultimately on one's personal views about the issues. Fulke and Goade advanced the standard Protestant arguments against the real presence in the sacrament and against transubstantiation; and Campion attempted to refute them with the standard Catholic responses. Unfortunately, however, we are prevented from hearing the arguments that Campion might have advanced. And with the exception of Campion's reference to Ambrose, we are prevented from hearing the views of the patristic authorities that he might have cited if he had been permitted. (We may only guess what they might have been from his lengthy commentaries on the Fathers which appear as the fifth and sixth reasons in his *Rationes Decem*.) Fulke's dismissal of Campion's many requests to present his side on the grounds that others, not they themselves, controlled their activities is too conveniently self-serving to be plausible.

In view of such overt machinations, I believe that the impartial modern reader is more likely to be receptive to Campion's responses than to be persuaded by the syllogisms of his opponents simply on the basic grounds of fairness. If there is or is not a real presence, a miraculous transubstantiation in the sacrament, what are the arguments for and against it? If we are not already theologically predisposed about the matter, we do not wish to be limited to the views of only one side. Let both sides be heard, and let us judge the reasonableness of all the arguments. The arrangements in place for this and the other debates, however, prevent us from hearing both sides.

As a result, and especially at this debate because it is so narrowly focused, the unfair arrangements become as much of an issue as transubstantiation does. We sympathize with Campion's position because, like him, we feel that we are being manipulated by some unidentified authorities, by some all-powerful Council, that had set arbitrary regulations that are never explained or justified. Of course, given the religious climate of the times, it is doubtful that Campion, even if allowed to present his arguments, would have swayed his audience in Hopton's quarters to his side; but the more detached modern reader would certainly like to hear them.

Fourth Debate

At the fourth and final disputation on Wednesday, September 27, 1581, Campion met two new opponents, John Walker and William Charke. Unlike their predecessors at the previous three debates, Walker and Charke were not generally considered to be among the most distinguished English divines. Neither had risen to prominent positions in the church, or in the government, or at the universities. Nor, except for their association with Campion, had either established a scholarly reputation as a controversialist. Rather, they were known primarily for their preaching and for their rigid Puritan views.

John Walker, a graduate of Cambridge (B.A. in 1547, B.D. in 1563, and D.D. in 1569), was presented a modest living in Suffolk. As proctor for the clergy of Suffolk at the convocation in 1562, he voted in favor of reforming rites and ceremonies, and he signed a petition for improved discipline. In 1564 he was licensed as a parish chaplain in Norwich, and with the support of Matthew Parker and the Duke of Norfolk, he was appointed in 1568 as canon at Norwich. There with the other Puritan clergy he protested against ornaments in the cathedral. In 1571 he was collated to the archdeaconry of Essex. Bishop Aylmer of London gave Walker a number of special assignments, one that included the collection of materials for a refutation of Campion's *Rationes Decem* as well as the task of disputing with Campion at the Tower.

William Charke (fl. 1580), Campion's other opponent, once a fellow at Peterhouse, Cambridge, had been expelled from the University in 1572 for preaching at St. Mary's that Satan had introduced the episcopal system. After his appeal to Burghley for readmission failed, he was appointed chaplain to Lady Cheney and later to the Duchess of Somerset. Apparently he recovered at least some of his lost prestige when in 1580 he was among the first to answer in writing Campion's "Challenge" with his publication *An answere to a seditious pamphlet. . . .*[99] This work attracted notice and advanced him as a candidate to serve, first, as an official notary at the disputations and, then, as a disputant on the fourth day. We learn also from Robert Persons in his *Defense of the Censure* that Charke not only annoyed Campion in the Tower but also followed along beside him on his way to execution with "proud words and merciless behaviour."[100] In 1581 Charke was appointed preacher at Lincoln's Inn, but in 1593 he was suspended by Archbishop Whitgift for his extreme religious views.

Although Walker and Charke were both visible and vocal reformers, as well as Cambridge scholars, neither had achieved the clerical stature of Nowell; nor had either gained the reputation of Fulke as a controversialist. Indeed, their aggressive but uninspiring performances at the fourth debate might suggest to some that Queen Elizabeth may have secretly hoped that the debates would bring discredit to both the Catholics and the Puritans alike and thus demonstrate the wisdom of her earlier decision to found the national church on religious compromise. From Walker's pointed opening remarks, we sense her growing impatience with the progress and the results of the debates. To Elizabeth, the debates must have become more than a distracting annoyance, for they publicized the existence of serious religious dissent in England; and religious dissent, if unchecked, could easily create dangerous political problems. The debates were going on too long; they were attracting too much attention; and there was no positive religious or political resolution in sight. Walker, it seems, became the witting or unwitting spokesman for her discontent.

In his opening statement (as reported in the Catholic but not the Protestant version), Walker informed Campion that he and Charke had been sent by the "Queen's Majesty" who, moved by "clemency"

---

[99] *An answere to a seditious pamphlet lately cast abroade by a Iesuite, with a discoverie of that blasphemous sect. By William Charke.* 1580 (STC 5005). For additional publications associated with Campion's "Challenge," see Milward, *Religious Controversies of the Elizabethan Age*, pp. 54–56.

[100] Simpson, *Life of Edmund Campion*, p. 382.

and "mercifulness," was "loath . . . to deal with vigor against you. . . . She hath rather win you by fair means than to show justice against you; but take heed lest her mercy be turned to vigor, through your own dealing. . . ." The threat was clear. Campion must either accept the dogma of the Church of England or face the "justice" of English law. As we know, Campion did not conform, and Elizabeth's "justice" was executed. But before that tragic outcome, we witness the final debate, which in many respects amounts to a reenactment of the first.

The morning and afternoon sessions of the fourth debate dealt with three topics: (1) the canon of the Bible, (2) whether the scriptures contained sufficient doctrine for salvation, and (3) whether faith alone justified. The first two were considered in the morning; the third, in the afternoon. This choice of topics by the Protestants is rather surprising, because, as we recall, the canon of the Bible and the "faith alone" issues had already been debated at length by Nowell and Day at the first disputation. In the Protestant account, no reasons are given for the selection of the topics. However, in the Catholic version Campion reminds Walker and Charke at the outset that their letter to him of Sunday, September 25, had stated that they intended to dispute "touching the authority of the holy scriptures," which he had taken to mean "the authority of the authentical scriptures" and not "which be authentical," or "whether all things necessary to salvation be contained in scripture." By hindsight, perhaps, the ambiguous wording, "the authority of the holy scriptures," could be understood in many different ways, but it is still puzzling to find that the Protestant disputants should have decided, if indeed the choice was theirs, to go back over ground previously covered. We can only surmise that the disputants themselves, or perhaps the members of Elizabeth's Council, must have felt that the Protestant positions on these topics had not been adequately presented by Nowell and Day.[101]

As was the case with the second and third debates, the Catholic

[101] Evidence that the Protestants felt that the debates had not been going in their favor may be found in Strype, who cites Thomas Norton's warning to Burghley that stricter regulations must be imposed. Norton suggested, for example, that all objections be recorded, read aloud, and acknowledged as accurate by the debaters before a reply be allowed. Norton himself was charged with keeping order at the fourth debate. See Strype, *Annals*, 2.2.360–64; and *Parker*, 3: 212–14.

and Protestant versions of the fourth debate are basically similar with regard to the order and substance of the arguments presented. Also, once again, we find that the more lengthy Protestant version purports to be a verbatim account, and the briefer Catholic version a summary. Also, once again, we find that each version emphasizes or minimizes certain points of argument that are favorable or unfavorable to Walker and Charke or to Campion. In other words, the reader is again left to choose the winner and the loser, for the Protestant version favors Walker and Charke, and the Catholic version favors Campion.

According to the Catholic version, after Walker's brief account of Campion's offenses (which sounds much like the later formal indictment made against him at his trial) and an introductory prayer, he raised the issue of Campion's accusation that Protestants had cut off certain authentic books from the scriptures. Although Campion objected briefly to what seemed a shifting of the topic, he listed the books that, he insisted, had been wrongly cut from the Old and New Testaments by Luther and Calvin. Walker argued that the authenticity of those books had been doubted long before Luther's time, but he denied Campion's request for books to document his claims. Walker then cited Origen's statement that some had doubted these books. Campion replied that Origen's statement did not mean that Origen himself had doubted them. When Walker cited Jerome's warning about the unreliabilty of apocryphal books, Campion distinguished between certain apocryphal books that were doubted and others that were heretical and remarked that Jerome had not objected to all of them.

We are, of course, already familiar with Walker's arguments. Similar ones had been advanced by Nowell and Day at the first debate. Walker simply cites a different set of authorities, and Campion responds essentially as he had before. This initial exchange about the canon of the Bible illustrates the redundancy that characterizes the fourth debate. Apparently, Walker and Charke were unwilling (or unable) to break new ground by addressing any of the other issues that Campion had raised in his *Rationes Decem*. Nor was Campion permitted to introduce them himself at the debate.

Charke next took over the questioning and attempted to set a slightly new direction. He cited two instances in scripture where, he claimed, internal evidence revealed that certain books were not authentic. First, he argued that because the author of Machabees had asked for pardon about what he had written, the book could not be accepted as canonical. Campion denied that the author's asking pardon for his style proved that the book was not canonical. Citing the analogy of Paul's statement about his own style, "Rude am I in speech," Campion argued that the request for pardon could have "proceeded of humility." He reminded them that style of expression must not be confused with doctrinal content.

Second, Charke then moved on to Judith, maintaining that her deliberate deception of Holofernes proved that the book was not authentic. When Campion pointed out that Jerome had praised Judith, Charke expressed doubt that Jerome had actually written the passage in question and went on to insist that her deceit was not compatible with the word of God. Campion defended her on the grounds that she had intended to deliver her people. When Charke cited a passage in which Judith prayed that her speech may deceive, Campion distinguished between material and formal fraud and cited, as similar examples, the Israelites' stealing from the Egyptians, and God's command to Abraham to kill his son Isaac. Finally, Charke observed that Judith and Machabees had been omitted from the canon by the Council of Laodicea. But Campion countered by pointing out that Laodicea had not been a general council and that it had listed only those books which had not been doubted in that part of the world. He added that the books had since been accepted into the canon.

The debate then shifted to the second topic: whether the scriptures contained sufficient doctrine for salvation. Walker and Charke maintained that they did, basing their argument on the grounds that the apostles had taught all things. Campion accepted their argument but qualified it to mean that the apostles had disclosed all things "either in general or special words written." He cited baptismal practices and the "proceeding" of the Holy Ghost from both the Father and the Son to illustrate that some accepted truths had not been stated specifically in the scriptures. He pointed out that some practices, on the authority of the scriptures themselves, were referred to the church for interpretation. When Charke called Campion's remarks about the "proceeding" of the Holy Ghost "extremely blasphemy," Campion challenged him to prove from scripture that the Holy Ghost proceeded from both the Father and the Son.

Charke cited scriptural evidence to show that the Holy Ghost proceeded from the Father, but he was unable to prove that the Holy Ghost also proceeded from the Son. The differences in reporting this issue about the "proceeding" of the Holy Ghost serves as a typical instance of emphasizing or minimizing a point at issue. In the Catholic version, Campion clearly wins the point; but in the Protestant version, Charke dismisses the point as inconsequential.

Charke next introduced the argument that if all things necessary were not in the scriptures, then the apostles either would not or could not include them. Both alternatives, he insisted, were blasphemy. When Campion agreed, again adding the qualification "either generally or particularly," Charke answered that the door could not be left open to "traditions." Campion argued that the Holy Ghost may deliver traditions to the true church and again cited authorized religious practices that cannot be proved from the scriptures. After they engaged in a brief exchange about baptismal practices, Charke cited a passage from Ignatius of Antioch who had said that the acts and preaching of the apostles should be written down to avoid future controversies. Campion explained that Ignatius had intended his own writings to supplement the writings of St. John, which had already been completed. Thus, Ignatius could not be understood to be opposed to traditions when he himself had written of them. Charke cited other passages from scripture and the Fathers (for example, John, Ambrose, Tertullian, and Basil) in support of his argument, but Campion placed each passage in its fuller context to support his own argument that some traditions were valid and needed no specific scriptural authority.

Walker began the afternoon session, dealing with the topic of whether faith alone justified, by questioning Campion as a parish cleric might drill a child at a catechism lesson. What was the etymology of "faith"? What was the subject of faith? What were the parts of man? In what part was faith? When Campion suggested that they were wasting time, Walker assured him that the questions were leading to a point. However, many questions later, after Walker had completed his catechetical exercise, the unknown writer of this Catholic account observed that nothing had been concluded. Walker's point is equally elusive in the Protestant version. Apparently to save his colleague, Charke took over the questioning.

Charke assured Campion and the audience that he could show

eleven places in scripture which "manifestly prove . . . that faith only doth justify." To Campion's objection that the statement "faith only doth justify" appeared nowhere in the text of scripture, Charke argued that it appeared in a negative sense; for, he claimed, eleven places state "that works do not justify." When he named the places, Campion established their general context. For example, he argued that St. Paul had emphasized faith over works because in dealing with the Jews and Gentiles he had to counter the importance the Jews had attached to "the performance of the ceremonies of the old law" and what "the Gentiles attributed . . . to the moralities." St. Paul, Campion insisted, had not discounted works. Rather, he had denied "works going before faith." Charke then advanced a specific argument to prove his point: Abraham, according to St. Paul, was justified though he had nothing to glory in. "Ergo, good works do not justify." Campion explained that St. Paul's intent had not been to exclude good works but "to prove that the ceremonies of the law did not justify" because Abraham had preceded the law. In fact, Campion continued, Abraham's belief in the coming of Christ could itself be seen as good work. Then they discussed the meaning of the "second covenant." Charke maintained it meant "faith only." Campion, urging a broader meaning, insisted it was "all the religion of Christ, which included faith, hope, and charity."

They moved on to consider the significance of the fact that the words "faith only" appeared in no scriptural text. Charke argued that because the words were contained in the sense of many passages, they "may be added." By way of analogy he reminded Campion that the text that orders us to honor God did not say "God only," though it was clearly understood by all to mean that. Campion agreed that we must honor God only, but he rejected the idea that justification implied faith only. Campion and Walker then engaged in a discussion of the various meanings of Abraham's faith, and Campion concluded that faith, when it was made manifest, may also be understood as a work. He cited St. James to prove that Abraham had been justified by good works.

Charke next turned to the Fathers to show that Basil, Cyprian, Ambrose, Jerome, and others had supported the belief that "faith alone justifies." Campion agreed that some Fathers had indeed mentioned "faith alone" but that, like St. Paul, they had used it in order to emphasize the importance of believing in the Christian religion, and he cited the analogy of missionaries who first preached about faith to the Indians in order that the natives might believe. Then, after they believed, one might teach them that they must also do good works. Charke concluded the debate with the argument that since Christ had taken our sins by imputation, our justification must be by imputation. Campion's final answer was that "we are justified by faith, hope and charity as causes which we have of the gift of God." When some of the spectators began to leave after Campion's answer, Charke "commanded the doors to be shut till after prayer." Thus ended the final debate.

Debates Conclude: Campion Tried and Executed

By the end of the fourth debate the reader understands more clearly why the authorities probably decided to end them. The debates were going nowhere. The most controversial scriptural and dogmatic topics (for example, the canon of the Bible and transubstantiation) had already been considered, and by the time of the final debate the arguments about these topics had become redundant. The introduction of other topics addressed by Campion in his *Rationes Decem* involved some obvious risks. For example, topics dealing with certain views expressed by the Fathers (Campion's fifth and sixth reasons) and with particular decrees issued through church councils (Campion's fourth reason) might have been introduced; but Campion had already demonstrated an impressive knowledge about the Fathers and councils, and he seemed quite anxious to say a good deal more about both. Also, to raise broad or narrow issues related to church history (Campion's seventh and tenth reasons) would surely have allowed Campion to lead his Protestant opponents not only into the embarrassing position of rejecting the ideals of their nation's Catholic past but also into condemning the sacred beliefs and traditions of their own ancestors.

Aside from the difficulty of finding new topics favorable to their cause, the authorities also faced the problem of finding new debaters to oppose Campion. He had already proven himself to be a formidable opponent for some of their most qualified men. To be sure, many English clerics were fine preachers and serious scholars, but highly qualified scholars who were also effective in the give-and-take of public debate were not plentiful in the clerical ranks of the Church of England. For example, Elizabeth's Regius Professors at Oxford (Humphrey) and Cambridge (Whitaker) had willingly accepted and carried out the charge of writing lengthy refutations of Campion's *Rationes Decem*, but neither was judged suitable to meet him in public debate. To match lesser scholars against Campion could lead to a disaster. Thus, the authorities ended the debates. Although Campion had neither been converted nor discredited, his opponents claimed victory.

For the seven-week period after Campion left Hopton's quarters at the conclusion of the fourth debate on September 27 until his arraignment at Westminster Hall on Tuesday, November 14, little is known about him other than that on October 31 he was cruelly racked for a third time. Having failed to win him over privately with promises of preferment or with tortures on the rack, and having failed to discredit him publicly with reports of his confessions or by the disputations at the Tower, Queen Elizabeth and her Council apparently had few options left. Catholic unrest in England was growing at a dangerous rate, and the steady flow of seminary priests secretly returning to England had to be stopped. To retain Campion in prison indefinitely or exile him not only would be counter to recently enacted laws, but would also be understood as signs of weakness on the part of the government in allowing Catholics to keep one of their leading spokesmen. Also, because Elizabeth was at this very time engaged in unpopular marriage negotiations with a Catholic prince (Alençon), leniency toward Campion would be sure to encourage Catholic hopes for religious freedom. With equal certainty, leniency would surely arouse Protestant feelings against her.

That Campion was admired by Elizabeth and by some of the highest-ranking members of her court must have made the decision doubly difficult. The Jesuit and his queen had been friends since the occasion of her formal visit to Oxford in 1566. At that time, Elizabeth had been so impressed with him as a bright young debater that she had recommended him to Burghley and Leicester; and, according to both Campion and the Spanish ambassador, she had called upon him as a speaker to ornament her court during his student days at Oxford. Leicester's bountiful patronage was acknowledged by Campion himself in the dedication of his *History of Ireland*. Sir Henry Sidney had protected him during his short stay in Ireland, and Sir

Philip Sidney had visited him when he was stationed at the Jesuit college in Prague. On hearing of his departure from England, Burghley had remarked that England had lost a jewel.[102] After his capture and imprisonment in the Tower, Elizabeth, Leicester, and Bedford had received him at a private interview in an attempt to win him over. Moreover, it is highly unlikely that the queen actually believed Campion and his fellow priests to be traitors.[103] Yet, at the same time, Elizabeth must have feared the unpredictable consequences of the priests' loyalty to their religious superiors in Rome. She could not afford to keep Campion and the others imprisoned indefinitely, as she had Mary Stuart and the Marian bishops. Because he had become the public embodiment of Catholic dissent against her, she would make him an example of English justice. Campion and his fellows would be tried in a court of law.[104]

The mass trial took place at Westminster Hall on November 20, 1581. Campion and his fellow Catholics were found guilty of treason. With Sherwin and Briant, he was hanged, drawn, and quartered at Tyburn on December 1, 1581.

---

[102] Waugh, *Edmund Campion*, p. 61.

[103] William Camden (1551–1623) writes in *The Historie of the Most Renowned and Victorious Princesse Elizabeth* (London: Benjamin Fisher, 1630), 3:11: "Yet for the greater part of these silly Priests she [Elizabeth] did not at all believe them guilty of plotting the Destruction of their Countrey: but the Superiours were they she held to be the instruments of this Villany. . . ." In the same work (2:106–109) Camden claims that he had known both Campion and Persons at Oxford. He describes Campion as "a sweet natural and most courteous man." But Persons was "a man of seditious and turbulent spirit." Camden's distinctions between the two men have been repeated often by later historians.

[104] See Appendix D.

[First Disputation]

[Morning Session]
Conference at the Tower

August 31, 1581.

The effect of such speeches, arguments and discourses as were had by Mr. Nowell, Mr. Day and other Protestants with Mr. Campion, Jesuit, and other seminary priests in the audience of some honorable, other worshipful and many common persons in the parish church of the Tower of London the 31st of August.[1]

(Margin. Note at the entry every Protestant had one of Mr. Campion's books [that is, *Rationes Decem*] in his hand.)[2]

First Mr. Nowell, as it might seem of modesty, signified to the assembly that it was Mr. Day his pleasure, though willingly he would have given place, that he should declare the cause of their meeting and enter the conflict with Mr. Campion, which he did in a prepared preamble containing this sense.

1. First, for that Mr. Campion had made an impudent challenge provoking them all to disputation in matters of religion, therefore and for that cause they were come to deal with him, and because he should not excuse himself that he was unprovided they were not to discuss in no other things than he had set down in his Latin book, entitled *To the Two Universities*.[3]

2. Secondly, that most shamefully he charged them of outrageous cruelty, whereas many thousands of his coat had been roasted, and

---

[1] Strype (*Annals* 2.2.361) states that the first disputation was held "in the Chapel of the Tower" which suggests St. John's rather than St. Peter's.

[2] This and the following marginal notes are Protestant interpolations.

[3] *To the Two Universities* is part of the subtitle of Campion's *Rationes Decem*.

so few of the contrary touched with death for the profession of their religion.

3. Thirdly, he read words out of Mr. Campion's book bearing this tenor: What moved Martin Luther, that flagitious apostate, to judge the Catholic Epistle of St. James to be a swelling and a strawy epistle, etc.[4]

Mr. Campion, when he supposed that his adversary had said, he addressed himself to answer the former points in manner following.

1. Unto the first briefly he answered that in his book he gave the causes why he so provoked his adversaries, adding moreover that it was not equal dealing on the sudden, being destitute of all the helps wherewith he made his book, to require of him an accompt of every particular therein contained, albeit he willed them to proceed, for that he would stand in defense of the same, though pressed and overcharged with such to too much disadvantage.

2. Unto the second he said what was done before our time by them of that time was to be answered and justified before God, yet never did they rack or practice that hellish torture against men as they do now, which rack, quoth he, is far worse than many deaths.

Reply. Then it was replied by Sir Owen Hopton, Lieutenant, how that he was scarce pinched and that it might rather be termed a cramping than racking.

Catholics. Whereunto Mr. Campion said thereof he himself could best report and be most truest judge, because he felt the smart, and so did not he, adding that his speech was general of others who were handled with greater rigor than he himself had been.

Here it was said that his companions and he were so used for matters of state and not for religion.

Let any man, quoth Mr. Campion, within this realm charge me with word or fact but concerning conscience and religion, and I yield to determination. Whereunto was made no answer. And then he showed that his punishment was for that he would not betray the places and persons with whom he had conversed and dealt with as

[4] Martin Luther (1483–1546), German theologian, was the leading and most influential Protestant reformer. He attacked church abuses (for example, indulgences) and revised the sacramental system. He advocated justification by faith alone through the merits of Christ and insisted that the Bible be the standard of faith and practice. Among his many writings are a catechism and a translation of the Bible into German.

concerning the Catholic cause, alleging an example of primitive Christians who chose rather to abide martyrdom than that they would yield up the books which Catholic pastors had given and distributed among them. Much more said he: I ought to suffer anything rather than to betray the bodies of those that ministered necessaries to supply my lack.

This being done and sundry other odd and by-speeches on both parts uttered, Mr. Nowell stopped and commanded silence from any longer speech, calling him, the said Mr. Campion as I remember, GLORIOSISSIMUM THRASONEM [most vainglorious boaster], with such other like terms of heat and choler, and spoke this for his part to Mr. Campion.

Nowell. Sir, this is the point you do belie Martin Luther, for he hath not the words wherewith you charge him, as that he called St. James' Epistle TUMIDAM ET STRAMINEAM [swollen and strawy]. And he brought in Martin Luther's text wherein it was not to be found, adding with many terms of asseveration that it was in no edition to be found in London, neither the Dutch or other edition. And therefore, he said to Mr. Campion with these words in Latin: IMPUDENTISSIME MENTIRIS [most impudent liar]. Thou dost lie most shamefully and impudently. Which term was thought of modest and charitable men very evil to become a gospeller's mouth. (Margin. This was done with charity.)

Campion. Whereunto Mr. Campion made this answer: first, that he did read the very text with those words cited and refuted by Doctor Lee, and moreover unto the books brought then in place, he said they were such as Luther's scholars and favorers after his death, ashamed of his shameless errors, had pruned and purged, leaving out many things which he left in writing.[5] Last of all, he said, if he might be licensed, he would procure from the Emperor, the Duke of Bavaria, as I think (Margin. These he termed to be the greatest states in the world, which was evil taken.), and other potentates of Germany, Luther's own copy, with those very words, to be sent to her Majesty. (Margin. Here Mr. Beale, clerk of the Council, would have

[5] Luther believed that Henry VIII's book *Assertio septem sacramentorum* had been written for Henry by Dr. Edward Lee (ca. 1482–1544), who afterward was appointed archbishop of York (1531).

had Mr. Campion sworn that he had read the same.[6]) And here Mr. Campion desired them to suspend their judgement until such time as trial could be made of that infallible truth wherewith his adversaries so much pressed him, calling to his fellow priests then present for testimony whether they had in Catholic writers of greatest credit read the same, which with words they affirmed justifying his assertion. Hereupon Luther's books, *De Captivitate Babilonica*, were brought, wherein Mr. Campion read much to this end and sense, viz.: many do affirm probably that the Epistle of St. James is unworthy of the apostolical spirit, whereupon he inferred that Luther leaned to those as by his words were proved, which justly other than by caviling could not be excused from blasphemy.

Contraries. Then his contraries in Luther's behalf said that he did no more than the ancient fathers eleven hundred years before had done, namely Eusebius, who termed it a bastard epistle, and that by many it was called in doubt even from the apostles' time.[7]

Campion. Mr. Campion answered that Eusebius did not so term it by giving his own judgement of it, but by some it was so taken, yet never universally doubted of or rejected; moreover, that until it was determined by common consent of the mystical body of Christ, that is, his church, being the living judge, it was not offensive to make doubt thereof; but after that it was so declared to be canonical, that it was blasphemy for Luther or any of them to doubt thereof.

Contraries. Then did the Protestants allege two epistles of St. Jerome, especially his *Prologus Galeatus* set before all bibles, wherein the books of Machabees were left out of the canon as also other, and accompted apocryphal.[8] To this also they added the witness of a

---

[6] Robert Beale was the brother-in-law of Francis Walsingham and served for a time as his secretary. He was a member of Parliament in 1574, appointed clerk to the Council, and sent by Elizabeth on diplomatic missions to the Continent. He was also a member of the commission that interrogated Campion.

[7] Eusebius (260–340) became bishop of Caesarea in 314. He is reported to have written forty-five works. Of those that have survived, the most influential have been *The History of the Church from Christ to Constantine* and *Chronological Tables*. In his *History* Eusebius does not include the Epistle of St. James as canonical; nor does he list it as spurious. In effect, by listing it as disputed he may simply imply that its authenticity had not yet been decided. See Eusebius, *The History of the Church from Christ to Constantine*, trans. G. A. Williamson (New York: New York University Press, 1966), pp. 134–35.

[8] St. Jerome (ca. 340–420), a towering biblical authority, prepared the Vulgate version of the Bible at the end of the fourth century.

Cardinal called Cajetan who taught that as concerning books of the scripture and the canon thereof that it was to be measured by that which St. Jerome had left as concerning the same.[9]

Catholics. Unto this the Catholics answered: first, unto St. Jerome that in his prologue he only wrote of the books of the Old Testament, wherefore it nothing made against the Epistle of St. James. Secondly, that true it was that he left out of the canon the books of the Machabees and others, but that was only out of the canon of the Jews, not their excluding them out of the canon of the church, which they proved by the authority of St. Augustine who flourished at the same time, who in his book *De Civitate Dei* expressly writeth this that the Jews receive not the Machabees in their canon, but that the church doth, which they confirmed again out of the same doctor, who in his book *De Doctrina Christiana* repeateth all the books of the canonical scripture wherein he listeth both the Machabees with the Epistle of St. James with others which in our days have been called again in doubt.[10] To this also they added the authority of the Third Council kept at Carthage where by consent of many holy bishops they were declared to be canonical scripture, moreover that this universal council was confirmed by the General Council held in Trullo, and therefore after such great judgment given by the whole church, to doubt of those books was no less than blasphemy.[11] Unto the Cardinal Cajetan it was answered he was but one man against whom they might oppose the whole Council of Trent defining these books to be canonical as their forefathers had done.[12]

Contraries. Here the Protestants labored to shift off the matter with a distinction, saying that canon was to be taken equivocally and that St. Augustine would have them in the canon, as out of which books doctrine for reformation of manner might be taken but no

---

[9] For a survey of Cardinal Cajetan's controversial writings, see Jared Wicks, S.J., *Cajetan Responds: A Reader in Reformation Controversy* (Washington, D.C.: Catholic University of America Press, 1978).

[10] St. Augustine (354–430), bishop of Hippo, was one of the most highly regarded of the Church Fathers. Currently, he is perhaps best known for his *Confessions* and *The City of God*.

[11] The Third Council at Carthage met from 393 to 424. The Trullan Synod (692) completed the work of the Fifth (553) and Sixth (680) General Councils. It met in the domed room (*trullus*) of Justinian II's palace at Constantinople.

[12] The Council of Trent (1545–63) responded to the spread of Protestantism by establishing many religious reforms in the Roman Catholic Church.

arguments for proof of matters of faith, and to show that this word *canonical* might be taken equivocally, they alleged Gratian who termeth the pope's decretals canonical writings.[13]

Catholics. Unto this the Catholics answered that true it was canon and canonically might be taken equivocally, but not in our former controversies, for that without distinction those books of the Machabees and St. James are no less numbered for canonical by St. Augustine than the four evangelists, and for that the second council above named declared them to be the true word of God and as the rest of the canonical scripture, wherefore they inferred that no less out of them than out of the rest arguments of faith ought and might be deducted, and to doubt of this after such sound determination were no less than blasphemy.

Nowell. And so Mr. Nowell then putting the priests that would have spoken in the cause to silence, and as oft calling them brabblers and using other terms which little edified, as IMPUDENTISSIME QUAMTES [most impudent as you are] with such like, when by the Catholics no such speech was uttered but upon the cause directly, saving that one Mr. Sherwin said unto him very boldly that he would not be of his religion one quarter of an hour to gain the value of the whole world and many such, etc., and then as Mr. Sherwin began to say. . . .

Nowell. Mr. Nowell showed by recapitulation what his party had said in the former points requiring the attention and judgment of the standers-by, who when he had ended—

Catholics. The Catholics requested that briefly they might also declare how they had answered them and their arguments, laying down strong grounds or reasons for their own cause, but with a commissioner's check silence was commanded, and so they departed and these were the especial things discoursed and argued upon in the aforenoon.

[Afternoon Session]

Protestants. Dr. Day. In the afternoon greater recourse was made unto the place, where when they were assembled, Mr. Day began to

[13] Gratian, a twelfth-century Camaldolese, or Benedictine, monk (d. ca. 1179), wrote the *Concordantia decretum Gratiani*, a systematic collection of patristic texts, conciliar decrees, and papal pronouncements unified by Gratian's own commentary. Little is known about his life.

allege out of Gratian a decretal epistle of Pope Leo IV to this effect that first the chiefest credit ought to be given to the evangelists than to councils, after that to the supreme pastors of Christ's church, and in the fourth place to the doctors consenting, which who so did not indifferently was to be accompted not to believe the four evangelists. Here he required to know how this "indifferently" was to be understood.

Catholics. To this by-question the Catholics answered that this word "indifferently" was not to be taken as though there had been no difference betwixt the evangelists and the rest, but that he which did not believe the church of Christ and Christ's chief vicar in the same and the doctors consenting, was to be accompted in such case as he which should deny the four evangelists, Christ himself setting down: If he hear not the church, let him be reputed a publican and heretic. And again: He that heareth you heareth me.

Protestants. To which last authority one of the Protestants said they used that text to serve all turns, but gave no reasons that in this case it was not rightly used.

Catholics. Moreover the Catholics yielded the difference which they made betwixt the holy scriptures and writings set down by councils, which was that they were bound to believe that every word in [the] testament was set down by the special direction of the Holy Ghost so that the writer could not fail in memory or otherwise slip in any small defect whatsoever, and therefore we were bound in the pain of damnation to believe the smallest things in the Bible, not so much but that Toby's dog had a tail, for that in scripture it is found that he wagged the same when young Toby returned from his journey [Tobias 11:9].

Protestants. This one example was carped at by a gentleman that had been brought up in Luther's schools, saying that it was NIMIUM SCURRILE [very scurrilous], which is to be referred to equal judgment. Now for councils, it was said that they had no promise of the Holy Ghost's assistance for every word or syllable which they should set down but only for the resolute definition of matters of faith.

Catholics. And the Catholics showed that they had not councils equal with scriptures, and yet that it was as great a fault to again say [gainsay] the one as the other, both having their authority from the Holy Ghost. As for councils, it was there proved by that we read in

13th of the Acts whereby the council called together by the apostles in the end it was defined thus, so it seemeth to the Holy Ghost and us, and thus much before they entered into any set questions.

Protestants. After this impertinent question was ended, they fell to debate, as Mr. Campion's book gave occasion, of their only faith, whether that did only justify, reading words out of his book where he said that with St. James' Epistle Luther was wounded, thrust through, with such like terms.

Catholics. Which he justified to be true, for that Luther himself said, howsoever it fell out with him in other questions, he would hold fast on his only faith, as on a sure and certain anchor against all temptests. And therefore St. James' preaching justification by good works shook him to shivers, and therefore he might well write of him in the behalf of St. James as he did.

Protestants. Well the Protestants said that there was no such cause why Luther should abide such danger by the Epistle of St. James, for that ancient fathers justified as much as he did and that albeit the word SOLA, only, were not to be found in scripture yet that it was to be found in the ancient fathers, whom they had brought with them, namely, St. Basil,[14] St. Hilary,[15] and one other in whom this sense of speech was read, that by the law that no justice was procured but by the only faith in Christ Jesus, so, say they, these fathers teach with Luther that faith only doth justify.

Catholics. The Catholics answered that most willingly they admitted those blessed fathers, but so that they were rightly understood, who they interpreted thus, that by the words there read, it did manifestly appear that the fathers compared the law and the works thereof with faith and therefore justly concluded by the law no justice could be applied but by faith only in Jesus Christ, neither this faith only in Jesus Christ to be the Protestants' only faith but that which St. Paul speaketh of in the 5th chapter to the Galatians where he saith that circumcision availeth nothing and uncircumcision profiteth nothing, but faith working by charity, etc. And then the Catholics out of St. Paul do reason thus against our "solafidians": that only faith doth justify; then faith without charity doth justify, but that

[14] St. Basil (330?–79?), bishop of Caesarea, a leading early Doctor of the Eastern Church, refuted the heretical teachings of Arius.

[15] St. Hilary (315?–57?), bishop of Poitiers, defended orthodox Christianity against the heresy of Arianism.

was contrary to St. Paul as the text alleged importeth; therefore, the bare only faith cannot justify.

Protestants. To this the Protestants said that the syllogism consisteth of four terms but without declaration of the same made no further answer.

Catholics. Again it was said by the Catholics that St. Paul most plainly in the first to the Corinthians, the 13th chapter, convinced their error where he taught if a man have all faith and have not charity, it nothing profiteth.

Protestants. Unto which the Protestants said that he spoke of the faith of miracles.

Catholics. But reply was made by the Catholic, Mr. Sherwin, that whereas St. Paul said if I have all faith, of necessity their only faith whereof they boast and brag of so much must be contained in that clause or else they must have no faith.

Protestants. And unto this silence was their answer.

Catholics. Then further did the Catholics conclude out of St. James his Epistle in the end of the 2nd chapter that works were to faith that which the soul is to the body; but the soul is the form and life to the body; so therefore the life of faith is good works and by consequence the cause of our justification, because our justification is nothing else but our spiritual life. Unto this was added the authority of St. Augustine, out of his book *De Fide et Operibus*, 15 capt., where he hath registered that this doctrine of justification by faith only was a heresy taught in the apostles' time, for refutation whereof he declareth that St. John, St. Peter, St. Jude, and St. James did write their epistles, wherein they so inculcate the doctrine of good works.

Now unto the party, one Mr. Sherwin, that is, proposed, it was only said that there should be another time for him to be dealt withal, who upon such speeches and other words of authority was often, as he openly declared, there abridged of liberty to speak, that he was both willing and able in the justifying of the Catholic cause and therefore severely inhibited to proceed in arguments which he many times began, at the length broke out in these words: Well, I will hold my peace, but withal will I hold my faith.

It happened in process of their disputation that by occasion incident there was talk of a text in scripture which forsooth must needs be viewed by Mr. Campion, and to make the matter pleasable, as the Protestants imagined, they caused a Greek testament to be brought unto him, which he refused to take, saying merrily to his contrary that it should be yours, at which doing many laughed, as condemning him of ignorance of the tongue, and therefore jestingly by the Protestants it was said, GRECUM EST, NON POTEST LEGI. [It is Greek, perhaps it cannot be read.] Whereunto Mr. Campion gave no answer but rested on a matter as a man unable by their judgments either to read Greek or understand the same. But it chanced not long after that the Protestants as they had provided afore were to allege a place out of St. Basil, the Greek Doctor, and again thinking to give the Catholics another bob they commanded again the book to be given to Mr. Campion that he might read, whom they derided as not able to do the same, but he took the book, having one of their ministry at his elbow, both read and gave the sense of the writer, and bade him bear witness that he was both able to read and understand Greek, whereat there was some admiration made among the Protestants, and he was demanded why he had not done so before, who mildly answered that the print was over small. Why, said they, had you not declared so much, for that had been sufficient.

The like trial made to another Catholic, to wit Mr. Sherwin, who by report of his fellows and other of his companions is very see [torn MS.] in the Greek and Hebrew tongue, yet he took the book and [torn MS.] openly did not read, which was imagined that he did to be accounted ignorant in the tongue or rather for that he was willed to hold his peace for that there should be another time for him to speak.

Catholics. Again one other grave man of the Catholic part, when talk was of St. Jerome's mind as concerning the authority of the Epistle of St. James, offered to speak, [but] by a gentleman Protestant brought up in Luther's schools, as he then affirmed, was before he could utter his mind condemned of ignorance. Let that fellow speak, said some of the Protestants, that he may shame himself and the cause also.

The words which this man uttered were these. St. Jerome's mind may quickly be known as concerning the authority which he giveth to the Epistle of St. James if it can be out of him showed, which may be easily done, that he allegeth sentences out of that epistle for the proof of matters of faith. This was that which was condemned before it was spoken. After some such grekes given,[16] Mr. Campion was willed to say what he thought of faith or what place his church gave unto the same, and then he entered into this determination.

Catholics. Whereas you require the declaration or protestation of my faith in this point, this I say that, in consideration of man's justification, in holy scriptures we read of justification IMPII, the justification of the wicked, as of a pagan or other person who is in the state of mortal sin. To this man I say and the Catholic Church doth teach that neither the works of the law, if he were a Jew, or the works of nature, if he were a gentile, should anything avail to his justification, but he must have it gratis, that is, freely of the mercy of God. Wherefore said he that spoke, if you by your SOLA FIDES [only faith], mean that SOLA only distinguisheth works of the law or works of nature before a wicked man be made the child of grace, I subscribe to you. Yet withal so that neither faith alone doth perfect man's justification, but faith as the foundation and entrance, and charity as the formal cause, so that in this kind of justification, he admitted no good works but added that a man so made the child of grace, by faith, hope, and charity, was then by observing the commandments and good works to grow further in justice, after the saying of the apostle in Apocalypse, QUI JUSTUS EST JUSTIFICETUR AD HOMINEM [He that is just, let him be more justified]. And so he said David was, after that Nathan the prophet had declared his sin remitted by good works more and more justified [2 Samuel 12:1–14], and this [torn MS.] that works proceeding from grace and charity in the regenerate man did merit life everlasting.

Protestants. But here Mr. Nowell said he would agree that good works were necessary, but could not admit that they did merit, for that no such word was to be found in scripture.

Catholics. Then the Catholics said that nothing was so familiar as a reward promised for our works, and mercies must needs have relation to merit, and albeit the word could not be found in scripture, yet there was no cause why he should deny it, the matter being so clear. For said he the procession of the Holy Ghost from the Father and the Son, the word, that is, consubstantial, is not there to be

[16] It is probable that "grekes" is a mistranscription of the word "creaks," that is, sardonic remarks. The basic sense of the word reappears in the modern expression "wisecracks."

found, neither this term TRINITAS, that is, the trinity, and yet all these are sound doctrines of belief. After this the Catholic said that he was not justly charged by Mr. Nowell, that he detracted from Christ's passion when he held this doctrine of merit of good works, for that they had the divinity only from the passion of Christ and proceeding from grace whereby the blood of Christ is applied to the soul of man; they did not detract from Christ's passion because all the worthiness of works was only derived from the same, but there stayed.

Protestants. Now they would not enter into that question because it was over late and so they departed every man his way and the prisoners to their old profession.

Reporter. One thing about the authority of St. James' Epistle I had forgotten which was that the Protestants did allege St. Augustine making only this distinction of the books to be read that some were canonical, as all such as were talked of before, and other apocryphal in which, because there were some things false, they were not to be read.

Mr. Hart. This place a pert Papist, for so I heard him termed, took and thanked his adversary for that he had made a good argument for proof of his party, for, said he, St. Austin [that is, Augustine] said apocryphal books only not to be read because so false things were in them; therefore, said he, all the rest were to be read after the mind of St. Austin because no false things were in them, and so he concluded that St. James his epistle being in the canon of the scripture was of like authority with the rest because it was of like truth.

[Second Disputation]

[Morning Session]

A disputation or conference had within the Tower of London on Monday being the 18th of September, Anno Domini 1581, wherein were assembled the Lord Clanricard, Sir Owen Hopton, Sir William Gorge, Sir Thomas Heneage, Sir Nicholas Poynds, besides others, Doctor Fulke, and Doctor Goade disputants, being sitting at a table, and for the said conference appointed, before whom and right opposite upon a stool was set Mr. Campion, Jesuit, having only his bible.[1]

Fulke. Then entered Doctor Fulke in speech as followeth. Let us pray, and therewithal kneeled down and the rest of the company.

---

[1] Aside from references to Owen Hopton, Lieutenant of the Tower, and the disputants themselves, this is one of the few instances in the manuscripts that the names of particular individuals present at a debate are cited. These are personages of some importance. For example, the Earl of Clanricard (Claurickard) had been brought back to England from Ireland in 1579 by Sir Henry Sidney to be questioned by the Council about the behavior of his rebel sons, Ulick and John, who had fought against each other and against England. Claurickard was detained in England until the summer of 1581 when his sons made peace and submitted to Elizabeth's authority. The Earl died soon after his return to Ireland in August 1582, and was succeeded by his son Ulick. See John O'Donovan, ed., *Annals of the Kingdom of Ireland by the Four Masters*, V (1854; New York: AMS Press, 1966), pp. 1709, 1725, 1745, 1771, 1773.

Sir William Gorge, a military man, was vice admiral of the fleet, fought against the Turks in Hungary, and was recommended to Elizabeth by Maximilian II. He was knighted about 1579 and named Gentleman Porter of the Tower. He is buried in St. Peter ad Vincula.

Sir Thomas Heneage (d. 1595) studied at Cambridge, sat in Parliament, and served Elizabeth as a gentleman of the Privy Chamber, treasurer of the Queen's chamber, and succeeded Sir Christopher Hatton as vice chamberlain of Elizabeth's household. Heneage was knighted in 1577, given valuable land grants, and appointed master of rolls and keeper of records of the Tower. He also sat on special commissions. Although a rival of Leicester's, he was a friend of the courtiers and a supporter of such religious figures as John Foxe and Tobie Matthew. His first wife, Anne, was the daughter of Sir Nicholas Poynds.

Sir Nicholas Poynds (Poyntz) (d. 1593) of Iron Acton served as sheriff of Glostenbury.

Mr. Fulke prayed to this effect, that it would please God to apply that solemn action to the confirming of the faithful in his fear, and to the converting or confounding in their own consciences of such as were blinded, obstinate, and served the God of this world, etc.

Campion. But Mr. Campion refused to communicate in prayer with them, saying he would pray by himself, which he did privately, and after his arising from his prayer, and when he was set down, he made the sign of the cross upon his forehead and breast, saying: IN NOMINE PATRIS ET FILII, ET SPIRITUS SANCTI [in the name of the Father, and of the Son, and of the Holy Spirit].

Fulke. Mr. Doctor Fulke by way of preface made the hearers acquainted with the state of the question, which he said was that Mr. Campion's own choice and parcel of his book, viz, of the nature of the church; wherein, said Mr. Fulke, you have accused us in following Calvin's definition therein, saying that we thereby have destroyed the substance thereof. And therefore by appointment we come to know whether you mean to persevere in your former assertion. Yea or no?

Campion. Campion prayed Mr. Doctor Fulke to signify his name. Who said, Fulke. Then Campion said: Mr. Doctor Fulke, so it is that in my book I requested disputations, and about a sennight past there came hither some who disputed with me about the first part of my book, they being thereunto prepared, and I brought hither altogether unprovided. There were at that time such as did note and afterwards reported our conference.[2] But I understand there be many things published thereof more than truth is, and that I am belied in print, so that I think it scarce good and just dealing, wishing I had at this time a notary on my part. Besides, at this time also I think it had been convenient I should have had notice of this our present meeting, which I had not.

Fulke. There is nothing published in print but that which is indifferent. But for your preparation wished, you have had as long warning as we had. For on Saturday last it was demanded of you what part of your book you would defend and have disputed. And you appointed this place whereupon this our present question is taken.

Campion. There came indeed unto me on Saturday one to de-

[2] The report of the conference refers to the Nowell–Day version of the first debate which was first circulated and later republished in *A true report* (1583).

mand the same, and I said then, as I say now, that I will either here or in the face of the university justify every part of my challenge in my book. But for this our question, I said that the first part of my book was already disputed of, and the second part of the book is in order next, that may be disputed, if you please. But I would the auditory should understand that I am brought hither unprovided, and my opponents ready furnished thereunto.

Fulke. Your time and ours is all one to this action.

Campion. The contrary doth appear by your heap of books ready prepared before you for the same. But I wish you would consider it to be God's cause which we have in handling, and I would you would dispute to have the truth known rather than to have victory. And if you did so, the better I came provided for the disputations, the better the truth should be sifted and discussed. But I hope the truth is so plain that it will suffice at this time to defend itself. Wherefore, Mr. Doctor, proceed in your purpose, for I trust that the disputations which I requested are yet to come. So after some words to this effect on either part, they descended to the question, which was, as Mr. Fulke said:

UTRUM ECCLESIA SIT VISIBILIS NECNE
[whether or not the church is visible]

Fulke. Whereupon Mr. Doctor Fulke began to frame an argument to prove that because the triumphant church in heaven is not visible, so the church is not visible.

Campion. But Campion, as appeared by his words, perceiving that he meant to take that argument, did say that it was altogether meant in his book of the church militant on earth, and not of the church triumphant in heaven.

Fulke. Calvin's definition is general, and therefore to be intended as well of those that be in heaven, as of those that be on earth, and those that are yet unborn, and you have generally found fault with that definition.

Campion. Calvin's definition is that the church is invisible, and he meaneth only the church militant here on earth. And although I did generally set it down in my book, as Calvin doth, yet my meaning was, as I have said before, only of the church militant on earth. And I spoke therein according to the common phrase of people, who speaking of a general thing, do yet mean a special. As for example, when I talk of a queen, you will intend a queen on earth and not a queen in heaven.

Fulke. Then you start from that which you said in your book, and you refuse to maintain the same.

Campion. No, I still stand to it, and I do but explain my meaning therein to be only of the church militant. And I am sure that the auditory doth not expect that we should dispute of the church in heaven, but of the church on earth, which is visible, and in such manner visible, as that one man may say to another, thou art of my faith, and I of thine, and we both are of one church. But at the last they did, after long intercourse of words, agree on the state of the question: whether the church militant be visible always or no.

Primary Arg.

Fulke. Then Mr. Doctor Fulke, saying he would reason with him dialectically, framed his argument in this sort. In time of Elias, the church was brought to such a scarcity that the prophet complained that there was left none of the faithful but himself alone.[3] So, the church is not always visible.

Campion. Mr. Doctor Fulke, thus you argue, and repeated it, and said: Thus I answer. You must understand this to be spoken in the schismatical country of Samaria, which was but a member of the whole church of the Jews. In which country of Samaria, although he said that he did know none but himself alone, yet it doth not necessarily follow but that there were more, as it is hard for one man to know all. And again, it is evident that under Achab [Asa] and Josaphat [Jehosaphat], two good kings, the true religion was professed and the true church known and visible.[4]

Fulke. What! Do you know where these words were spoken?

Campion. They were spoken by the prophet being persecuted, as he was in his journey from Samaria towards Juda, on the Mount

[3] The following biblical references to the Elias account refer to the King James (KJ) and to the Douay-Rheims (D-R) translations. KJ: 1 Kings 19:10; D-R: 3 Kings 19:10.

[4] The manuscript mistakingly names Achab for Asa. See KJ: 1 Kings 16:29ff.; D-R: 3 Kings 16:29ff. Additional differences in spelling between the two translations are: KJ: Ahab and Jehoshaphat; D-R: Achab and Joshaphat.

Horeb in the wilderness. And therefore you must understand that the prophet did mean that he knew none in Samaria, though the state of Juda were well known unto him. And hereupon Campion did add an example of himself being heretofor at Geneva, where he did not know any of his own religion. Yet, he said, he knew well that there were of them many thousands in Spain, and France, etc. And although at the time of the said complaint of the prophet, the exercise of religion was not permitted, yet is it not consequent but that there were then many that were of the church, as there were here Protestants in the time of Queen Mary, and at this present there are Catholics.

2 Arg.

Fulke. In the time of Manasseh and Achaz [Ahaz], the temple of the Lord was polluted, the sacrifice omitted, and the high priest committed idolatry upon the altar.[5] So, the church was not then visible. For Mr. Fulke said that they were persecuted.

Campion. At that time as in other ages, the high priests did submit themselves to the humor of their princes, and open idolatry was committed in the temple, by reason whereof the sacrifices were omitted, yet it did not follow but that one faithful man did know another. And the Jewish Church differed from the Church of Christ in this, that the Jewish Church had but one place, which was the temple, appointed for the sacrifice. But the Church of Christ hath many places, and lawful for the administration of their sacraments and rites; for it is lawful, and so used in time of persecution, to administer the sacraments abroad in the field, in chambers, and secret places. And I doubt not but that there be many in England that would run twenty miles to hear a Mass, even as in time of Queen Mary they did to their communions. And what, I pray you, was that which did cause the said omission of sacrifice in time of Manasseh and Achaz [Ahaz]? It was, you say, persecution. And who were they that were persecuted? The faithful. So then, you confess, the church is best known when it is persecuted. And in discoursing of the nature and quality of the church, Campion alleged that it was an inseparable quality unto the church to be visible.

[5] Manasseh is described in KJ: 2 Kings 21:1–18 and 24:3; D-R: 4 Kings 21:1–18 and 24:3. For Achaz [Ahaz], see KJ: 2 Kings 16; and D-R: 4 Kings 16.

3 Arg.

Fulke. Against which saying Mr. Doctor Fulke made his argument thus: If visibility be an inseparable quality of the church, then it is an inseparable note of the same, but it is not an inseparable note. So, it is not an inseparable quality.

Campion. I deny your major and your minor. The major I deny because you confound a note and an accident, which in proper sense ought not to be confounded, for they betoken several things, even as the notes and qualities of a way do differ. For the qualities of a way are to be straight, ready, short, and gain [that is, direct]. And yet is none of these a note of the way, but the note of the way is to turn on the right hand or on the left hand, to go by such a cross, such a windmill, which notes being taken away, the way yet remaineth. Your minor I deny because I affirm that it is a note of the church.

Fulke. For the maintenance of his major he proved the property of speech by an argument A DIVISIS AD CONIUNCTA [from distinctions to agreements] thus: It is by your confession a note, and it is inseparable. So, it is a note inseparable. And for the maintenance of his minor: If it be a note, it may be known. But it may not be known. So, it is not a note.

Campion. It may be known.

Fulke. If [it] might be known, it might be seen, but it may not be seen, Ergo.

Goade. It may not be known.

Campion. It may be seen.

Fulke. Fulke proved his minor thus out of Chrysostom,[6] who after many words concluded: QUOD ECCLESIA TANTUMMODO DINOSCITUR EX SCRIPTURIS [because the church is known only from the scriptures].

Campion. That is like to this argument: I believe in God only. So, I do not believe in the church.

Fulke. VISIBILE NON EST SCRIPTURA [scripture is not visible].

[6] St. John Chrysostom (ca. 349–407), a leading Father of the Eastern Church, was noted for his eloquence and for his many religious writings, including commentaries, epistles, and treatises. He served briefly as patriarch of Constantinople until his banishment by Empress Eudoxia.

Campion. Campion denied that for, saith he, this is scripture: Thou art the son of the living God.

Fulke. That is not a scripture.

Campion. Visibility is contained only in the scriptures.

Fulke. But how do you answer Chrysostom who is so directly against you?

Campion. Campion answered that the scope of Chrysostom was to show the difference as trial between the primitive church and that church. For when the apostles did true miracles, those miracles were noted as the true church, but since the faithful ceasing to do miracles, the knowledge of the true church is to be had by the scriptures, wherein is contained that the church is visible. And Campion said that Chrysostom did only exclude miracles in those words.

4 Arg.

Goade. So after some variance in exposition of that place, whether visibility were the scriptures, etc., Mr. Doctor Goade began his argument out of the New Testament, as followeth: In the time of our Savior Christ, the scribes and pharisees sat in Moses' chair, yet the church rested in our Savior Christ. Ergo, the church was not then visible, as you have said.

Campion. You make an argument for me. Although the church were then beginning, yet Christ preached openly in the temple, and there were a number that believed, as Mary the Virgin, Mary Magdalene, Joseph of Arimathea, John the Evangelist, and many others that stood about the cross, which either openly or secretly acknowledged the true religion and were known one to another.

Goade. You said before that the property of a visible church is to have a place of resort, wherein the sacraments may be ministered, which could not be done at that time, nor afterwards in the time of persecution under Diocletian,[7] when Christians were kept in prison and martyred, and had no public place for resort for service and sacraments.

Campion. I do not say that the church should always be in pomp and prosperity. Yet I doubt not but the members of the same were known one to another, and known also to them that did persecute

[7] Diocletian (245–313) was the emperor of Rome from 284 to 305.

them, howbeit they believed not as they did. For in the time of persecution under Diocletian certain escaped the prison, as Silvester and others; as in time of Queen Mary many did, and in this Queen's time do.[8]

Goade. You meddle too much with the state of this time.

Campion. I mean as well Queen Mary's time, as this present time.

Goade. Whereas you say that the church is so visible that one member knoweth another, that cannot be; for the faithless do not know the faithful, according to the saying of St. John. The world doth not know us.

Campion. I answer that the faithless do know the faithful, although not to their salvation, even as I do know you to be a Protestant, and you me to be a Catholic. And for the place in St. John, it is to be intended, as I said before, NON SCIUNT EOS, UT OPORTET, PER FRUCTUM [they know them not, as is proper, by their fruit].

Goade. DEUS TANTUM NOVERIT QUI SUNT EIUS [God alone knows who are his own].

Campion. True it is that DEUS TANTUM NOVERIT QUI SUNT EIUS, that is, God alone knoweth by election who are his. And seeing you yourselves do call your church a congregation of the faithful, and the angels in heaven cannot be called a congregation of the faithful because they are in heaven, but must be a company in earth, as your meaning is, and so visible. Ergo, you mean the church visible.

Fulke. What! Is all the church visible?

Campion. Not all at one time by one man in one place, as it is not possible for me, being in this chamber, to see all men or all Catholics in all places. But yet it is possible for a man being in Spain to see Catholics there, and so there the church is visible.

Fulke. The church is a congregation of the elected.

Campion. Can you say any one man to be elected? This man, or that man? Which if you can not so say, then cannot you show any one man to be of your church. How then, I pray you, answer you the scripture, or can you say with the scriptures: DIC ECCLESIAE [tell it to the church]? Whereupon Mr. Goade somewhat pausing, Mr. Campion said: Mr. Doctor Fulke, now help him with an answer if you can.

---

[8] St. Sylvester was bishop of Rome from 314 to 335.

Fulke. What then? Another time shall serve, for it is not your part to oppose.

Goade. And thereupon Mr. Goade proceeded as followeth: I will urge you with the strongest argument, which is taken to maintain your side to prove your own opinion, which is out of the 5th book [chapter] of Matthew: VOS ESTIS, etc. [you are, etc. . . .].

Campion. I can show you a stronger; the place you mean is very good.

Goade. If you refuse this, I will take yours.

Campion. No, I will not refuse it, but since as we come hither for the glory of God and the sifting out of his truth, rather than for victory in argument, it were good we should have in question the most forcible text, whereby the truth might be the sooner debated and discussed. Also, the place which I would show you is literal and plain, and so more familiar to the audience. And yours, although it is very good, yet is it allegorical.

Goade. Then bear witness, my masters, that he refuseth the place which Hosius and other of this side do esteem as most strong.[9]

Campion. No, you cannot witness that, for I will admit it, lest we should lose our argument. And, therefore, frame your argument and you shall be answered.

Goade. The place above mentioned of St. Matthew hath these words: NON POTEST CIVITAS SUPRA MONTEM POSITA ABSCONDI [a city placed on a mountain cannot be hidden]. You say this is intended as spoken to the whole church, and we affirm it was only spoken of the apostles.

Campion. It was spoken of them in two degrees, as well in respect that they were of the faithful, as in respect that they were apostles in their function. And this is not particularly spoken unto them in respect of their function only, wherefore not like other places of scripture, which import of a special reference to their function, as

[9] Stanislaus Hosius (1504–79), born in Cracow, Poland, became a leading churchman during the Counter Reformation. He was nominated bishop of Culm in 1549 and in 1551 was transferred to the see of Ermland in East Prussia. He was the spirit behind the Catholic movement to stem the tide of Protestantism throughout Europe. He combated heresy, rallied the clergy, convoked synods, and opened schools and colleges for the training of priests. His *Confessio Catholicae Fidei Christiana* . . . went through thirty-two editions in his lifetime. He was called the "second Augustine" and "hammer of heretics." Pius IV sent him on diplomatic missions to Vienna toward reopening the Council of Trent. He was created cardinal in 1561.

ITE ET BAPTIZATE [go forth and baptize], and many other places which are only proper to their function. But the circumstance of this place and the plain words of the text do evidently prove these words above mentioned to pertain to them in both the degrees, as I have already said. For mark the words precedent spoken to the apostles in the same chapter: VOS ESTIS SAL TERRAE ET LUX MUNDI [you are the salt of the earth and the light of the world.]: meaning by this word, SAL, the apostles, and by TERRAE, the rest of the church. Likewise meaning by LUX, the apostles, and by MUNDI, the rest of the church. Howbeit by these words the apostles and the church are severed, yet in the text immediately following it is said: NON POTEST CIVITAS, ETC., wherein the apostles are considered in both their respects, as I have said above. As oftentimes by naming the principal of anything, the inferior parts be included. As for example, in this word PATERFAMILIAS [head of the family] is included the whole family, even so speaking in this place to the apostles, as the chief of the faithful, he included the remnant, having no other words to prove he spoke generally of the apostles, as he did in the other places before, so that it is evident by the circumstance of the text that Christ meant the whole church.

Goade. I will urge you with two doctors, which are Chrysostom and Jerome, which do explain this place to be meant of the apostles, as I have alleged. And because Mr. Goade could not readily turn to the places, it was appointed they should be prepared against after dinner.

Campion. I would, Mr. Goade, that you and I might shake hands together of St. Jerome's religion, that we might meet together with him in heaven.

Goade. I will not be of man's religion further than he is of Christ's.

Campion. Therein do you well, for we must not be of Paul, Cephas, or Apollo further than they are of Christ. And having thus ended, Mr. Campion wished that he might urge the other place before by him mentioned, which he said was a stronger.

Goade. Although it be contrary to the order of disputation and to our appointed conference, yet I will admit it, therefore show the place.

Campion. It is taken out of the 18th chapter of Matthew, where it is said: SI PECCAVERIT IN TE FRATER TUUS, CORRIPE EUM, SIC SI TE NON AUDIERIT, DIC ECCLESIAE [if your brother trespass against you, reprove him, and if he will not hear you, tell it to the church]. Whereupon thus I reason: seeing these words, DIC ECCLESIAE, are always to be executed in the church of God, ergo it must be always visible.

Goade. I will distinguish of your antecedent, for it must be executed when there is a visible face of the church, but not always as when the members thereof are afflicted, and the congregation unknown.

Campion. This was a remedy for all ages; then seeing the malady is continual, the remedy must be in like manner continual. As for example, offense betwixt brother and brother do continually chance, whereupon he must exhort him privately and after show the church, as he is counseled by his text. Ergo, the remedy in all ages must be executed. And I pray you, before Luther his time, whither or to what pastor should one resort for this continual remedy, seeing for many hundred years there was none at all known of this religion.

Goade. It cannot be had in persecution.

Campion. In vain was it then of Christ commanded that this remedy should be always executed, seeing it cannot be executed in time of persecution. For although persecution be in one place, yet this complaint may be done in divers other places. As for example, the Protestants in Queen Mary's time being persecuted in England, yet they might have this remedy in Germany where their religion was used. And although every one cannot attain to this remedy, yet the remedy is in being as good and available. As for example, if a man make a feast for all comers thereunto, yet two or three being restrained by imprisonment or otherwise may die for hunger, and yet the remedy in being and to be had, although not to them.

Fulke. The remedy may be good although not applied, as a remedy in apothecary's shop may be good, although it be not used.

Campion. That proveth the remedy to be in being to all such as could come by it.

Fulke. And thus having in manner ended the forenoon's disputation, Mr. Fulke said after divers intercourse of speech that ECCLESIA is sometimes taken for COETUS FIDELIUM [assemblage of the faithful].

Campion. ECCLESIA is nowhere taken for the church invisible only.

Fulke. Yes, for to believe in the church is an article of our faith; and faith is invisible; ergo, the church is invisible.

Campion. Although faith be invisible, yet OBIECTUM FIDEI [object of faith] is visible. And to believe in Christ is an article of our faith. Will you conclude, therefore, that Christ could not be seen when he was here on earth in his natural body? Mr. Campion urging them to reply against these answers, Mr. Fulke and Mr. Goade said that he vaunted himself too much and hath deceived them of the opinion of modesty, which they conceived and heard of him. Whereunto Mr. Campion replied that for humility he would be contented to kiss their feet; but in the truth of Christ I must not by humility give you place; for the scripture saith: NON SIS HUMILIS IN SAPIENTIA TUA [be not humble in your wisdom] and uttered other texts to that purpose, saying that he must not betray the truth by using too much humility; and thus they ended, declaring what should be their question for the afternoon, viz.: WHETHER THE CHURCH MILITANT OF CHRIST MAY ERR IN MATTERS OF FAITH.

[Afternoon Session]

After dinner the company there assembled were about the number of 60 persons, and the same order used as was before noon, and the place out of Chrysostom, which Mr. Goade did urge before noon against Mr. Campion, was read, and expounding the text of the 5th of Matthew before alleged by him, which in effect was that St. Chrysostom did expound the place CIVITAS SUPRA MONTEM POSITA to be spoken to the apostles.

Goade. And with that Mr. Goade said: You see, Mr. Campion, that Chrysostom doth hold contrary to your opinion.

Campion. St. Chrysostom doth not say that Christ speaking there to the apostles did speak to them as apostles in respect of their function, but speaking generally as may be intended as well that he meant his speech to them as they were of the faithful, and not in respect of their function. And unless St. Chrysostom had said that Christ spoke to them in respect of their function he proveth nothing for you no more than for me.

And having thus answered, Mr. Fulke began his argument as followeth, touching this question:

WHETHER THE MILITANT CHURCH OF CHRIST MAY ERR IN MATTERS OF FAITH

1 Arg.

Fulke. I will urge you, Mr. Campion, with this argument. That that is incident to every member is incident unto the whole; but to err is incident to every member; ergo, to the whole.

Campion. I deny your major.

Fulke. My major is a place of logic which cannot be denied.

Campion. There is no such place; and although there were, yet it cannot hold in this point; for Christ promised the special assistance of his Holy Spirit unto the whole Church, to lead her into all truth, which was not promised to every singular member thereof. For it is manifest that divers members thereof have fallen from the church and so have erred.

Fulke. Such were never of the church; for if they had been, they had remained thereof still. For as St. John saith: EXIERE DE NOBIS, QUIA NON FUERE EX NOBIS [they went out from us, because they were not of us].

Campion. These words EXIERE DE NOBIS do manifestly prove that they were once in the church, or else they could not have gone out from us. And although the text saith further QUIA NON FUERE EX NOBIS, that is to be intended of those that be of us by election. For Wicliff and Arius were once of the church, and yet after did fall from the church because they were not thereof by election.[10]

Fulke. Arius had never faith; for if he had, he could never have fallen from the church.

---

[10] John Wycliff (ca. 1328–84) was an English reformer whose attacks on church doctrine, especially transubstantiation, led to his being condemned as a heretic in both 1380 and 1382.

Arius (ca. 250–ca. 336), a North African priest and theologian, was a successful preacher until his heretical teachings about the subordination of Christ led St. Alexander, bishop of Alexandria, to excommunicate him in ca. 321. Arius reasoned that if the Son were really the Son of God there must have been a time when he did not exist. His views were refuted by St. Athanasius and condemned at the First Council of Nicaea (325).

Campion. Not so, for so long as he remained in the church and did believe as the church did, so long was he of the church. For like as a father that hath many children in his house, of which some are very disobedient and perverse, yet during the time they obey his commandments, and he doth allow them for his sons, so long are they to be accompted his sons until for their disobedience and wickedness they be cast out, and then no longer may they be accompted his sons. Even so during the time that they were of the Catholic Church and did believe, as the Catholic Church did believe, they were of the church until for their false opinion they were cast out.

Fulke. That is not so. For if he be once of the church, he shall never be cast out.

Campion. How then doth the scripture say: EIECIT ILLOS IN TENEBRAS EXTERIORES [he cast them out into exterior darkness]?

Fulke. If he be once the son of God, he is heir, as St. Paul saith, and never can become the son of the devil.

Campion. David was the son of God, and yet by a most horrible sin committed against God by adultery and murder became the son of the devil in that fact, till by repentance he had reconciled himself to God again.

Fulke and Goade. We deny that David was ever the son of the devil.

Campion. St. John saith: QUI FACIT PECCATUM, SERVUS EST PECCATI [whoever sins is the servant of sin], but David FECIT PECCATUM; ergo, FUIT SERVUS PECCATI ET PER CONSEQUENS SERVUS DIABOLI, for that fact [David sinned; therefore, he was the servant of sin and, as a consequence, a servant of the devil].

Goade. Every sin of frailty doth not make a man SERVUS PECCATI but those which proceed of malice or want of grace.

Campion. What! Did not David's sin proceed of malice in committing that fact [act?] with Bathsheba and in killing her husband Uriah? It is clear it did, and so it doth in committing of most of the capital offenses which always do include malice.

Fulke. We are from our question.

Hopton. And therewithal Sir Owen Hopton, the Lieutenant of the Tower, said: I must needs tell you that you are departed from the state of the question.

Fulke. And with that Mr. Fulke began to prove the question as followeth and said that every particular man hath the spirit promised him. And for proof thereof alleged the place: NISI QUIS RENATUS FUERIT EX AQUA ET SPIRITU SANTO, etc. [unless one be reborn by water and the Holy Spirit . . .].

Campion. That is only meant of baptism in which the Holy Ghost doth work remission of sin and not any assurance of their steadfast continuance in the truth, as it is to the church.

Fulke. You are deceived. Original sin is not taken away by baptism.

Campion. That is very strange. For shall not an infant after baptism be saved? For what, I pray you, shall let [that is, prevent] him?

Fulke. I will not enter into the judgments of God, but I think if he be reprobate he shall not be saved.

Campion. Then may a child by your opinion be without baptism as well as have it, seeing it neither worketh remission of original sin, neither furtherest to salvation, which is a strange position and contrary to express scripture.

And after certain speeches uttered, they left this argument, and partly also because they had departed from the state of the question; and so Mr. Goade commenced a new argument as followeth.

2 Arg.

Goade. I will urge you thus: every particular church, as the Church of the Corinthians and Galatians, may err; ergo, the whole church may err.

Campion. Campion, repeating his argument, answered his antecedent and denied his consequent. And for the antecedent said that the whole Church of the Corinthians did not err; for St. Paul doth not say that all did err, but certain; for the text doth mention but of QUIDAM [certain], which can not imply all. The which Mr. Goade did likewise grant. And although St. Paul did speak generally, O STULTI GALATAE, QUIS VOS FASCINAVIT [O foolish Galatians, who hath bewitched you], yet he did not mean that all did err, but did speak after the manner of a preacher, rebuking the whole assembly for some particular sins, as whoredom and the like, not meaning thereby that all were faulty in that sin, but only certain, or the most part.[11] And as for your consequent, it doth nothing follow; for al-

[11] St. Paul (Galatians 3:1) reads: "O incensati Galatae, quis vos fascinavit. . . ."

though a particular did or may err; yet it doth not follow that the whole should err, no more than of error in one man, it should follow the whole to err, as I have showed in Mr. Doctor Fulke's argument.

Wherewith, Mr. Doctor Goade being belike satisfied, proceedeth in sort as followeth.

Goade. The Church of Rome hath erred in matters of faith. Ergo, the true church hath and may err.

Campion. Repeated the argument and prayed Master Lieutenant to put him in mind of the question, which is, whether Christ's militant church may err. And now, you see, Mr. Goade doth prove that the true church hath erred because the Church of Rome hath erred, whereas you all know it to be a question whether the Church of Rome be the true church or no.

Goade. You believe the Church of Rome to be the true church. Then if we may prove error in the Church of Rome, we do prove the true church may err.

Campion. Not so, for first you must grant the Church of Rome to be the true church; and then if you prove error in it, you must prove error in the true church.

Goade. We will suppose for this time that it is the true church.

Campion. Suppose it you, and I will believe it. And although it be not the question, yet lest the audience should be disappointed, I will maintain it; and then in this manner must be your argument. The Church of Rome is the true church, and that church hath erred. Ergo, the true church hath erred. And then I would have you prove your minor.

Goade. Thus I prove it. The Council of Trent hath erred in affirming matters of justification to be inherent in ourselves; ergo, the church hath erred.

Campion. The Council of Trent did not affirm the cause of justification to be inherent in us, as the Pelagians did, but as given from God of his mere mercy unto us, and so to be said inherent in us, as faith, hope, and charity whereby we are enabled to work our own justification, which are not of us, but in us by the special mercy and free gift of God.[12]

[12] Pelagius, a fifth-century British monk, taught that man is the author of his own salvation. His teachings were attacked by St. Augustine and condemned by the Church.

Goade. That which justifieth must be perfect and answerable to the law of God.

Campion. It must be perfect according to the perfection which God requireth at our hands; for God doth not require such an exquisite perfection as should satisfy the rigor of the law, because by his passion he hath delivered us from the bondage and curse of the law.

Fulke. Man's justification groweth by performance of the law, which is not possible for any man to perform. Ergo.

Campion. The law may be fulfilled by this means: in loving God above all things, and thy neighbor as thyself, which a man may well do by the grace of God.

Goade. Note this absurdity, for no man can keep these commandments.

And therewith some in affirming the same did hiss.

Campion. Because there was a hiss given in that I said the commandments might be performed, I beseech you give me leave to explain my mind how the commandments may be performed, and that is: to love God with all his heart so far forth as it is required at his hands, that is, to love him above all things, to prefer him before all other riches, to forsake all things for his sake, so that he would renounce the world and also his life, to cleave and stick to God. And the other, to love his neighbor, that is to be understood to prefer him before any riches, and withal to be ready to pleasure him in that that lieth in him. And in vain was it commanded to be performed, if it were impossible to be performed. And all this may be performed by the special assistance of almighty God. And, I pray you, let this be noted.

Fulke. It was not Christ's meaning in giving these commandments that they should be performed, but that we seeing our own infirmities by them might be still moved to call for mercy.

Campion. Then might Christ as well tell us that we might not perform them, and so bid us call for mercy, as to command us to perform them, seeing by your reason we may not. But the contrary doth appear in that he commanded it must be performed. For unjust were that father which would command his sons to do certain things which they cannot perform, and withal meaneth that they should not perform it, being plain contrary to his commandment. For how can his will be known but by his express words?

Fulke. No, that cannot be the meaning; but as I have alleged it before, seeing that it is impossible to perform them, every cognitation and temptation being a sin.

Campion. That is strange, that every temptation is a sin, whereas the scripture saith: BEATUS VIR QUI SUFFERT TENTATIONEM [blessed is the man who suffers temptation], and by your reason he is MALEDICTUS [cursed]. And withal it followeth of your position that if one come to the Queen's jewel house and is tempted to steal, if he do resist the temptation, he doth offend in resisting, which is strange in my conceit.

Fulke. It may be strange among the Jesuits, but nothing strange among the servants of God.

Goade. How doth the opinion of justification inherent stand with the opinion of St. Paul, who saith we are justified in Christ?

Campion. We are justified in Christ by these means, that is, part in Christ and part in ourselves. In Christ his passion and his mercy, and in us faith, hope, and charity, of the gift and mercy of God, and so inherent in us.

And having so answered, Mr. Fulke began as followeth.

3 Arg.

Fulke. The general councils may err; ergo, the church militant may err.

Campion. General councils cannot err in matters of faith.

Fulke. It appeareth by St. Augustine against the Donatists, the second tome, that provincial and general councils may err and be reformed, for his words be these: EPISCOPI NONNUMQUAM AB ARCHIEPISCOPIS CORRIGUNTUR; ARCHIEPISCOPI A CONSILIIS PROVINCIALIBUS, & PROVINCIALIA PLENARIIS; & IPSA QUOQUE PRIORA POSTERIORIBUS EMENDANTUR, & EXPERIMENTO QUOD CLAUSUM EST APERITUR [some bishops are corrected by archbishops, archbishops by provincial councils and provincial councils by plenary; the earlier may be amended by the later, and by experiment what was hidden may be revealed].[13]

[13] The Donatists, against whom Augustine wrote, were members of a rigorous sect of Christians in North Africa (311–431) who protested against the consecration of Caecilian by Felix, a *traditor* bishop. The Donatists, named for Donatus, a rival to Caecilian, believed that the validity of the sacraments depended on the spiritual state of the minister and that all who joined their sect must be rebaptized.

Campion. It appeareth not by St. Augustine that councils may err in matters of faith or in their decrees thereof, for the word EMENDANTUR doth import no less. And error cannot properly be said to be amended; nor heresy cannot be said to be amended; wherefore he intendeth that councils may be expounded or explained in matters of faith, and so amended, but in matters of discipline or manners to be changed and ordered according to the difference of places and times, as appeareth by other words in the same place, which be EXPERIMENTO QUOD CLAUSUM EST APERITUR, which cannot be for matters of faith, whereof there is no experience, but only in matter of fact; and in matters of fact we do not deny but the church may err. As if a council should condemn a man of a crime whereof he was not guilty, therein or in the like perchance they may err. And seeming herein to be satisfied, Mr. Goade proceeded.

4 Arg.

Goade. One general council is contrary to another. Therefore, the one hath erred.

Campion. This is the only argument that was yet moved worthy the answering. And I deny that one general council is contrary to another.

Goade. The Councils of Nicea and Constantinople did decree one against another concerning images.[14] Therefore, the one hath erred. But because Mr. Goade did not remember what Council of Nicea, the first or the second, neither whether it was the first Council of Constantinople or the second, that day they proceeded no further.

The next day after the disputation Mr. Goade showed the councils.

Campion. Whereunto Campion answered that the second of Nicea being general did condemn that Council of Constantinople being but an assembly or conventicle of a certain sect called the ICONOMACHI [iconoclasts], assembled without lawful authority; and in the book which they showed, he alleged it was not alleged as a council, but recited by the author showing it to be annulled and con-

[14] Constantinople (754) condemned worship and veneration of images; decrees regarding images that were made at Constantinople (754) were set aside at Nicaea (787).

demned as of no authority for the cause before said. Whereunto they did seem to agree.

5 Arg.

Goade. The Council of Constantinople erred in that they decreed to take the cup from laity, contrary to the scripture: BIBITE EX HOC OMNES [drink all of this].

Campion. These words were only spoken to the apostles being present, and none which were of the laity, for any thing that may appear. For by OMNES was meant all that were present, as if a man should say to a company, Drink you all, or every of you; or let this cup go through you all.

Fulke. How say you then by these words of St. Paul to the Corinthians, I.11:28: PROBET [AUTEM] SEIPSUM HOMO, & SIC DE PANE ILLO EDAT, & [DE] CALICE BIBAT [let a man improve himself by eating the bread and drinking from the cup]. These words EDAT & BIBAT be the imperative mood, and so all men commanded both to take and drink both kinds, and you deny them.

Campion. These words of St. Paul do not command all men to take or to drink, as you say, but do import that such as do receive both kinds, SEIPSOS PROBENT [let them improve themselves]. For find you by those words that we are commanded once or twice or at all any time in this life to receive either the one or the other; but only such as do receive SEIPSOS PROBENT. And yet are we bound to receive once a year, at the least by the commandment of the church, although not commanded in scripture; and so you see we are bound to certain commandments not mentioned in scripture, which is contrary to your doctrine.

Fulke. Do you say the scriptures do command both kinds not to be received?

Campion. Not so neither, for I do allow that both kinds may be received so that a man do it with humility and by license; for so have I seen myself. And I confess that in the primitive church it hath been said to have been received sometimes under one kind, and sometimes under both; and so may be received again at the appointment and discretion of the church. And withal it is no matter of faith whether the laity do receive under both kinds, seeing the body doth comprehend both. But notwithstanding, in the institution of the sacrament it was requisite that both should be used, because it did prefigure the passion of Christ. And the church doth retain both still in the sacrifice of the Mass, being the figure of his passion.

6 Arg.

Fulke. Innocent the Third, Bishop of Rome, decreed that infants could not be saved without receiving the sacrament of the altar, and vouched out of his notebook for proof thereof, St. Augustine, *Contra Pelagianos*, lib. 2, cap. 4.[15]

Campion. You show no other authority but your notebook. Therefore, I think St. Augustine hath no such place that expressly proveth that Innocent did indifferently decree that of necessity infants ought to receive that sacrament, but only showed the practice of the church allowed of at that time, and withal this proveth nothing the question we have in hand.

7 Arg.

Goade. Peter, whom you affirm to be the head of the church, did err, and was therefore reprehended of St. Paul in the first to the Galatians, and therefore, the church hath erred.

Campion. What is this to our question? Notwithstanding, I deny that Peter did err in any matter of faith. And therefore the place was read; and Mr. Campion answered that St. Paul did reprehend St. Peter for eating and companying with the Jews, and segregating himself from the company of the Gentiles, which was no matter of faith, but only of manners and conversation, as appeareth by the text, which doth call it but dissimulation; and withal, it was but for frailty, fearing the Jews; for the text saith: TIMENS EOS QUI EX CIRCUMCISIONE ERANT [fearing them who were circumcised].

Fulke. Think you not, Mr. Campion, that Peter thought it a matter of conscience?

Campion. I know not. It might be that Peter was of opinion that it was lawful for him to keep company with the Jews, only so yielding something more thereby to their weakness, which St. Paul, being

[15] Innocent III (1160–1216), pope from 1198, greatly enhanced the power and the authority of the Roman Catholic Church.

more strict, did not allow of, as if one Catholic should hold that it were lawful to be conversant with Protestants, and another doth hold the contrary. Which opinions, being only but touching conversation, is no matter of faith. St. Jerome also doth think that St. Peter was not reprehensible in that act, although St. Augustine should seem to be of the contrary opinion.

Goade. Take heed of dissuading men from companying together, lest you incur the danger of some statutes.

Campion. I hope, Mr. Goade, you came not to threaten me. I say nothing but that some men are of opinion that Catholics ought not to be conversant with Protestants. What then of this?

Goade. I do not threaten you, but do friendly warn you to take heed for your own safety.

Fulke. You see, Mr. Campion, that Paul did reprehend Peter whom you call the head of the apostles, whereas you hold that no man may reprehend the pope.

Campion. We do hold that every man may admonish and reprehend the pope; yea, the poorest friar that is may admonish him.

Fulke. Gratian saith that no man may reprehend the pope, although he did carry a hundred persons by his example to hell.

Campion. There is no such place in Gratian, nor in any other approved author.

Fulke the next day did show the place of Gratian.

Campion. The meaning of the place is that no man may judicially reprehend the pope, nor examine him; but that no man may charitably reprehend him or admonish him, the text doth not import. For a subject may charitably reprehend his prince, although not judicially reprove him.

8 Arg.

Fulke. The Council of Nicea, the second, decreed that angels had bodies, which is a great error, and for proof he vouched his notebook, which was to this effect that: QUOD JOHANNES MONACHUS DIXIT NON ESSE CORPORIS EXPERTES, etc. [which Joannes, the monk, said are not devoid of bodies].[16]

[16] In the authorized edition of 1583 (*A true report*) Fulke states that Johannes, bishop of Thessalonica, read at the Second Council of Nicaea that angels are "not altogether without bodies, and invisible." Tharasius, archbishop of Constantinople, agreeing with John, said, "we must paint the Angels also, seeing they may be circumscribed, and have appeared as men. . . . The holy synod said, yea my lord" (N2).

Campion. You still allege for authority your notebook, which no man of judgment ought to allow. But to answer the place, I say it is not the decree of the council, but the opinion of that Johannes Monachus, whose opinion is there recited. And although the place were the decree, as it is not, yet it doth not affirm that angels have such bodies as we have, but certain airy substances, as it may appear by the place. For it doth not follow because ASSUMUNT SIBI CORPORA [they assume bodies to themselves] that therefore they have bodies; but it rather followeth they have none, because they do assume other bodies, which they could not, if they had bodies of their own, the which he inferred upon the sight of the book the next day of their disputation. And further, admitting all that you do allege, yet this thing being no matter of faith, but a thing indifferent to be believed, it maketh nothing to prove your argument that the church may err in matters of faith. For I doubt not but many good men that be now in heaven were of opinion that angels had bodies, as Athanasius and others whom they hold there to be of that opinion.

Fulke. It is no matter of manners, and what is it then?

Campion. It is, if it be admitted, a little fault and no error in faith; for, I pray you, is it a matter of salvation or damnation to believe that they have bodies or lack bodies?

Fulke. It is no matter of salvation nor damnation, I grant, but yet matter of faith.

Campion. That is a strange thing, to be a matter of faith, and no matter of salvation. Show me one such matter of faith. Here hath been many strange paradoxes granted this day. I would they were noted: That a thing may be a matter of faith, and no matter of salvation. That baptism taketh not away original sin. That if a man be once of the church, he shall never be out of the church, and so fall from the church. That every temptation is sin. That David in committing adultery and murder was not in that act the servant of sin.

Fulke. I can show you many matters of faith which be not matters of salvation, and thereupon showed the matter in question, that is, whether the angels had bodies.

Campion. That is no example. But, Mr. Fulke, it standeth upon you to prove that the church may err in matters of faith; for so you say in your book against Mr. Doctor Bristow. I would you would maintain it.[17]

[17] In 1574 Richard Bristow, professor at Douai, published his *Motives to the Catho-*

Fulke. I am to maintain my book by another way.

Campion. I am called forth to maintain my book here, and why should not you in the like sort maintain yours? But you are not able to maintain it. I will prove that you hold divers blasphemies in it. Wherefore send it to this worshipful gentleman, meaning the Lieutenant of the Tower, and I will against the next day show the things that I have said; or I would you would maintain it against me in Cambridge.

Fulke. You shall have my book, and I know there is nothing therein but that which I am able to justify. The next day of their disputation, Mr. Fulke in the forenoon delivered Mr. Campion a book, the which all the time of their disputation he held in his hands without looking thereon.

Campion. But in the afternoon he told Mr. Fulke that he desired his book against Bristow, and that he delivered him another book against Heskins and Saunders [Sanders], which he never meant nor desired.[18]

Fulke. How could I know your mind or intent?

Campion. I demanded expressly your book against Bristow, and so ended for that point.

9 Arg.

Fulke. It appeareth by a prayer used at the end of every council that they may err, wherein are these words: IGNORANTIAE PAR-

like Faith (STC 3799) and, in 1576, a revised edition entitled *Demaundes to bee proponed of Catholickes to the Heretickes* (STC 3801). Fulke replied in *Two Treatises written against the Papistes* (STC 11458), written in 1568–69 but not published until 1577. Bristow's *A Reply to Fulke* (STC 3802) appeared in 1580, the same year as Fulke's *A Retentive, to stay good Christians, in faith and religion, against the motives of Richard Bristow* (STC 11449). Fulke's next work in the exchange, *A Reioynder to Bristows Replie* (STC 11448), was published in 1581, the year of Bristow's death. See Milward, *Religious Controversies of the Elizabethan Age*, pp. 39–43.

[18] Thomas Heskyns (fl. 1566), a Dominican priest, defended the Mass in *The Parliament of Chryste* (STC 13250) in 1566; Fulke responded in *D. Heskins, D. Sanders, and M. Rastel* (STC 11433), a work published in 1579. See Milward, *Religious Controversies of the Elizabethan Age*, pp. 7, 12–13, and 16–17.

Nicholas Sanders (Sander) (1530–81) was an Oxford graduate who left England after Elizabeth's accession and went to Rome, where he earned a doctorate in divinity and was ordained by Thomas Goldwell, bishop of St. Asaph. In 1561 he accompanied Cardinal Hosius to the Council of Trent and on missions to Prussia, Poland, and Lithuania. From 1565 to 1572 he was a member of theological faculty at the University of Louvain, where he was authorized to grant English priests faculties

CAS, & ERRORI INDULGEAS [spare ignorance and make allowance for errors] which words do imply that they may err.

Campion. You show us nothing but your notebook for proof of any such prayer to be used. But admitting it to be true, as you report it, yet that doth not imply that necessarily they may err in matters of faith, but in some small errors, as in matters of fact or negligence, which might have overslipped them. As for example, the council might err in accusing a man of some crime or fault, who perchance was guiltless of the same. For do you suppose that the Council of Trent would have used that prayer if they had thought it to imply necessarily that they might err in matters of faith, whereas their meaning is contrary; and to expound it contrary to their meaning is a hard exposition. And further, the word IGNORANTIAE doth not imply errors in faith, no more than where David saith, IGNORANTIAS MEAS NE MEMINERIS DOMINE [O Lord, remember not my ignorances]. And yet he did not mean thereby errors in faith.

Fulke. The prophet there meanest of his ignorances, but here the council said, ERRORI INDULGEAS, which must be intended of errors in doctrine.

Campion. Although it be so, yet it is to be intended errors of fact, and not errors of faith. And I refer my further answer when you show the place. And the next day of the disputation the prayer was showed forth by Mr. Fulke; to which Mr. Campion answered that the prayer was to forgive those their errors which had made any objection contrary to the truth established in that council, as it doth always chance before any matter in controversy be determined, divers objections be made to the contrary, thereby to sift out the truth the better, as in this present controversy betwixt us. And let this answer be noted.

Ult. Arg.

Goade. Goade did urge this argument: The church hath taken away an article of our faith, ergo, the church hath erred.

---

for absolving cases of heresy and schism and to prohibit Catholic attendance at Anglican services. In 1573 he visited Madrid and received a pension from Philip II. He was sent by the pope to Ireland to incite Irish chieftains to rebellion; he is alleged to have died of cold and hunger in the Irish hills. For a brief summary of his writings, see Milward, *Religious Controversies of the Elizabethan Age*, pp. 11–15.

Campion. God forbid.

Goade. I do not say directly, but by a mean, for by a mean and implication it denieth the ascension of our Savior into heaven, which we find expressly in our Creed. Ergo.

Campion. I deny the antecedent.

Goade. They say that he remained here upon the earth, because he is really in the sacrament; ergo, not in heaven.

Campion. I deny your consequent, for it followeth not that because he be present in the sacrament that he is not in heaven. For we do not suppose him tied to the condition of a natural body, as appeareth by the miracle of his ascension, which contrary to the nature of any earthly body sweeping downwards towards the earth, mounteth up to heaven by like degrees as we go upon the earth, and did enter the highest heavens which are as hard as crystal, without any breach or violence offered to the same.

Fulke. That which you say of the hardness of the heavens is against Trismegistus' opinion, which you cannot defend against the philosophers of Cambridge.[19]

Campion. I will defend it against any philosopher. And further, I add that it was impossible for a natural body to walk upon the water, and to enter into a closed house, the door being shut, as we find that Christ hath done.[20]

Goade. We say that the doors did open at his entry, as they did unto Peter in the Acts of the Apostles, when the angel delivered him out of prison [Acts.12:5–11].

Campion. We find it expressed in that text that the doors did open unto Peter, and after did shut again; but we find no such express mention of Christ. And I hope you will not deny this to be a miracle.

---

[19] Trismegistus, a celebrated Egyptian priest and philosopher, is reported to have translated the written tablets of Mercury (Hermes), and thus is credited with the restoration of wisdom, especially the arts and mathematics. He gave his ingenious interpretations of the inscribed symbols to the care of the priesthood. He is said to have been the author of many volumes on universal principles, on the nature and order of celestial beings, on astrology, on medicine, and on other topics.

It is interesting to note that Campion had actually debated this topic during his student days at Oxford.

[20] Accounts of Christ's walking on the water are found in Matthew 14:22–27, Mark 6:45–51, and John 6:16–21; on Christ's entering the closed house, see John 20:19–23.

Fulke. I confess it to be a miracle, although the text import it not so much; for it was a miracle of the divine operation that the doors yielded unto our Savior Christ.

And therefore for the better understanding thereof he read the text; and therewithal they offered to him a Greek Testament, which Mr. Campion received but read not, but recited the words in Latin, saying that the Greek words imported no more. Wherefore they might use the common language which was Latin, until there were any cause to appeal to the Greek, and then he returned to the book again.

Fulke. The Greek is the original language wherein the apostles did write, wherefore the fittest for this time and controversy.

Campion. The text hath that Christ entered CLAUSIS IANUIS. Therefore, the doors did not yield unto him.

Fulke. What is the tense of this Greek word?

Campion. Answered that it was an aorist.

Fulke. Read the text, and said it was preter perfect tense, and that it was in Latin as much as CUM FUISSENT CLAUSAE [when they had been closed].

Campion. You say it is a preter perfect tense, which is all one. Here hath been a great glorying in vaunting oftentimes of the Greek text, and I have been divers times offered to read the same, as though I could not read it, which I am loth to say, it is very childish. Yet be you sure, when time shall serve that we shall have need of the Greek, you shall find that I have sufficient to prove and justify my cause. And the Latin words are these: CLAUSIS IANUIS, as I said before, which if they differ from the Greek, then may some controversy arise about understanding the Greek. But insomuch as they differ not, I think the Greek needless to be read. And by these words, CLAUSIS IANUIS, it is manifest that the doors were not open but shut; and therefore he must needs come through the doors or walls. You will not say that he came in by a juggling trick. Luther, who was as great an enemy to me as you are, thought it a very strange and monstrous opinion to say that Christ was not really in the sacrament.

Goade. Luther confessed consubstantiation, but not transubstantiation. There is a place in St. Augustine, though I cannot call it to memory, that there is no miracle wrought in the sacrament.

Fulke. The place is this: MIRUM QUOD EST IN SACRA-

MENTO STUPOREM NON HABET [the wonder that is in the sacrament is not bewildering].

Campion. There is no visible miracle to make the astonishment of the senses, the wonder being hid under bread and wine. And sure I am that St. Augustine hath no such place that there was no miracle in the sacrament. But St. Chrysostom saith in these words speaking of the sacrament: O MAGNUM MYSTERIUM [O great mystery], affirming that at the time of the celebration the angels to be present.

Fulke. You seem not to have read St. Augustine.

Campion. Seeing you charge me with ignorance in St. Augustine, I challenge you before this company to dispute with you in St. Augustine in the University of Cambridge.

Fulke. I am ready if I be enjoined thereunto; but I marvel not at your confidence in challenging me, who have challenged all the learned in the whole kingdom.

Campion. To prove that the sun is sun, and the day is day, I dare challenge all the whole world. And I pray you, seeing I have been pressed to answer all this day, that either now or the next time I may be admitted to oppose also.

Fulke. We are therein to be directed by others. Wherefore if it please them so to appoint, we shall be well content.

FINIS

[Third Disputation]

[Morning Session]

Before they began disputation, Sir Owen Hopton willed Mr. Campion to acknowledge the mercifulness of our gracious Queen towards him, in granting him so much liberty as to come to the trial of his demand. Whereunto Mr. Campion answered as followeth.

Campion. I do protest that I came hither with a mind resolute, and I come hither as one not of a suspended mind, or doubtful, but wholly resolved in matters of faith. These parties, my adversaries that come hither, come to reform me, and I come hither to reform them. And withal I humbly acknowledge my prince's great benevolence towards me. And as for you that are come to confer with me, I give you hearty thanks. And as I take the cause of your coming in good part, so I do request you to take mine. And therefore, IN NOMINE, etc. [in the name, etc.]. At your pleasure proceed to argument.

Fulke. Then Mr. Doctor Fulke said: Let us begin with prayer. The effect whereof was that God would give them understanding to make manifest his truth, to the utter subversion and confusion of heresy and falsehood.

Campion. I have prayed before I came; wherefore you may proceed, if you please.

Fulke. At our last conference, Mr. Campion, you answered our arguments with multitude of words, similitudes, comparisons, and distinctions. Whereupon it was reported that we could say nothing. But this day, Mr. Campion, we mean to cut you shorter.

Campion. No sir, but if my words have offended you, I will be briefer.

Fulke. Before we come to our arguments, we will discharge our credit and show certain places we vouched at our last conference, because Mr. Campion doubted whether there were any such place or no, for that we had not the books in present which are added to the last disputation, in their proper places, as they were alleged. Then he showed forth a decree of Innocent III, alleged by St. Augustine, that infants could not be saved without receiving the sacrament of the altar.

Campion. I answer, as I did before, that the decree of Innocent was not indifferently spoken as simply necessary, but only allowed it as the practice of the church at that time.

Fulke. Then the place of the Second Nicene Council, Art. 5, was alleged by Mr. Fulke to prove that the council erred in decreeing that angels had bodies.

Campion. I confess that the council holdeth that they be not altogether EXPERTES CORPORIS [without bodies], for they do ASSUMERE CORPORA [assume bodies]. And will you conclude, because the council holdeth, that they assume bodies, ergo they have bodies? It is a fallacy. Tratius [Thrasius] in the council saith, APPARUERUNT SICUT HOMINES [they have appeared as humans]. And in what bodies they appear, in the same they may be painted.

Fulke. Said further: It appeareth the councils may err, for that they use this prayer in the end of the council: UT IGNORANTIAE PARCAS ET ERRORI INDULGEAS [that you may spare ignorance and make allowance for error].

Campion. I answer that the prayer proveth not that the council may err but is made to the end that God may forgive those who have made any objections contrary to the truth established in that decree. As it doth always fall out that before anything in controversy be established, many objections are made to the contrary, and in the end the truth be confirmed as, for example, the question in controversy betwixt us.

Fulke. Then upon occasion of an argument made by Mr. Doctor Goade in the last disputation of Paul's reprehension of Peter, for keeping company with the Jews, and severing himself from the Gentiles, Mr. Fulke out of Gratian vouched a canon that no man may reprehend the pope.

Campion. Any man may admonish him, as a poor subject may admonish his prince, but no man may examine him, or judicially reprehend him.

Fulke. Mr. Campion, you said that I held in my book that the true church might err. Here is the book. Show me the place.

Campion. Give me leave to peruse your book, and I will show you the place at after dinner.

Fulke. Whereupon Mr. Fulke delivered his book to Mr. Campion, and said: I do not hold that the church may err generally but in some respects.

Goade. Mr. Doctor Goade, upon occasion of an argument in the last conference that the church might err vouched that the Council of Nicea was against the Council of Constance [Constantinople], and brought now the book.

Campion. What Council of Nicea?

Goade. What council? said Goade. I had it in my paper, but I cannot find it. I will remember the council, and bring the book against the next conference; and hereupon he brought the book and showed that the Council of Constance disallowed of images which the Second Council of Nicea did allow.

Campion. The Second Council of Nicea, being general, did condemn the Council of Constance, being but an assembly or conventicle of a certain sect called ICONOMACHI, assembled without lawful authority; and in the book that you show, it is not alleged as a council, but recited by the author to be disannuled and condemned as of no authority for the cause aforesaid; but you cannot show me a general council lawfully assembled to be contrary in themselves.

Goade. Upon the occasion of the last conference said that the Council of Trent hath erred in that it holdeth the matter of justification to be inherent in ourselves, and thereupon inferred that the church might err, and would have showed the book.

Campion. Discharged him of that, and confessing the words, he answered: The Council of Trent did not affirm the cause of justification to be inherent in us, as the Pelagians did, but as given from God of his mere mercy, and so to be said inherent in us, as faith, hope, and charity, whereby we are enabled to work our own justification, and so to be said not of us, but in us, by the special mercy and gift of God.

Then went they to the question, which was: whether Christ were really present in the sacrament.

Fulke. You hold, Mr. Campion, that Christ is really present in the sacrament.

Campion. I do so.

Fulke. This cup is the new testament in my blood, which is shed for you, etc., ergo.

Campion. Your place is the 22 of Luke, verse 20, where the Greek hath: This is the cup, the new testament in my blood; and not: This cup is the new testament, etc., for the word EST is neither in Greek or Latin, neither doth this place any way convince me.

Fulke. You may not appoint me my place, Mr. Campion. My place is out of the first to the Corinthians cap. 10, ver. 16. And then my argument is this. The cup is the new testament. The natural blood of Christ is not the new testament. Ergo, the natural blood of Christ is not the new testament.[1]

Campion. Your argument hath 4 terms: the cup is the cup of the new testament; and by the cup, metonymically, St. Paul meaneth that which is contained in the cup.[2]

Fulke. I grant.

Campion. Let this be noted that in your argument be four terms, and I marvel you will make such an argument being doctors of Cambridge.

Goade. Look how Christ was present to the fathers of the old testament in the sacrament, so he is present in ours. But Christ was not really present to them in theirs, ergo not in ours.

Campion. I deny your major.

Goade. They received the same substance, ergo the same presence. And to prove that they received the same substance, the scripture is plain, the first to the Corinthians, cap. 10, ver. 4 [3]: where it is said, EANDEM ESCAM MANDUCAVERUNT, etc. [they ate the same food].

Campion. I deny your antecedent, EANDEM ESCAM, is the same according to the spiritual effect, for Christ had not then taken upon him the substance of man; he only delivered the figure thereof,

---

[1] Fulke's syllogism seems to be either misreported or mistranscribed in both the Catholic version and *A true report*, where it reads: "The cup is the new testament. But the natural blood of Christ is not the cup. Ergo, the natural blood of Christ is not the cup."

[2] Campion's point is that Fulke uses "cup" in two senses: (1) figuratively, for Christ's blood, and (2) literally, for the chalice.

as the place where they were baptised in a cloud, they received the same which we do; ergo will you say it was water. The Israelites did believe in the same Christ. Abraham did believe in the same Christ. Ergo, by your reason he was incarnate to Abraham as to us. The fallacy of your argument consisteth in these words, "the same," for they believed in the same Christ, they did eat of the same bread, drink of the same rock, but in a mystery, and ours in verity.

Goade. Austine [Augustine] *De Utilitate Credendi* his judgment upon St. John, cap. 21, ver. 20, is that theirs is the same with ours in substance. His words are these [words are omitted in the MS.].[3]

Campion. It was the same in end, for that it gave to them the same effect, to them by hope, to us in truth. And Augustine is to be intended in respect of the end and effect, as is said, AGNUS INTERFECTUS EST AB ORIGINE MUNDI [the lamb was killed from the beginning of the world], that is, in effect. And thus you see the absurdity of your argument.

Fulke. Whatsoever is in the sacrament is insensible; but Christ his body is not insensible; ergo, Christ's body is not in the sacrament.

Campion. I deny your major.

Fulke. The major is Epiphanius and here is Epiphanius in Greek, read it.[4]

Campion. It needeth not. I understand the place very well. Epiphanius maketh not for you, but clear against you, for he saith: we must not believe our eyes, for that which we see hath the form of roundness; but faith must instruct us touching this sacrament as, for example, I see this book; you are Doctor Fulke; yet I do not see the substance of you nor of the book, but the accident of both.

Fulke. Is this your answer?

Campion. This is my answer.

Fulke. Your answer is absurd, and you understand not Epiphanius.

Campion. It is my answer. Reply if you can.

Fulke. The meaning of Epiphanius is that the substance of the sacrament is insensible.

[3] According to *A true report*, Augustine's words are: "Those sacraments were in signs divers, but in the thing signified are equal. Hear what the Apostle sayeth. All did eat the same spiritual meat, indeed the same meat spiritual. For touching the corporal meat, they did eat one, & we another; but they did eat the same spiritual meat that we do."

[4] Epiphanius of Constantia (Salamis) (ca. 315–403), a Church Father, opposed Arians and Origenists. Fulke's allusion is to Epiphanius's *Ancoratus* (374).

Campion. His meaning is that only the outward form is insensible.

Fulke. Your answer is no answer. You know not what you say.

Campion. There is no cause why I should forbear you. I am the Queen's prisoner and not yours. And if you use such words, I will return them.

Goade. If Christ be naturally in the sacrament, he is upon earth; but Christ is not upon earth; ergo, Christ is not in the sacrament.

Campion. I deny your minor.

Goade. If Christ were upon earth, then he should be sought for upon the earth. But he is not to be sought for upon the earth. Ergo, he is not upon the earth.

Campion. I deny your minor that Christ is no way to be sought only upon earth.[5]

Goade. He is to be sought for only in heaven; ergo, not in earth.

Campion. I deny your antecedent.

Goade. The antecedent is St. Paul's to the Colossians, cap. 3, verse 1, where he willeth us to seek Christ above, and not beneath. Whereupon I conclude that if Christ were to be sought for upon earth, then the apostle had done evil in teaching us the contrary; but the apostle hath not done evil; ergo, he is not to be sought for upon earth. And the drift of the apostle is that we should not seek Christ by ceremonies.

Campion. St. Paul his meaning is that he is not now to be sought for here on earth in bodily presence, as he was before his ascension, that men may eat and drink with him, but he is to be sought for as he is present, that is, in the sacrament by mystery.

Goade. Your affection must needs be only there where Christ is bodily present; but Christ is only bodily present in heaven; ergo, your affection must be only in heaven.

Campion. I deny your major and minor proposition. And first to your major that our affection must only be where Christ is only bodily present. But that cannot be true, for when I read the Bible my affection is there, and yet Christ not bodily present there. Therefore, prove that we must seek Christ only where he is bodily present; for we must seek him divers ways, as in purity of life and

---

[5] This passage is more clearly stated in *A true report* (1583) which reads: "I deny your minor. He is some way to be sought upon earth in the sacrament, but not by his ordinary presence."

holy conversation. We must seek him in the sacrament, as he is present there. Also we must seek him by mortification and, as it is said, we must die with him, rise with him, and ascend with him, so we must seek him by affection. He is miraculously here present in the sacrament and visibly present in heaven.

Goade. All your answers are insufficient.

Campion. That is my answer; let it be put down; and let the learned judge of it.

Goade. Well then, I will leave this argument.

Fulke. If Christ be present in his natural body, then in his true body; but Christ is not present in his true body, ergo not in his natural body.

Campion. I deny your minor.

Fulke. If in his true body, then his true body should be in the cup; but his true body is not in the cup, ergo he is not present in his true body.

Campion. I deny your minor.

Fulke. The minor is Chrysostom and recited the place; the effect whereof was to declare of the death of Balthazar for abusing the holy vessels, etc.: IN QUIBUS NON EST CORPUS DOMINI [in which is not the body of the Lord].

Campion. St. Chrysostom his meaning is of the vessels of the old law and not of the cup of the new testament.

Fulke. The meaning of St. Chrysostom is of the vessels of the new testament, as appeareth by the word EST which is the present tense.

Campion. But admitting St. Chrysostom spoke of the chalice of the new testament, yet his meaning was not to exclude Christ his true and natural body from the chalice, but only that we should not abuse those sanctified vessels, wherein the body of Christ was after the sacrament ministered.

Fulke. Chrysostom there remaineth a mystery, which proveth that the sacrament is not taken out.

Campion. The mystery in common speech may be said to be there, though the sacrament be ministered, because the vessels are sanctified to such holy uses.

Fulke. What a mystery in the cup after the administration! That is a foolish answer.

Campion. Write that down for my answer. You urge me with Chrysostom; Chrysostom maketh not for you. I would you would answer me in Chrysostom.

Fulke. Write and I will answer you.

Campion. If you will not answer in disputations, I will join with you in writing, if I may be permitted to have books and things necessary for that purpose. And I request you, Mr. Fulke, that you will be a means unto the council for the same.

Fulke. There is no cause why I should be a means unto the council for any such as you are.

Campion. Where Catholics are in credit with the state, they can procure so much, and no doubt you may, if you please, but it is not for your advantage.

Goade. If Christ his body be in the sacrament, then it should continue upon earth; but it shall not continue upon earth; ergo, he is not in the sacrament.

Campion. I deny your minor.

Goade. Christ himself hath said that he will not be bodily present upon earth, Matthew. 26., ver. 20 [11].

Campion. Christ his meaning is that you shall not have him as you have the poor in visible conversation.

Goade. He is in no sort to be sought upon the earth; ergo, not in the sacrament.

Campion. I deny your antecedent.

Goade. The antecedent is Augustine, 5. tract., tom. 9. upon St. Matthew, SURSUM EST DOMINUS, DONEC SECULUM FINIATUR. Ergo [the Lord is above until time ends].

Campion. What do you infer of that place? I said it is spoken of his visible conversation, and not of his miraculous presence in the sacrament; for his presence in heaven doth not take away his sacramental presence in earth; for Augustine acknowlegeth his presence with every good man in prayer, which your argument, if it were true, would take away, and only include his visible conversation.

Fulke. If Christ be naturally present in the sacrament, then he is present in truth; but he is not present in truth; ergo, he is not naturally present in the sacrament.

Campion. I deny your minor for he is present in truth.

Fulke. The minor is Gratian out of the common law; the effect of the words were that the heavenly bread which is set upon the table is called the body of our Lord but improperly.

Campion. He meaneth no such thing as you would have him, but only that it is improperly called the body of Christ, in respect of the accidents which appear in our eyes.

Fulke. Gratian he taketh it for the whole sacrament, and calleth it PANIS CAELESTIS [heavenly bread].

Campion. It is called PANIS in respect that it was bread a little before; and it is called CAELESTIS in respect of the consecration, and SACRAMENTUM in respect of both.

Fulke. Except it were taken for the whole sacrament, it could not be compared to baptism; but St. Augustine compareth it to baptism; ergo, it is taken for the whole sacrament.

Campion. St. Augustine in this place doth compare the signs and accidents of both the sacraments, which is no simple comparison, but so made.

Fulke. That which he speaketh of is the body of Christ.

Campion. He termeth the accidents the body of Christ, but improperly, as I may say this is a book, and yet I see but the accidents.

Goade. If Christ be present in the sacrament in his natural body, then hath it the properties of a natural body; but it hath not the properties of a natural body; ergo, he is not present in his natural body.

Campion. I deny your minor.

Goade. If it had the properties of a natural body, as it is in the sacrament, then it should be only in the sacrament, and in no other place at that instant; but at that instant his body is in heaven; ergo, it hath not the properties of a natural body.

Campion. It is present in the sacrament miraculously, not naturally, but yet a true body, though the quality be suspended for that time, like as the three children in the fiery furnace did not burn, and yet it was against the property of quality of the fire not to burn.

Goade. Augustine and Theodoret, in his 3. dialogue, do prove the body of Christ to suffer circumscription of a place.[6]

Campion. It is not necessary that Christ's body being in the sacrament miraculously should suffer circumscription, and you might as

[6] Theodoret (ca. 393–ca. 458), bishop of Cyr, theologian of the school of Antioch, and church historian, was engaged in the Nestorian controversy about the nature(s) of Christ (that is, divine and human). As a church historian, he extended the historical work of Eusebius from 323 to 428.

well jest at the ascension of Christ and deny it, for if it had the properties of a true body, it should PETERE DEORSUM [fall downward].

Goade. If he be present in body, then hath he two bodies.

Campion. One body in two places, you argue philosophically, and not theologically. And now seeing that I have answered your doctors, obtain me leave to show forth my doctors, and I will show you arguments that you can never answer, and plain places affirming that the same body which was born of the Virgin Mary is really in the sacrament.

Fulke. Cannot answer. There is no doctor that maketh for you.

Campion. No, you cannot answer, and herein I challenge you for the credit of your cause and, if you distrust not in it, to procure me a day to dispute.

Fulke. We cannot.

Campion. You will not.

Fulke. We will not make such suit for any such as you. If Christ were really in the sacrament, then should his body be eaten of the wicked; but they do not eat his body; ergo, his body is not in the sacrament.

Campion. I deny the minor.

Fulke. The minor is out of St. Augustine, *De Civitate Dei*, cap. 35. I remember not the words.[7]

Campion. His meaning is that the wicked receive not his body to salvation because they receive it unworthily, as when a Jew receiveth baptism for money, or some other filthy lucre or gain and not for the love of Christ. He receiveth true and perfect baptism but to his damnation, except he afterwards repent and believe, which if he do, he shall not again be baptised, but the first baptism shall now work in grace. So as he may be said to believe, though he have received the sacrament of baptism, not to have received baptism, because he

[7] *A true report* (1583) cites this reference to Augustine as lib. 21, cap. 25, and supplies his words: "Therefore neither is it to be said that these ungodly men do eat the body of Christ, because they are not to be accompted in the members of Christ; for, to omit other things, they can not be at one time both the members of Christ and the members of an harlot. Finally, he himself saying, 'He that eateth my flesh and drinketh my blood dwelleth in me and I in him,' showeth what it is, not so far as a sacrament may go, but in very deed to eat the body of Christ and to drink his blood."

hath not received the effect of baptism, but damnation instead of salvation. So the wicked receive Christ, not with faith, but to their damnation. That is, they receive not worthily or in grace.

Fulke. If the wicked eat the sacrament, they eat REM SACRAMENTI [the sacramental thing]; but they eat not REM SACRAMENTI; ergo, the wicked eat not the body of Christ.

Campion. I answer that RES SACRAMENTI is taken two ways: for the body, and grace; as it is taken for grace, they receive it not.

Fulke. Christ is not received but by grace only; the wicked receive him not by grace; ergo, the wicked receive him not.

Campion. I deny your major; they receive his body, though not worthily and in grace.

Goade. If they should eat the body of Christ, then sacramentally, but not sacramentally. Ergo.

Campion. I deny your minor.

Goade. If sacramentally, then forever, but not forever, ergo.

Campion. I deny the consequent of your major, for any man may receive the body of Christ, and not be saved; for do you hold that if one eat your communion worthily, that then he shall be saved?

Fulke. If Christ be present, then in an immortal and glorified body, but in none of these, ergo.

Campion. Christ is present in a glorified body.

Fulke. This body which is in the sacrament is the same which Christ gave to his disciples; but that which he gave to his disciples was not a glorified body; ergo, Christ is not present as in a glorified body.

Campion. I answer to your major: he gave the same in quality and substance, but not in condition, for that it was not then glorified, as it is now; but now being glorified, we receive the same body glorified. And your argument containeth a fallacy in this word *the same* A FIGURA DICTIONIS [by a figure of speech], as QUICQUID HERI EMISTI, HODIE COMEDISTI; CARNES CRUDAS EMISTI, ERGO, CARNES CRUDAS COMEDISTI [whatever you bought yesterday, you eat today; you bought raw meat; ergo, you eat raw meat]. And yet we make not our argument, as you take it, that because it is glorified, therefore it is present, but because Christ said, HOC EST CORPUS MEUM [this is my body].

[Afternoon Session]
After Dinner

Fulke. Mr. Campion, can you show me the words you spoke of in my book?

Campion. This is not your book which I demanded. I would have seen the book which you wrote against Mr. Allen his scroll of articles, whereunto Mr. Bristow replied.

Fulke. Would you have us know what book you meant. I hold not that the true church may err in matters of salvation.

Campion. It is no great matter for the book, for everyone that hath read it doth know that you hold that the church erred in teaching prayer for the dead, and invocation of saints which you cry out on in the pulpit, saying that it is idolatry. And do you make it no matter of salvation to teach or not to teach idolatry? Then they fell to the questions of transubstantiation.

Fulke. You hold that there is transubstantiation, which we will impugn.

Campion. I hold that after the words of consecration, there is transubstantiation.

Fulke. Our saviour Christ did drink the same cup, which his apostles did drink; but that which Christ drank was wine; ergo, his apostles drank wine.

Campion. I deny your major supposition that Christ did drink wine after he had consecrated it.

Fulke. The major is St. Matthew, cap. 26., ver. 29.: I will drink no more of this wine, till I drink it with you in my father his kingdom. Ergo, he did drink of the same wine.

Campion. It doth import but that he did drink indifferently [that is, indefinitely] of wine, and he referreth his speech in those words to the eating and drinking he had tasted of before, for all that which was brought was wine, and the place proveth only that he consecrated wine, and the meaning of the place is that he will not drink any more in this life. And the place maketh for me, for it proveth that it retaineth the appellation of wine, he consecrated in wine, he delivered wine consecrated, ergo wine. I deny your argument. Prove that and reply in a syllogism.

Fulke. You shall hear what Chrysostom saith: QUANDO HOC

MYSTERIUM TRADIDIT, VINUM TRADIDIT [when he gave this mystery he gave wine.] That which he delivered was the sacrament; but he did deliver wine; ergo, wine was the sacrament.

Campion. He delivered wine consecrated.

Fulke. He delivered wine consecrated, ergo wine; the doctor speaketh exquisitely [specifically or exclusively] of wine.

Campion. The doctor speaketh to avoid the consecration in water only, which certain heretics in his time held, and not exquisitely of wine, but calleth it wine, because it was wine a little before, as it is said: The rod of Moses eat up the rods of the sorcerers; and yet was it not a rod at that time, but a serpent; but it is so said because it was a rod a little before.

Fulke. When Moses wrote, then it was a rod.

Campion. He speaketh of it at that time, when it did eat up the serpents, at which time it was not a rod, but called a rod.

Fulke. Your answer is avoided already.

Campion. I refer my answer to the consciences of the indifferent hearers.

Goade. The apostles of Christ did eat the substance of bread after the consecration; ergo, after the consecration there remaineth bread.

Campion. I deny your antecedent.

Goade. That which Christ gave, they did eat; but Christ gave bread; ergo, they did eat bread.

Campion. NEGO MINOREM [I deny the minor].

Goade. That which Christ took in his hands he did distribute; but he took bread in his hands; ergo, he did distribute bread.

Campion. I answer to your major out of St. Ambrose, li. 4, DE SACRAMENTIS, cap. 4. The words were these: TU FORTE DICIS, PANIS MEUS EST USITATUS, SED PANIS ISTE PANIS EST ANTE VERBA SACRAMENTORUM, UBI ACCESSERIT CONSECRATIO, DE PANE FIT CARO CHRISTI [you say my bread is common bread, but the bread itself is bread before the words of consecration; as soon as consecration occurs, from bread it becomes the body of Christ]. And Ambrose proveth these words to be operatious [that is, forceful and plain].[8]

Goade. We confess a great change, but no transubstantiation. Is it

[8] St. Ambrose (340?– 97), bishop of Milan and celebrated Church Father, wrote many exegetical treatises. He received St. Augustine into the church.

not a mighty efficacy for us by eating of bread to feed on Christ? The doctor his meaning in that place is only to put a difference between that bread and common bread, and he calleth it PANIS, ERGO NON CORPUS [bread, therefore, not body].

Campion. The doctor his words do import a transubstantiation; for he saith: DE PANE FIT CARO CHRISTI [of the bread is made the body of Christ].

Goade. St. Paul in the first to the Corinthians, cap. 10, calleth it bread. His words are these: The bread which we break, is it not the partaking of the body of Christ?

Campion. It retaineth the appellation of two causes, one for the outward form or accidents of it, the other for that it was bread a little before, as MORTUI SURGUNT [the dead rise], and yet they were not dead when they rise, but because they were so a little before; CLAUDI AMBULANT [the lame walk], and yet when they walked, after Christ had healed them, they were not lame, but it was so said because they were so a little before. And I did show you before in what respect it was called PANIS [bread], and in what respect it was called CAELESTIS [heavenly].

Goade. We are all partakers of the same bread; therefore, it was bread.

Campion. I have showed you before two causes wherefore it is called bread, and I add a third, for that it feedeth our souls. And in this sense Christ himself in the 6th of St. John calleth himself bread, where he saith: PANIS QUEM EGO DABO CARO MEA EST [the bread that I shall give to you is my flesh].

Goade. The apostle saith: We are all partakers of the same bread.

Campion. After it is sanctified, we are all partakers of the same bread.

Fulke. What is broken after the bread is consecrated?

Campion. Can a substance be broken?

Fulke. Cannot bread be broken? St. Paul saith FRANGIMUS [we break], and therefore, it was bread.

Campion. The accidents of bread may be broken, but not the substance. As when I break a stick, the substance is not broken, but the accidents; so the body of Christ in the sacrament is not said to be broken, but divided, and yet the whole body delivered to everyone.

Fulke. There is something material in the sacrament, which goeth the way of all meats; ergo, it is bread and wine, and cited Origen upon the 15th of Matthew, the effect of the words was that whatsoever goeth into the mouth and goeth into the belly is voided; ergo, that which is consecrated is voided.[9]

Campion. The accidents, quality, and quantity go into the stomach: and there being altered, as other meats, they go into the belly; but the sacrament remaineth no longer than the SPECIES remain uncorrupted.

Fulke. In what predicament is MATERIA?[10]

Campion. MATERIA taken indifferently is in no predicament; but as it is taken for SUBSTANTIA, it is taken in the predicament of SUBSTANTIA; and so the quality thereof in the predicament of quality; and these accidents of bread, in that they have a miraculous and substantial or material being without bread, which is their proper subject, go into the body; and as they feed and are digested in the stomach, so they are cast out of the belly, when they are digested.

Fulke. Natural philosophy and logic are beholding unto you. Whatsoever is the matter of bread is the substance of bread.

Campion. Not so. But whatsoever is the material substance of bread is bread.

Goade. I will prove that the substance of bread and wine do remain.

Campion. Prove that.

Goade. That which overthroweth the nature of the sacrament is not to be admitted in the sacrament; but transubstantiation overthroweth the nature of the sacrament; ergo, it is not to be admitted in the sacrament.

Campion. I deny your minor.

Goade. It taketh away the elements; for St. Augustine saith:

---

[9] Origen (185?–254?), one of the leading thinkers of the early church, is best known for his textual and exegetical criticism of the Bible in which he emphasized the allegorical method of scriptural analysis.

[10] Aristotle attempted to define or describe how many and what particular things may be predicated of any subject in the analysis of judgments. He proposed that there were ten categories or predicaments: (1) substance or being, (2) quantity, (3) quality, (4) relation, (5) place, (6) time, (7) posture, (8) having or possessing, (9) action, and (10) passion. See his *Categories* in *The Complete Works of Aristotle* I, trans. J. L. Ackrill (Princeton, N.J.: Princeton University Press, 1985), pp. 3–24. See also W. David Ross, *Aristotle* (1923; London: Methuen; New York: Barnes & Noble, 1964), pp. 20–25.

ACCEDIT VERBUM AD ELEMENTUM, ET FIT SACRAMENTUM [the word came to the element, and it became a sacrament].

Campion. It doth not take away ELEMENTUM; for the SPECIES of bread and wine supply the place of the element, in that they have a miraculous being in the sacrament, without their proper subject.

Goade. It taketh away that which is earthly, for it taketh away the wine, and it must have an earthly substance.

Campion. FORMA A FIGURA [form from figure] be RES TERRESTRES [earthly thing], but prove that it must have an earthly substance, QUANDO VERBUM VENIT AD ELEMENTUM, FIT SACRAMENTUM PER AUGUSTINUM CONCEDO [when the word came to the element, it became a sacrament, according to Augustine, I concede], but that doth not prove that it remaineth an earthly substance, or that it ceaseth to be an earthly creature to the receiver, as the accidents thereof be, the elements be not gone, there remaineth the analogy of bread, to make the receiver to know the operation of the sacrament, which is to feed, as the quality of bread do feed.

Goade. You wipe away the earthly substance.

Campion. It taketh away the substance, SED NON ELEMENTUM [but not the element]; it remaineth in the sacrament, UT ELEMENTIUM PROPORTIONE [as an element by analogy], but not in substance.

Goade. There must be a substance of the element to feed.

Campion. I deny that.

Goade. What doth feed then?

Campion. That which remaineth which be the accidents.

Goade. Do the accidents feed?

Campion. I say that the accidents always feed, and not the substance; and the substance doth nourish by the accidents, UT PROXIMA CAUSA [as the proximate cause]. And I would I were in the university to prove this against you.

Goade. What can the accidents without the substance feed?

Campion. The want of the substance of bread is supplied with the presence of Christ's body miraculously; for if the substance of matter were suspended, the accidents would wet; even so the substance of bread being taken away, the accidents would nourish. I would I might have a day to show my doctors concerning this matter.

Fulke. That which Christ gave to his disciples was bread; ergo, bread remaineth.

Campion. I deny it was bread.

Fulke. They were pieces of bread; ergo, bread.

Campion. They were not substantial pieces of bread.

Fulke. Cirellus, upon St. John, cap. 10, saith: DEDIT FRAGMENTA PANIS [he gave pieces of bread].[11]

Campion. I have answered this argument before; for there is no diversity between the whole and the piece. What diversity is there between this argument and your argument before? Whither is the force of your argument in this word *bread* or a *piece*?

Fulke. Either he gave bread or not bread; and the doctors say he gave bread; ergo, etc.

Campion. He gave bread by appellation but not in substance. I have answered your authorities. I beseech you in the way of charity to let me have a day to show forth my authorities, to prove that the same body is delivered in the sacrament, which Christ did take of the Virgin Mary. The most of your arguments consist in bread by appellation.

Fulke. I will never oppose myself to you, and there is no doctor that maketh for you.

Campion. I challenge you before this honorable company to answer my authorities. You cannot answer the doctors that I shall allege.

Fulke. I will urge you with the place of Gelasius, where he saith we have known that after consecration some have retained PORTIONEM CORPORIS CHRISTI, etc. [a portion of Christ's body].[12]

Campion. It is LOCUTIA POPULARIS [popular speech], and is as much to say as that the signs are broken under which the body of Christ is comprehended, and yet the body is not broken, but wholly given to everyone. You might as well jest at the incarnation of Christ.

[11] Cirellus [Cyrillus], that is, St. Cyril of Alexandria (d. 444), bishop, theologian, and prolific writer, was deeply involved in the lengthy Nestorian controversy. He also concentrated on biblical exegesis and anti-Arian polemics. *A true report* cites Fulke's reference here to Cyrillus as: "Ioh [John], cap. 4."

[12] Gelasius, forceful pope from 492 to 496, engaged in doctrinal controversies with the Eastern Church and became a strong advocate for papal supremacy. Many of his letters and treatises on religious matters were excerpted and published in canonical collections and thus became widely known.

Fulke. Do you call it a jest? It is according to your speech the other day that Christ came in by a juggling trick.

Campion. I trust that be recorded, as I spoke it. I spoke not so.

Fulke. What say you to that same bastardly Epistle of St. James where he saith we ought to keep the fragments of the body of our Lord?

Campion. My last answer serveth for this place.

Goade. If there be transubstantiation, it is grounded upon some place of scripture; but it is not to be grounded upon any place of scripture; ergo, there is no transubstantiation.

Campion. I deny your minor.

Goade. If upon any part of scripture, then upon this place of scripture: HOC EST CORPUS MEUM [this is my body]; but not upon this place; ergo, etc.

Campion. NEGO MINOREM [I deny the minor]. And yet you do not dispute properly, for you turn to the question handled before dinner. And if the audience do think it meet to turn to the question handled before, proceed and I will answer you.

Goade. Would you be rid of this argument? Can you not answer it?

Campion. I gave you 4 or 5 answers the other day; and yet if you will needs have this, I will give it to you; but it is not to the question properly.

Goade. If upon this place of scripture, then upon the sense; but not upon the sense; ergo, not upon the place.

Campion. Upon the sense.

Goade. It is a figurative kind of speech; ergo, not proper.

Campion. In that it is figurative, is it not proper?

Goade. Tertullian, lib. 4, *Contra Marcione*, saith that CHRISTUS ACCEPIT PANEM ET DISTRIBUIT, DICENS, HOC EST CORPUS MEUM ID EST FIGURA CORPORIS MEI [Christ took the bread and distributed it, saying, this is my body, that is, a figure of my body].[13]

Campion. Tertullian, in this place disputing against certain here-

[13] Tertullian (160?–225?), a non-cleric and early church theologian, is said to have laid the groundwork for Western theology and is regarded as the major theologian of the West until Augustine. He held rigorous Montanist views on discipline, and wrote on a broad range of religious subjects: apologies for Christianity, treatises on Christian life, and anti-heretical works.

tics who denied that Christ had a true body, answereth in this place the objection of the heretics who saith that Christ gave a figure of his body, whereupon Tertullian thought he might invincibly conclude against the heretics who affirmed that Christ delivered a figure of his body, that therefore he had a true body, which was only that which Tertullian in that place labored to prove.

Fulke. I have not heard such an answer. It is no good answer.

Campion. You cannot improve this answer. If you do not know this answer, you are not so conversant in our books as you might have been. For Tertullian in that place bringeth divers figures of the old testament to prove that Christ had a true body, and in the end upon the heretic's own words when he confesseth that Christ had a body. And where he saith, ID EST FIGURA CORPORIS, ID EST is not in exposition of CORPORIS, the comma must be made at ID. And this is my second answer.

Fulke. Augustine, ep. 23., NON ENIM DOMINUS DUBITAVIT DICERE, HOC EST CORPUS MEUM, CUM SIGNUM DEDIT CORPORIS SUI [for the Lord did not hesitate to say, this is my body, when he gave a sign of his body].

Campion. DEDIT FIGURAM [he gave a figure]; and yet he gave his body, for every substance hath a figure; and that is a figure which is presented to the eye; and the external figure is called SIGNUM, this is, Christ; and yet the roundness is not Christ, and yet I see Christ; and that doth St. Augustine mean.

Fulke. Here Mr. Fulke urgeth St. Augustine in the words following. The words I remember not.[14]

Campion. St. Augustine there disputed against the heretic who thought that because the blood is called ANIMA, that if he should eat the blood, he should eat ANIMA. It is called the soul because the soul is present in the blood. And so the bread is said ANIMA as the presence of the body of Christ; and the wit is called the brain because it is there most present.

Goade. Theodoret writeth that the elements of bread and wine remain.

[14] Augustine's words as reported in *A true report* are: "For of that which is written, that the blood of a beast is the soul of it, beside that which I said before, that it pertaineth not unto me what becometh of the soul of a beast, I can also interpret this commandment to be made in a sign; for our lord doubted not to say, 'This is my body,' when he gave the sign of his body."

Campion. Theodoret writeth against Erenistes,[15] the heretic, and minded to confute his opinion who did think that the divinity of Christ did take away his body; but he argueth that if Christ's bodily presence could stand together with the figures of bread and wine, in like manner his divinity might stand together with his humanity, and his humanity not to be absorbed by his divinity. Substance is not here taken SPECIFICE, but GENERICE, and it is taken for entity, which is being; neither is nature in that place taken for SUBSTANTIA. This place of the doctor by his discourse doth prove the real presence in the sacrament directly.

Goade. The elements remain in their nature and substance.

Campion. They remain not in their natural substance.

Goade. That which doth nourish our bodies remaineth; ergo, the natural substance remaineth.

Campion. Nature sometimes is taken for the external signs, as quantity and quality; and so is it here. Heat is the nature of the fire, and is therefore the substance; the elements may remain therefore and not the substance.

Goade. Christ doth honor the sacrament with grace, and taketh not away the substance.

Campion. The substance doth not remain.

Goade. That which doth nourish remaineth; ergo, the substance remaineth.

Campion. NEGO ARGUMENTUM [I deny the argument]. The accidents do nourish, and every substance doth nourish by the accidents and not of itself, and so the accidents is PROXIMA CAUSA [proximate cause].

Goade. Can the accidents nourish without substance?

Campion. It may nourish as, for example, if it pleaseth God to take away the substance from water, the accidents would wet; and even so would the accidents of fire burn; and I say that the absence of the substance of bread is supplied by the presence of Christ's body.

Fulke. I will urge you with the authority of Gelasius, where he saith that the bread and wine do go into a divine substance, and yet they do not leave their own natural substance.

---

[15] This reference to Erenistes appears to be a scribal error. Theodoret wrote *Eranistes* in 447 against Eutyches, who taught that Christ had one nature. This reference should probably read: "Theodoret writeth *Eranistes* against the heretic. . . ."

Campion. This place of Gelasius and the other of Theodoret have all one answer; for their discourse is both against one sort of heresy; and substance is there taken GENERICE, viz., for a being; and the thing that they both go about to prove is that the humanity of Christ is not absorbed by his divinity, as the heretic they write against would have had it. And yet the bread and wine is transubstantiated and hath a being transcendent.

Goade. There remaineth substance in one of the elements; ergo, no transubstantiation.

Campion. NEGO ANTECEDENS [I deny the antecedent].

Goade. There remaineth wine; ergo.

Campion. I deny that there remaineth wine.

Goade. Cip., ep. 2, li. 3, proveth that the wine remaineth where he saith, DICO VOBIS, etc.: MEMINIS ESSE VINUM QUOD DOMINUS OBTULIT, etc. [I say to you, etc.: remember that it was wine which the Lord offered, etc.].[16]

Campion. He doth not say that Christ doth call it wine after consecration. He proveth only that Christ did consecrate in wine, and that whosoever should after consecrate by his example should consecrate in wine and water, and not in wine only, for it is CALIX MIXTUS [mixed cup].

Goade. Ireneus saith there doth remain a thing after consecration; ergo, the elements remain. His words are these: JAM NON COMMUNIS PANIS EST, & [indeed it is not common bread].[17]

Campion. That thing is accident and is found in nine predicaments, and the accidents be earthly, and so it may be said the RES remaineth.

Goade. Invisible grace is a substance, because Christ who is grace is a substance; and so then by your reason, the sacrament should consist of two substances.

Campion. I deny your argument. Neither doth invisible grace always go with the sacrament; for Judas received Christ but not grace;

[16] *A true report* cites this reference as: Cyprian, epist. 3, *ad Caecilium*. Cyprian (ca. 205–53), bishop of Carthage, was influenced by Tertullian but showed greater moderation in his own writings. He wrote many letters and treatises on a wide variety of doctrinal subjects (for example, church unity, baptism, and virginity), which earned him the reputation of being one of the founders of Latin theology.

[17] Ireneus [Irenaeus] (ca. 130–ca. 200), bishop of Lyon, biblical theologian and writer against heresies, is perhaps best known for developing the ecclesiastical concept of authority. He was highly regarded by both Roman Catholics and Protestants for his views on authority and for his commentaries on the Bible.

but Peter received both. And thus this argument ended. Mr. Campion said, I have been thrice opposed, and now it were reason I should be once opponent.

Goade. Christ is not present in a natural body; ergo, not in a true body.

Campion. I deny your antecedent.

Goade. By senses his presence cannot be proved; ergo, he is not present in a natural body.

Campion. I deny your argument, for Chrysostom willeth us not trust our senses in this sacrament.

Goade. Christ made the proof by senses when he said, Feel my wounds; ergo, we may use the same.

Campion. That is a very good argument to prove that Christ had a body, and the body of Christ in itself is sensible. And it followeth that if it may be felt, it is a body, but not contrariwise; for it may be a body, though it be not felt nor seen; and often times he suspendeth those qualities, as in this sacrament he doth. And it is read, EVANUIT EX OCULIS EORUM [he disappeared from their eyes]. And in another place, TRANSIT PER MEDIOS EORUM [he passed through the midst of them] and was not seen, etc. And yet at those times he had a true body, and so he may be present and not seen nor felt; but whether the cause be in our eyes, or it pleaseth him to suspend his natural quality, it lieth not in our knowledge.

Goade. If the apostles had been taught this kind of doctrine concerning the resurrection, they would not have believed it.

Campion. It pleased him to give his body to be felt to them, and it was necessary, for that there was then some question or doubt of his resurrection.

Goade. It is necessary that you prove such a sensible feeling of Christ his body in the sacrament.

Campion. The apostles were thoroughly instructed in this sacrament by Christ's institution, neither did they make any doubt of it afterwards, and therefore it was not necessary. And it may be a true body, although it be not seen nor felt, as I said before.

Fulke. I will urge you with one authority and so make an end, for the time is past already. Ireneus saith: It is not the sacrifice which sanctified the man, but the sacrificer; ergo, no transubstantiation.

Campion. Ireneus speaketh of the offerer, Christ; and he meaneth that the sacrifice doth not sanctify, without it be received with purity of conscience.

[Fourth Disputation]

[Morning Session]

A disputation in the Tower in Sir Owen Hopton's hall, being Lieutenant, 27 September 1581. Doctor Walker and Mr. Charke of the part Protestant and Mr. Campion, Jesuit, of the other part, one Mr. Norton, barrister, for notary.

Doctor Walker by the way of preface uttered speeches to the effect as followeth.

Walker. This man, having departed this realm, hath joined himself to the man of Rome, our common enemy Antichrist, and now hath returned again into this realm, where he hath wandered from place to place through the greatest part thereof; and in the north country he hath sown such sedition that they now cry out of him and curse him; and now he hath proceeded further and hath charged us most impudently and falsely with mangling and cutting of the scriptures; and in this little pamphlet (holding Mr. Campion's book up in his hand) hath most boldly challenged us, slandering us in most bitter and spiteful terms, calling us LUTHERI CATULOS [Luther's young whelps] with such other, etc. But as for me, I will neither defend Luther, nor Calvin, nor Beza, nor Zwingli.[1] For I am neither

[1] John Calvin (1509–64), French theologian, was one of the most influential of the Protestant reformers. Rigid dogmatism and strict discipline characterized his religious views. These views were officially adopted at Geneva where for a time he established a virtual theocracy. His many written works include his *Institutes of the Christian Religion*, which define his theological views.

Theodorus Beza (1519–1605), French theologian and reformer, was a colleague of Calvin's at Geneva. His works include a translation of the New Testament and *Ecclesiastical History of the Reformed Churches of France, 1531–1563.*

Ulrich Zwingli (1484–1531), Swiss religious reformer, emphasized scriptural authority in his preaching and writing. He cited many practices as unscriptural, such as adoration of saints, images, and relics, and the selling of indulgences. Under his influence, Zurich became a theocracy until civil war broke out among the cantons and he was put to death.

a Lutheran, a Calvinist, a Bezian, nor Zwinglian. I am only a man of God and a free Christian of Christ whose doctrine I do and will by his grace profess and maintain, and his holy scriptures which bear testimony of him, and wherein are all things sufficiently expressed which do appertain to our salvation.

Then he said: Let us begin with prayer. And he prayed to the effect that it would please God that they might deal in this present conference with modesty and sobriety and reverently in the fear of God to the establishing of his truth and confounding of errors, etc.

After prayer ended, he said: Howsoever matters have been handled and disputed before, I beseech you now that we speak of these matters and dispute of them, as it becometh us. And SI QUIS MALE AGENDO ALIQUAM VOLUPTATEM CEPISSET, IS MALE AUDIENDO ILLAM AMITTAT [if anyone takes pleasure in doing evil, let him lose it in hearing evil]. And now it hath pleased the Queen's Majesty to send us to see whether your doctrine be sound and true, or corrupted, according as your writings are. The clemency of the prince and great mercifulness doth herein appear, and how loath she would be to deal with vigor against you, as she might justly do. She had rather win you by fair means than to show justice against you; but take heed lest her mercy be turned to vigor, through your own dealing, for QUAMDIU ABUTERE NOSTRA PATIENTIA CATELINA, etc. [how long will you try our patience, Catiline, etc].[2] Then holding up Campion's book in his hand, he said: So little as this pamphlet is, yet it hath bred great trouble. But according to the Gospel, Matthew 18.: VAE ILLIS PER QUOS, etc. [Woe unto those through whom, etc.]. Well, you have accused us for following Luther and Calvin in cutting off from the canonical scriptures divers books, and therein you have accused both them and us wrongfully, for those books which they reject be not canonical, neither do they reject those which you report them to have done.

Campion. Upon Sunday last I received a letter from you both, whereby I did understand that you were in mind to dispute with me touching the authority of the holy scriptures, for even so were the words of your letter which I intended to be touching the authority of the authentical scriptures, and not to call in question and to dis-

[2] Walker alludes to and paraphrases Cicero's remark to Catiline in the First Catilinarian Oration.

pute which be authentical, neither whether all things necessary to salvation be contained in scripture, for that were to dispute of the sufficiency of scripture and not of the authority, which question you now seem to bring in. But, I pray you, let us not trifle the time away. Dispute upon which of these questions you will. I say that Luther hath cut off certain books of the New Testament, namely, the second and third epistles of St. John, the second of St. James, the epistles of St. Jude, the 2 epistles of St. Peter, the epistle to the Hebrews; also Calvin hath cut off seven books from the Old Testament, namely, Baruch, Tobias, Judith, Sapientia [Wisdom], Ecclesiasticus, and 2 of the Machabees, and herein hath done wickedly. And infirm [refute] you this position if you can; for otherwise if you will dispute of the authority of the scriptures according to your letter, you must admit them to be canonical, which you mind to dispute upon.

Walker. I think they have not cut them off; for in doubting of the authority of them, they have not cut them off, if they did doubt of them.

Campion. We come to dispute. You must not, therefore, stand upon "if" and "and"; for they do not only doubt of these, which is blasphemy; but they do reject them; and I hold that to doubt of them now is blasphemy. Infirm this position.

Walker. I do not know whether Luther doubted of these books. I have not read all his works; but whether he did or not, it is not material; for he might justly do so seeing they were doubted of so many hundred years before his time, as I shall show you.

Campion. You make the matter very doubtful whether Luther doubted of these books or not; for indeed to doubt or reject them is contrary to the Church of England now. Yet notwithstanding, since we cannot agree of the question, I will show you plainly that he did not only doubt of but rejected them, if you will let me have the books which I noted in the margin of my book; and if I cannot show it, then I will yield to you and take the shame thereof, if you will let this stand as a issue betwixt us.

Walker. I cannot let you have those books you speak of. But do you always hold it blasphemy to doubt of the truth?

Campion. It is not always blasphemy to doubt of the truth; for often times although a thing be true, yet it is not known for a truth, and so long a man may doubt; but after it is confirmed by the church for a truth, then to doubt is blasphemy, as now Remigius doth of the Epistle of St. James.

Walker. What, was that epistle always true and canonical or no?

Campion. In itself it was authentical, but yet doubted of, as it doth appear by the Council of Constantinople where it was agreed for canonical, and after that confirmed for canonical by the Council holden at Trullo, as appeareth by Saint Augustine, in li. 3., *De Doctrina Christiana*, cap. 8.

Walker. I will show you that these books were doubted of many hundred years ago, even by those authorities which you like the best of, by the old doctors.

Campion. I do principally rely and cleave [cling] unto the scriptures, and request your proof out of them; and next unto them to the church and doctors, whose authorities you must need use and stay upon, for that the other faileth of proofs herein.

Walker. I will see what you can say to Origen, who is plain for this matter; and I doubt whether he allowed of these scriptures for canonical. He read the places of Origen, whose words were to this effect that some men did doubt of these scriptures.

Campion. Origen maketh for me, for he saith that some doubted, wherein they did not well, as the Lutherans do now; neither did that prove that Origen did doubt thereof, although some did, which I do not deny.

Walker. I would know whom you call Lutherans.

Campion. You know that well enough.

Walker. If they doubted, it is another matter.

Campion. It is a blasphemy in them to doubt of them.

Walker. I told you before I am not a Lutheran.

Campion. I do not say that you are.

Walker. I do not maintain all Luther's doctrine. And you do unjustly accuse us in calling us LUTHERI CATULOS.

Campion. I would gladly you would dispute upon some question that our coming hither and troubling this worshipful auditory might not be altogether in vain; dispute either of the books of the Old Testament or of the New. Calvin hath done evil in cutting seven of the books of the Old Testament, the names whereof I have before rehearsed, which were DE SINCERO CANONE, from the number of the canonical books.

Walker. You shall hear what St. Jerome saith in his book, *Ad Laetam*

De Institutione Filiae, and the words were: CAVEAT AB OMNI APOCRYPHA [beware of all apocrypha], and what say you to the second book of the Machabees, cap. 12, where it is said: SANCTA ERGO ET SALUBRIS EST PRO DEFUNCTIS ORARE [it is therefore holy and wholesome to pray for the dead]?

Campion. Let me first answer St. Jerome's place, and then let us come to the other, or else we shall breed confusion. First, therefore, you must understand that this word APOCRYPHA is taken with the doctors two manner of ways: one is for the books which were doubted of sometimes; the other is for certain heretical books which were spread amongst the people, as the prophecy of Enoch, and the testament of Jacob, and such others which were spread abroad for scriptures and received of the common people, and against these doth St. Jerome write and giveth a caveat to Leta to take especial heed of them. For do you think he would have forbidden her the reading of Ecclesiasticus and the book of Wisdom, which are so full of godly and virtuous counsels to direct her to the perfection of good life? And St. Jerome saith in PRAFAT. REGIUM [Preface to Kings] that these books NON SUNT IN CANONE HEBREORUM [are not in the Hebrew canon]. But in another place he saith that they be in CANONE CHRISTIANORUM [in the Christian canon]. And as for the books of the Machabees, they are to be holden for canonical, for any thing that I can see yet to the contrary.

Walker. I am not bound to believe them.

Campion. If they be canonical, you are bound to believe them; and your reason is not good to say that you are not bound to believe them; ergo, they are not canonical. For that is PETERE PRINCIPIUM [to assume what is to be proven]. You must prove first that they are not canonical; and then you are not bound to believe them; otherwise you are.

Charke. St. John saith: EGO ET PATER UNUM SUMUS [I and the Father are one], wherein he showeth there can be no contrariety of spirit in God; but the writer of those books doth ask pardon, which he should not have done if it had proceeded from the same spirit of whom he did ask pardon.

Campion. The author doth ask pardon of his speech, if he have not set down the matter in as apt and convenient words as he should have done so good a matter, like unto the speech used by St. Paul when he saith, RUDIS SUM SERMONE [rude am I in speech]; and yet there was no contrariety of spirit in Paul; neither in the author of these books; for the pardon was craved only in respect of the style.

Charke. You fall a little into your waste words.

Campion. Dare you say that there is any letter added corruptly by him who was the Son of God?

Charke. That holy pen doth ask pardon for his writing which, if it had been of God, it ought not to have done; and thus I will prove it. Whatsoever is the word of God, either touching the word or touching the matter, is full perfect and sound and needeth no pardon. But this needeth pardon. Ergo, this book asking pardon is not of the Holy Ghost.

Campion. I answer your minor. In itself and for itself, it needeth no pardon. But for circumstances in respect of dainty hearers it may ask pardon of the style; and this humility was of the Holy Ghost, as that of St. Paul was where he said, RUDIS SUM SERMONE.

Charke. The apostle of purpose useth that which you call rudeness of speech. Wherefore, he would not crave pardon of that.

Campion. Neither this nor St. Paul's speech in themselves had need of any pardon, but for the causes I have before showed you.

Charke. Whatsoever is without cause is waste. But you confess this desire of pardon to be without cause. Ergo, it was waste.

Campion. It was not waste in that it proceeded of humility. There was cause, for that the style was simple.

Charke. Your answer is vain and ridiculous, and I tell you that the style is a good round style and would have served to have expressed the matter without any pardon craving.

Campion. And I tell you that he thought it was but a simple style and needed to crave pardon for the causes before alleged. Reply against this answer.

Charke. Well, let us see how well you will defend the book of Judith to be canonical which is so replenished with examples of vice, for in the 9th Chapt. of that book you shall see what filthy terms that unchaste Judith doth use where she prayeth to God UT HOLOFERNES CAPITATUS LAQUEO OCULORUM SUORUM IN ME [that Holofernes may be caught in the net of his own eyes in me].

Campion. I marvel not now though you rail against me, since you are not ashamed to call Judith an unchaste woman. Truly herein you scandalize me greatly, for I would not for all the riches in the world have said so much of that blessed saint. Also St. Jerome was far from your mind, for in his preface upon that book he praiseth her highly for her great chastity and willeth all others to do in like sort and to follow her example, and therewithal calleth her CASTITATIS EXEMPLUM [an example of chastity].

Charke. Well it may be a question betwixt you and me, whether ever that Bible and the preface were of St. Jerome's doing; but let that pass. I say it is not agreeing to the majesty of God, his word, for a woman to pray that a man be taken in the snares of her beauty, coming not as a wife, but so did Judith. Ergo, etc.

Campion. The Holy Ghost was the cause and the provoker of that action which Judith did and intended, and thereby she did know the better to bring her purpose to pass, and that was by decking herself in the best order she could, and so by that means she might be a cause to turn the wickedness of Holofernes to the delivery of his people, which was also the effect of her prayer and not, as you say, that he might be occasioned to sin by her. And truly it grieveth me very much to hear that most chaste Judith so wickedly slandered.

Charke. I protest it before God that I have spoken it and do think it with great quietness of conscience. Well, you shall hear another place out of the same book and chapter: the which doth evidently declare that this book hath not proceeded from the spirit of truth. Then he read the place. The words were: ET PRAESTA UT SERMO MEUS SIT FRAUDI ET VULNERI, etc. [and grant that my speech deceive and wound, etc.]. These words were not in Campion's book which he said was of St. Jerome's translation.

Campion. It was not properly in his [her] nature fraud, but for the external show only so that it was materially fraud but not formally.

Charke. What! Are you driven to such narrow distinctions already? I trust you shall be brought further shortly.

Campion. This difference is very apparent, for in truth it was materially fraud, and so was it materially stealing that the Israelites did take away other men's goods, coming out of Egypt, so was it material murder when God commanded Abraham to kill his son Isaac, but not formally, for God would not have commanded Abraham to do that when as before he had given him a contrary commandment, and commanded upon such pain to observe it. And I say there is no diversity where a thief killeth one by the wayside, and where a man is orderly and by law judged to die and so executed. Touching the material death for both of them are a taking away man's life from him, but the form, that is, the circumstance with all the things thereto belonging, doth make the diversity apparent. And reply you to this diversity.

Charke. Well, I need not for I trust every man seeth how frivolous it is. But I need not to stand upon this, for you shall see this book and divers others left out in the Council of Laodicea, can. [canon] 59, where all the books of the canonical scriptures are set down and rehearsed. But yet this book and the Machabees and divers others be left out; and reading the canon they were not there rehearsed, you may so hear your own councils have not taken these books for canonical, for otherwise they should not have been left out here.

Campion. The Laodicean Council was particular. It doth only rehearse those books which were then undoubted of in that part of the world where the council was held; and this proveth no general doubt; for particular councils do rehearse these books which were received and known for canonical with them; and it followeth not, because they received no more, that we might receive no more; and some doctors in their writing do rehearse those books only which were undoubted of in that part of the world, where they lived, Eusebius, [of] Caesarea, and St. Cyprian who was vouched for that purpose by Master Doctor Walker; but this doth nothing prove but that we ought to receive them and not to doubt of them as they did, seeing they have been received by the church, by whose only authority all scriptures have been known, and received for true and canonical scriptures; for otherwise you might with as great reason doubt of any part of the New or Old Testament at your own pleasure.

Then they argued upon another question which was moved in the beginning of their disputation which was whether all things necessary to salvation be contained in the scriptures, and that was before said to be the sufficiency of scriptures, whereunto Master Charke replied as followeth.

Charke. The apostles did teach all things UNA VOCE [with one voice] which were necessary to salvation. Ergo, they did write all things.

Campion. I deny your argument.

Charke. Thus I prove it. What care the apostles had to the

churches present, they had to the churches to come; but they had care to teach the churches present to open all the counsels of God to them. Ergo, they left the same written which was sufficient, no doubt, to salvation.

Campion. I answer your minor. They had the same care of the church to come as it was expedient; but it was not expedient to write all and every syllable they spoke; and yet notwithstanding, they have disclosed to all their posterity all the truth of God and so much as is necessary to salvation, either in general or special words written.

Charke. It is well you will sometimes yield. Now I have gotten somewhat of you, for you do agree with me, for you have given a greater wound to your own side than you or a hundred such as you can cure. The pope will give you little thanks for this day's work.

Campion. You have gotten nothing.

Charke. What! Did not you say that sufficient to salvation is contained in scriptures, and yet it was not necessary that all and every syllable, as you said, should be written they spoke?

Campion. I said that it was not necessary that all they spoke should be written, and yet sufficient is written to salvation, either in general or particular terms.

Charke. You said all and every syllable, and so let it be written down.

Campion. Well, put in all and every syllable, if you will, as lawyers do; but I will show you how all things are contained in scriptures necessary to salvation, either generally or particularly; for herein you think you have gotten some advantage. St. Augustine, writing against one Cresconius,[3] saith that it cannot be vouched out of scriptures by plain words that heretics' children should not be rebaptized; and many more things in like manner may be added, as that infants should be baptized before they believed, the proceeding of the Holy Ghost from the Father and the Son, that baptism is a sacrament, and preaching is not, and yet commanded at one time, and that the eucharist is a sacrament and washing of feet is none, and yet both commanded to us at one time. These and such like cannot be proved expressively by scripture, not by express words; but for

[3] Campion's reference is to Augustine's *Contra Cresconium grammaticum Donatistam* (405–406).

these we are referred by the scriptures unto the church as in that place where it is said: let him hear the church, obey the pastors; if he do not hear the church, let him be to thee as a heretic, and many such like places. And by this means all things necessary to salvation are contained in scriptures.

Charke. O blasphemy, because you did take me so short touching Judith wherein you seemed to triumph. I will now requite you, and you shall not now start back from that you have said, which is that God the Holy Ghost, the third person in trinity, cannot be expressly proved out of scripture which is extremely blasphemy.

Campion. I did not say so. You mistake my words. Gladly you would take some advantage if you could. I said that you could not prove the proceeding of the Holy Ghost from God the Father and from God the Son, with divers others things which I rehearsed before, by any express place of scripture; and I trust this is no blasphemy. Prove any of these by scriptures.

Charke. They may be gathered out of divers places of scripture.

Campion. Well then, I have said no blasphemy as you charged me withal; but because you say they may be gathered out of scripture, show me one equivalent place of scripture to prove the proceeding of the Holy Ghost from the Father and the Son.

Charke. In the 15 of John it is said: EGO MITTAM VOBIS A PATRE SPIRITUM VERITATIS QUI A PATRE PROCEDIT [I shall send to you from the Father the Spirit of truth who proceedeth from the Father.]

Campion. That proveth that he proceeds from the Father only and so that proveth against you. But you must prove a proceeding from the Father and the Son, in which you must note the effect of the word *proceeding*; for where we do believe that the Son is not made nor created but begotten of the Father, wherein this *begotton* is only effectual, so the proceeding of the Holy Ghost from the Father and the Son the word *proceeding* is only effectual. But, Mr. Charke, you need not trouble yourself, for this hath been a controversy between the Greek and the Latin Church discussed, because the learned men of the Greek Church could find no plain place proving the proceeding of the Holy Ghost equally from the Father and the Son, and I doubt not but among them there have been as learned as you are.

Charke. Comparisons are odious and needless here. But the apostles have left nothing out which appertaineth to salvation.

Campion. I grant in such sort as I have said with interpretation of the church: and with these general commandments observed, namely, obey the pastors, hear the church, and such like, always supposing a true church.

Walker. I have been these two or three days turning and seeking of books to prove that all things necessary to salvation are contained in the scriptures; and now by this subtle shift and distinction he hath avoided all; for it is the practice of them to preach and teach one thing; and when they come to defend it, to deny it and maintain another thing.

Campion. What I have said I have always taught, and it is the common opinion of all Catholics.

Charke. Well, I will pluck you from that distinction.

Campion. Do if you can.

Charke. All matters of salvation are manifestly contained in the scriptures; ergo, particularly.

Campion. I deny your argument. For manifestly is either in general or particular terms to be manifest, as this is manifest: believe the church; and under this are all things, which be not written generally, commanded, and so manifest, but yet not particularly.

Charke. If any thing be obscure and not manifestly written by the apostles, it is either because they would not or could not write it otherwise; but to say they could not is blasphemy; and to say they would not argueth malice in them. Ergo.

Campion. All things are contained manifestly either generally or particularly.

Charke. It is not manifest to leave a door to traditions, for that is to leave a way to heresies.

Campion. To leave a way to traditions, which the Holy Ghost may deliver to the true church, is both manifest and secure; and because you reject all traditions, prove some of these things which I have showed you before. Let me hear how you will convince me by scriptures that children should be baptized before they believe. Suppose me to be an Anabaptist. Let me hear how you will convince me.

Charke. Baptism and circumcision are of one nature, and the one doth represent the other. Ergo, etc.

Campion. The Anabaptist denyeth your argument for two causes: the one for that he ought to believe before he be baptized, and the other because he should not be baptized before the 8th day which is observed in circumcision.

Charke. The 8th day was not material, for it doth appear that some have been 40 years old before they were circumcised.

Campion. It is very material seeing it is so commanded in the law that it should be the 8th day. And although some were not till 40 years circumcised, it was not because it was indifferent, but by reason of some extraordinary occasion that they might not.

Charke. Well, we will not begin a new disputation of this matter, but proceed to our own question. How say you of Ignatius?[4] And [he] showed forth the Greek text, and thereof there read it to this effect, as far as I could conceive it, that it was necessary that such things as were either done or preached by the apostles should be written for the avoiding of controversies which might arise in the church.

Campion. The meaning of the place is this: Ignatius was St. John's scholar and was OCULATUS TESTIS [eyewitness] of many things done and said by St. John, which as then was not written; and being taken at Pathmos and carried to Rome, there to be executed, he wrote divers epistles in which he did write of these things, whereof he was OCULATUS TESTIS, they being then unknown to others. And lest by his death, being then at hand, they should be altogether unknown, he thought it necessary to commit them to writing. The which is his meaning in that place vouched by you, and not that such traditions delivered to the true church from the apostles and generally known and recited should not be allowed. And with all these things that Ignatius wrote was no scripture, for St. John's Gospel was then written, so that nothing was written by him other than such as may be accompted for a tradition; neither was this of Ignatius superfluous, no more than it was after the writing of the Old Testament to write the New Testament, or after the writing of the gospel, to write Paul his epistles.

Charke. When the apostles did preach, they did prove their doctrine out of Moses and the prophets.

Campion. Although sometimes the apostles proved the coming

[4] Ignatius (d. ca. 110), church prelate and martyr, was a disciple of St. John's. His letters supply information about the early church and emphasize the importance of the church hierarchy.

of the Messiah and other things by scriptures, yet not always. For sometimes with miracles and sometimes with both; and if that had been sufficient which was then extant, the rest that was written after was superfluous.

Charke. St. Ambrose saith, li. 1., 4 cap: CORR. QUICQUID NON AB APOSTOLIS TRADITUM EST SCELERIBUS PLENUM EST [what was not handed down by the apostles is full of wickedness].

Campion. St. Ambrose did write against certain which fathered false traditions upon the apostles and were carried under their names, whereas indeed they were none of theirs, which ought to be rejected; but such traditions, as the true church hath received from the apostles and believed, are not to be rejected. And this was uttered of the comparison of the traditions of the Catholics and the heretics.

Charke. Christ taught all: for he said, EGO VOBIS DOCUI OMNIA QUAE A PATRE ACCEPI [I have taught you all that I received from the Father]. And the apostles did write all that Christ taught. Ergo, all things necessary were written.

Campion. NEGO MINOREM [I deny the minor].

Charke. It is said in St. John, cap. 20, HAEC SCRIPTA SUNT SIC UT VITAM HABEATIS [these things have been written so that you may have life]; and by that it doth appear they put all things in writing.

Campion. Not so. For although St. John saith that HAEC SCRIPTA SUNT, yet he doth not say that all things are written; and as I have said before, I will grant that all things necessary to salvation are written either in general or in special words.

Charke. Tertullian against Hermogines biddedst him to prove his opinion out of scripture, and doth condemn the traditions alleged by him.[5]

Campion. Hermogines, being an heretic, fathered a bastard tradition upon the apostles and alleged it against Tertullian; and Tertullian calleth him to prove his opinion by the true scripture, seeing his tradition alleged was of us no credit; for Tertullian doth not argue it is not true because it is not written, but willeth him, seeing that tradition is not of credit because it is a bastardly tradition, to prove it by the true scripture.

[5] Tertullian's polemic *Against Hermogenes* countered the view that God created the soul from preexistent matter.

Charke. St. Basil, in his exercises, cap. *De Fide* [*On Faith*], was read in Greek to the same effect that the place of Tertullian was, as I could understand.[6]

Campion. Whereunto Mr. Campion said that he would expound St. Basil by another place of St. Basil's which, as he said, was more plain; but Mr. Charke would not be answered so, for he alleged that chapter was no payment; but to that effect as to the place of Tertullian, Mr. Campion answered and that St. Basil's meaning was to reprove them that rejected and disallowed of the true scripture and cleaved only to traditions, or to such scriptures as were then forged and devised.

Charke. I profess before God that Basil meant no such thing.

Campion. I deny your protestation and do affirm that his meaning is, as I have said, to revoke some from their errors in the foresaid matter.

Charke. It is a manifest apostasy to dissolve things that are not written sithen it is written that: OMNES MEI AGNOSCUNT VOCEM MEAM [all who are mine recognize my voice].

Campion. I grant to dissolve and reject those things that were written by the Spirit of God, and to bring in new devices of their own to be a manifest apostasy, but to allow traditions delivered by the apostles and hitherto received, that to be apostasy, I deny.

And thus they ended this forenoon's disputation.

[Afternoon Session]

At afternoon about two of the clock returned Doctor Walker and Mr. Charke; and after prayer made by Mr. Charke, Doctor Walker began some speeches touching this question: AN SOLA FIDES JUSTIFICAT [whether faith alone justifies]. Mr. Campion, on the other part respondent alone, answered him. Their speeches grew to this issue: so far forth as they did not exclude charity, as a cause efficient (in us inherent by the merciful gift of God) of our salvation, and faith, hope and charity to be not only three distinct virtues, but three

[6] St. Basil (330?–379?), bishop of Caesarea and Doctor of the Church, defended the Nicene Creed against the followers of Arius.

causes of our salvation necessary to the justification of every man, and given us free from God.

Walker. Then Doctor Walker said: It is long since I left the university, but yet I will try you in logic and philosophy. Then they tendered him many demands, as followeth. You say that faith, hope and charity are given us of God, and that is true. But how long do they remain with a man?

Campion. They remain till a man have lost them through his own sins and iniquities.

Walker. Well. But first what is faith and the etymology thereof?

Campion. According to the grammarians it is called FIDES, A FIENDO, QUIA FIT QUOD DICTUM EST [faith, from *fiendo*, because what is said happens.] And it is otherwise defined with the divines that: FIDES EST RERUM SPERANDARUM ARGUMENTUM NON APPARENTIUM [faith is the hope of things not apparent], according to St. Paul.

Walker. Is not faith before hope and charity? It is the ground. Ergo, it goeth before all things that come after it.

Campion. I grant that in nature it goeth before them; but it doth not justify before they come.

Walker. You must remember that PRIUS and POSTERIUS [before and after] be diversely taken in logic.

Campion. Therefore did I answer you in nature and in order too, if you will.

Walker. Therefore, it is most excellent.

Campion. I deny your consequent, for divers things that be after in nature be before in dignity.

Walker. Is not faith RADIX [root] and FUNDAMENTUM [foundation] without the which the other cannot stand; and yet will you prefer them before faith?

Campion. The tree and fruit be more worthy than the root, and the whole building more excellent than the foundation. And so the reasons you produce make utterly against you, as the meanest here may easily conceive. Besides that, the reason is flat contrary to St. Paul who saith: HORUM AUTEM MAIOR EST CHARITAS [the greatest of these, however, is charity].

Walker. Here meant St. Paul an historical faith. And I pray you is not OMNIS CAUSA EFFICIENS, PRESTANTIOR EFFERTUM [the whole efficient cause, full superior]?

Campion. Prove that St. Paul meant such a faith. And faith is a cause antecedent, but not efficient; it is the foundation of everlasting life, and a sure argument of my belief.

Walker. Well, I will go further with you. What is SUBIECTUM FIDEI [the subject of faith]?

Campion. Man is SUBIECTUM FIDEI to whom God hath bestowed that grace whereby he is elevated to acknowledge his goodness, and upon that he is called FIDELIS [faithful].

Walker. Of what parts doth a man consist?

Campion. Sir, what maketh this to the purpose? This only spendeth the time.

Walker. You shall know anon whereunto it tendeth. Answer me.

Campion. Man consisteth of body and soul.

Walker. Of which chiefly?

Campion. Of the soul.

Walker. In whither of these parts are faith, hope and charity?

Campion. In the soul, by the organ or instrument of the body.

Walker. The soul hath many POTENTIAS [powers]. In which of them is faith, as his SUBIECTUM IN QUO VERSATUR [subject in which it resides]?

Campion. In his INTELLECTUM, being illuminated by grace, because that part was most specially corrupted by error.

Walker. You answer well. But further, what is OBJECTUM FIDEI AD QUOD RESPICIT [the object of faith to which it reflects]?

Campion. Truth inspired from God.

Walker. ETERNA VERITAS EST DEUS, ERGO DEUS EST OBIECTUM FIDEI [God is eternal truth, therefore God is the object of faith]?

Campion. God, as he is to be understood of us, is the object of faith; and as he is good and eternal bliss, he is the object of hope; and as he is to be beloved only for himself, he is the object of charity.

Walker. God is incomprehensible, but so much as he hath revealed of himself, as his omnipotency in creation, his wisdom in preserving, and his goodness in governing, and so much we apprehend.

Campion. To apprehend these things effectually is sufficient, and it is fruitless only to grant them to be true unless we do apply them to our salvation through the passion of Christ.

Walker. It is true, as it is said, Rom. 4, NON HESITANS FIDE [not hesitating in faith].

Campion. I grant we must not doubt, but keep a firm and an assured faith, as Abraham did of whom that text is meant.

Walker. Well, what is the subject of hope?

Campion. The soul of man.

Walker. In what place of the soul is hope?

Campion. It is most properly in VOLUNTATE [in the will].

Walker. What is OBIECTUM SPEI [object of hope]?

Campion. The good of the life to come.

Walker. What was the object of Abraham's hope?

Campion. The same as of all other men, and specially the coming of the messiah, as we do believe that he is already come.

Walker. What was promised to us in Christ?

Campion. Salvation and eternal life.

Walker. The man that hath faith and hope hath a desire to enjoy God's promises.

Campion. When God hath lightened man's heart with charity, then hath he that desire steadfast.

Walker. What is the subject of charity?

Campion. The affection of man.

Walker. What is the object of charity?

Campion. God as he is to be believed, QUATENUS APPETITUR IN SE [insofar as he is desired in himself]; and the order of our justification is thus first to believe, then to hope, and last to love God.

And having thus answered all these questions, thinking that Doctor Walker would have inferred something, they paused a while; but Mr. Charke, seeing him to conclude nothing, began as followeth.

Charke. If there be anything specially labored and therewithal plain and evident in all the scriptures, it is this profession: SOLA FIDES JUSTIFICAT [faith alone justifies]. And here I protest in the Lord that in the behalf of this audience to whom, as Campion lately said but feignedly to the doctors, I am ready in the Lord God to do all the service I may. I will allege 11 places out of the scripture which do manifestly prove it to be the plain and true sense of God's word that faith only doth justify.

Campion. This position, that faith only doth justify, is not in all the word of God.

Charke. There are eleven places negative that works do not justify. And with that did capitulate the places as followeth: Rom. 3:28, etc.[7]

Campion. Of all your places there is none that doth probably prove your position. And because you do generally vouch them, I will answer them generally. The cause why St. Paul urgeth faith so much was because he was troubled with two kind of people, the Jews and the Gentiles. The Jews thought they might not be justified without the performance of the ceremonies of the old law, and the performance thereof was the cause of their election. And likewise the Gentiles attributed so much to the moralities,[8] thinking them to be the cause of their election, to avoid which errors was the scope of that epistle to the Romans, and to exclude works going before faith, and not to exclude works done in grace after faith. And this is my answer generally to those places alleged, reserving their several answers to every place incidently as they are alleged.

Charke. The end of all works were [is] that God might be glorified; and so was the work of Abraham and of all others; for else God should be disappointed of his end; but Abraham, as it is said in St. Paul, hath nothing to glory of. Ergo, neither for works going before faith, nor after.

Campion. Before circumcision and the covenant Abraham was just; therefore, the Jews might not glory in their works; for the scope of St. Paul in that chapter was to prove that the ceremonies of the law did not justify because Abraham who was before the law was just, and therefore that they might be justified without the law as Abraham was.

Charke. Well, answer this argument. Abraham hath nothing left to glory in. Ergo, good works do not justify.

Campion. I deny your argument; for the apostles showeth that

[7] The following additional references are cited in *A true report*: Romans 3:20, 21; 4:6, 13; 9:11; 11:6; Galatians 2:16; Ephesians 2:8–9; 2 Timothy 1:9; and Titus 3:5.

[8] Regarding justification, the disputants make the same distinction as Paul does in his Epistle to the Romans. The Jews expected to be justified by keeping the revealed law of the Old Testament, whereas the Gentiles relied on reason and founded their beliefs on the natural law. The disputants, of course, agree that the laws of the Jews and the moralities of the Gentiles were superceded by the New Testament.

Abraham was justified by works done in grace, as expecting the coming of Christ, and doth exclude works done void of Christ, and no other. Wherefore, prove your argument.

Charke. Abraham had all his works of Christ. Ergo, the works, that you say were excluded, were of Christ.

Campion. No works of Abraham were excluded. All the works he did were in Christ, and by these he was justified. Ergo, by Christ. And this was the meaning and the scope of the apostle.

Charke. You affirm contradictory to the Holy Ghost.

Campion. You do me open wrong in so affirming; and if you do not repent you of these words before you die, you must answer for them.

Charke. Abraham believed, and that was counted unto him for righteousness.

Campion. True it is he believed the messiah to come and looked for him, for it is said: CREDIDIT ABRAHAM DEO ET REPUTATUM EST EI IN IUSTITIAM [Abraham believed in God, and he is reputed justified]. This believing was a good work; MEDITARI FIDEM [to practice faith] is a good work and meritorious; and Abraham was not justified by works that went before faith, but after.

Charke. Proceeding to a new argument said these words before, that all the Romanists, if they had any modesty or shame, should never be able to breathe against certain arguments which I have to propound touching this matter. Thus he proceeded. Whosoever is justified is justified EX FORMULA FOEDERIS [out of the form of the covenant]; ergo, by the form of the first or second covenant; but not by the form of the first; ergo, by the form of the second, which is by faith only.

Campion. I grant your argument in this sense that faith only doth justify as it is distinct from the old law, but not as distinct from charity, which you must prove before your position can be granted.

Charke. The effect of the second covenant is faith, and we are justified by it. Ergo, not by works.

Campion. The second covenant is all the religion of Christ, which includeth faith, hope and charity; and also EUCHARISTA is PARS NOVI TESTAMENTI [the Eucharist is part of the New Testament] which by your reason should be excluded.

Charke. The covenant of the law is mixed with the covenant of the gospel; but that is not mixed with the covenant of the law; ergo, not with the gospel.

Campion. I answer your minor. The old law is not of faith; and as it is a naked commandment, it is a burden; so it is not of faith, so it doth not give the justice which is of Christ. And as it is the covenant of the old law, given from Moses, it is not mixed with the New Testament. But as it is of the law eternal, it is mixed with the New Testament, for he saith: MANDATUM NOVUM DO VOBIS, UT DILIGATIS INVICEM [I give you a new commandment, that you should love one another].

Charke. Although this word SOLA FIDES [faith alone] be not expressly mentioned in scripture, yet it is the sense thereof, and may be added; for whereas it is commanded, in the 6th of Deut.: DEUM TUUM ADORABIS [you shall honor God], Christ in the gospel doth expound it: DEUM TUUM SOLUM ADORABIS [you shall honor your God only]. Even so when it is said that FIDES JUSTIFICAT, we may add that SOLA FIDES JUSTIFICAT.

Campion. The word ADORABIS doth imply an honor done to God only, which is called LATRIA. And therefore, Christ doth very well expound it so; but justification doth not imply a justification by faith only; and therefore, you may not add "only" to the text.

Charke. Good people, you shall hear what a notable error the papists have grounded upon these words LATRIA and DULIA, whereas the words be of so new affinity, the one to the other, that they can bear no distinction. They make LATRIA an honor due to God, and DULIA an honor due to saints, which is a very gross distinction and an erroneous opinion.

Campion. I pray you, Mr. Charke, doth not the English word make the same distinction, for can I properly say adore my prince? No. But I ought to say adore God, and honor and serve my prince, so that now, Mr. Charke, let this be a question between us tomorrow, whether honor be done to saints; and in the forenoon, oppose you, and I will answer; and let me in the afternoon oppose, and answer you, if you will; and then shall it be tried.

Walker. We that are Christians are justified by the same means that Abraham was justified; but Abraham was justified by faith and nothing else; ergo, we are justified by faith and nothing else.

Campion. I answer your minor. Like as Abraham being just was made more just by a living faith, so the children of Abraham being justified do increase it and are made more just by a living faith.

Walker. Whether are we justified by the same means that Abraham was?

Campion. We are by the same means.

Walker. Abraham was justified only by faith; ergo, so be we.

Campion. I deny your antecedent.

Walker. CREDIDIT ABRAHAM DEO, ET REPUTATUM EST EI IN IUSTITIAM [Abraham believed in God, and he was reputed justified].

Campion. It is the proper office of faith to give credit to God, but to give credit effectually is the office of faith and charity.

Charke. Faith as it is a work, it doth not justify; but as it apprehendeth, it is a work; ergo.

Campion. Because this is difficult, I must be driven to speak of it scholastically, but I trust there are some here that can understand my meaning. There is in man a habit which doth include faith, and the act interior of this is to believe preceding, as INTELLECTU [in perceiving]. And the act exterior is to profess that faith and to make it manifest, which act is a good work and meritorious. And this I gather out of St. Paul who saith: CORDE CREDITIS, ORE SIT CONFESSIO AD SALUTEM [you believe with your heart, with your mouth let there be confession unto salvation] and to a man already justified, to believe is a good work, and RIMINARE FIDEM [to examine faith], is a good work also.

Charke. You cannot prove that out of scripture, that faith is a good work.

Campion. It is St. James. And [Campion] would have turned the place, but Mr. Charke said: Campion, make syllogism. And he turning the place of St. James, read a little, and made this syllogism: He that was justified by faith was justified by a good work; but Abraham was justified by faith; ergo, etc.

Charke. I deny your major.

Campion. The major and minor are both out of St. James.

Charke. And with that Mr. Charke interrupted him saying, You must not be opponent.

Campion. But notwithstanding he uttered his proof of the minor as followeth: St. James saith that Abraham was justified by his good works; and what were the good works, it followeth in the text: CREDIDIT ABRAHAM DEO, ET REPUTATUM EST EI IN JUSTITIAM; and so you see, Mr. Charke, that faith is a good work.

Charke. Omitting [Admitting?] this, said: Campion, I do yield to you in one thing, that you have one of the stingingest styles that ever I read, which is the only thing you brought to England with you; for as in every part of your book you taunt the professors of the gospel most bitterly, so do you not in any one thing deal more injuriously than to charge us so oft and bitterly with inducing this new doctrine, SOLA FIDES IUSTIFICAT. To the full instruction of this audience, I will manifestly show that it hath been delivered to us from the ancient fathers, as Basil, Cyprian, Ambrose, Jerome and others, so that this is no new doctrine of ours.

Campion. I will grant that some of these fathers, having to deal with pagans and Jews, as St. Paul had, for abolishing of their Jewish ceremonies and the Gentiles' moralities, to which they attributed too much, did sometimes use these words, that only faith in Christ did justify, meaning thereby Christian religion, and excluding paganish and Judaical ceremonies; whereas Luther now by his position of SOLA FIDES IUSTIFICAT doth exclude charity; and herein doth the difference consist betwixt the doctors then and Luther now. For it is a fitter speech among the Jews and Gentiles, who do not believe, to say SOLA FIDES IUSTIFICAT than among Christians who believe already; for I myself, if I were sent to such places as many of the Society (whereof I am) are to convert the Indians, I would, and I am sure they do, tell them that it is the only way to salvation, to believe in Jesus Christ; and when I could get them once to believe, then go would I yet further with them and tell them that they must do good works, which was the proceeding of these doctors whom you name.

Charke. Campion, are not you ashamed or do you not blush to abuse this audience, saying that they meant by faith, Christian Religion? But to make your folly more manifest, did not St. Paul who urged faith, as these doctors did, write to the Romans, Corinthians and others who were Christians?

Campion. Yes, but to such Christians among whom some were that said without circumcision they could not be saved, as in the 15th of the Acts it appeareth most manifest, where it is said: ET QUIDAM DESCENDENTES DE JUDAEA, DOCEBANT FRATRES: QUIA NISI CIRCUMCIDAMINI SECUNDUM MOREM MOYSI, NON POTESTIS SALVARI [and some coming down from Judea, taught the brethren: That except you be circumcised after the manner of Moses, you cannot be saved]; for the avoiding of which was the cause that St. Paul did urge faith so much.

Walker. Mr. Campion, I will allege you a place out of a doctor of your own side named Sadoletus, a cardinal, surely a man right well learned.[9] The place was read where Sadolet seemeth to say: We may not bring of our own works to justification. And all the strength of his argument stood upon a similitude, which was that a man, saith Sadolet, that goeth to fetch water out of a clear fountain, the more puddle water he bringeth, the more shall his clear water be troubled; even so the more we bringeth of our own works to justification, the more shall our justification be thereby polluted.

Campion. Shall we be driven now to spend our time upon Sadolet who was but within this 40 years a late writer? But notwithstanding I will not refuse him, for I say that Sadolet, speaking of works before faith, I think he did reasoneth nothing amiss; for such works which goeth before faith are available nothing to justification but only such as cometh after faith.

Charke. The Lord of his great goodness and justice hath showed and manifested this argument with which by the grace of God I will now urge him withal, to the confusion of him and all adversaries of the gospel, which he nor they shall ever be able to answer. Sanctification and justification are two distinct and sundry things; ergo, good works in sanctification in justification have no place.

Campion. Smiling at this argument said: Is this your doughty argument that cannot be answered? Take this answer. I deny your argument. Prove it.

Charke. What! Do you scoff? You know not where you are nor into what place you are brought. I doubt not but you shall be brought to a place where you shall learn better to behave yourself.

Campion. I have a terrible adversary of you, Mr. Charke. But what doth this prove your argument?

Charke. Whatsoever is of sanctification is not of justification; but good works be of sanctification; ergo, not of justification.

Campion. I deny your minor. For good works be not only of sanctification; for sanctification and justification be subordinate; and good

---

[9] Jacopo Sadoleto (1477–1547), bishop of Carpentras and a distinguished classical scholar, argued vigorously for reform within the Church. His most controversial work is titled *In Pauli Epistolam ad Romanos commentariorum libri tres* (1535).

works do proceed of both; and the one doth follow the other; for whosoever is justified is sanctified.

Charke. Because the time is far spent, I will end with such an argument as neither you nor any of your side shall ever be able to answer. It is this: Christ dying for us had no sin in him really that caused his passion, but only by imputation. Right so, the justification we have by the passion of Christ proceedeth not of any real cause in us, but only by imputation. Ergo, not for any good works inherent in us we are justified. Then looking aside upon the people, he said: This is an argument which all the world cannot answer. And herein we must praise the wisdom of the Holy Ghost, who hath ministered to us such an argument for the furthering of the gospel and confounding the enemies thereof. And therewithal there was a great murmuring amongst the people, and some of them did hiss before the argument was either repeated or answered.

Campion. This is your argument. Christ did take our sins by imputation.

Norton. Ergo, said Mr. Norton, the notary, it followeth that our justification must be only by imputation. And in this manner Norton did disturb the repetition of Mr. Campion and his answer twice or thrice, until he was commanded by Sir Owen Hopton, Lieutenant, to hold his peace, and to hear the answer.

Campion. Then Mr. Campion repeated the argument as followeth. Christ did take our sins by imputation; ergo, our justification is by imputation. This I answer: your similitude holdeth.

Charke. And here Mr. Charke said: What, do you call it a similitude!

Campion. Well, your analogy be it. It holdeth so far as it is possible to hold, and that is that Christ had our sins only by imputation, for he could not be sinful. But it holdeth not of our part that we cannot be capable of his justice, but by imputation only; for we may have the causes of justification inherent in us through his merciful gift, and so to have justice inherent, and not only by imputation. And here you see that your analogy doth not hold in this part.

Charke. Our sins were of force by imputation to cause the passion of Christ; therefore, his righteousness by imputation is of force to justify us.

Campion. I do not dispute whether the justice be of force by imputation to justify us, but in what order we are justified, whether by justice inherent or else by imputation. And I do say that we are justified by faith, hope and charity, as causes which we have of the gift of God; and therefore may be said his justice, because we have it from him; and it may be said a justice because it is in us. And this opinion you must impugn if you will impugn anything.

Charke. All your answers are set down and I hope the audience do now see how foolish they are. Therefore let us all thank God. And some being ready to depart, Mr. Charke commanded the doors to be shut till after prayer, which was to this effect: to thank God that he hath at this time brought this solemn action to such success, to the confirmation of the faithful and the confusion of the enemy, etc., which being ended all departed.

FINIS

Appendix A
Scudamore MS Add. 11055[1]

[Afternoon Session of Second Debate]

(A true copy of some disputations in the Tower as it was gathered and given out by some papist, but most falsely and untruly.)

Disputations had between Ed. Campion, Jesuit, Dr. Fulke and Goade, Ministers, this present Monday the 18 of September, 1581, in Sir Owen Hopton his parlor in the Tower.

Question. Whether the Catholic Church can err or no.

Fulke objecteth. Whatsoever is incident to every particular is incident to the whole, but to err is incident to every particular. Ergo, to the whole.

Campion. I answer that particular members of the church cannot.

Fulke. The greatest part of the Corinthians and all of the Galatians did err. Ergo, the Catholic Church may and did err.

Campion. I answer that all the Galatians did not err; and if they did, yet it cannot follow that the universal church did err.

Fulke urgeth these words: O INSENSATI GALATAE [O foolish Galatians].

Campion. I answer that it was but a custom and manner of preachers to speak unto all in general although they were not all fault worthy.

Fulke. The Church of Rome is the true church; but the Church of Rome hath erred. Ergo, the true church may err.

Campion. Do you believe that the major proposition is true?

Fulke. I suppose it.

---

[1] As with the other manuscripts, I have regularized spelling, placed Latin quotations in upper case and interpolations in parentheses, enclosed translations and editorial comments in brackets, expanded abbreviations, and modified punctuation for clarity.

Campion. Well do you suppose it, and I will believe it, and then prove the minor.

Fulke. It hath erred in matters of justification, and I will prove it. The Council of Trent doth attribute part of justification to that which is inherent in ourselves. Ergo, etc.

Campion. I answer that it is in us but not of us.

Fulke. That which doth justify us must be perfect and answerable to the law of God.

Campion. I answer that it must be perfect so far forth as God requireth, which is no more but to love God above all things and one's neighbor as oneself and that we may do in this life in so much as we prefer neither riches nor any worldly things, whatsoever they be, before the love of God. Which answer Fulke not liking replied and said it was impossible for any man living to observe the law; and therefore, when Christ willed us to love God above all things, it was but a manifestation of one's sins whereby we might be moved to crave for mercy and not his meaning we should observe these, for that (as he said before) it was impossible.

Fulke. General councils may err. Ergo, the church. I prove that. St. Augustine saith that general councils may be corrected by these words: The writings of all may be corrected.

Campion. I answer that the writings of bishops may be corrected and a general council may be amended, that is, more fully declared, and not amended in matters of faith but of conversation.

Fulke. The Council of Constantinople and the Council of Nicea disagreed in allowing of images. Being asked whether it were the second of Nicea or of Constantinople, they could not tell so that argument made no show.

Fulke. The whole church of St. Augustine's time did err in holding that infants should necessarily communicate. August. lib. 2, cap. 4, *Contra Pelag.*, QUI PUEROS DEFINIVIT, etc. [who defined boys, etc.].

Campion. I answer that it was not the necessity of the church in that time.

Fulke. St. Peter erred in a substantial matter of faith for St. Paul said he did not well.

Campion. I answer that it was not a matter of faith but an indiscretion.

Fulke. The general councils now holden do confess they may err.

Ergo, etc. I prove it: the form of the general council of the Pope do now confess afore God and the world UT IGNORANTIAE PARCAS UT ERRORI INDULGEAS [that you spare ignorance and make allowance for error].

Campion. I answer that it is meant of those errors, or general errors inherent to the frailty of man and not errors of faith.

Fulke. The second Council of Nicea doth decree an error that angels had bodies.

Campion. I answer that it was not decreed but a discourse; neither is it a matter of faith.

Fulke. SACRA SYNODUS DIXIT: ETIAM DOMINE [the holy synod said: Yea, my lord].

Campion. I answer that he saith nothing but that they are invisible substances and not bodies.

Fulke. St. Paul commandeth us to receive under both kinds which your church forbiddeth. Ergo, etc.

Campion. I answer that you can never prove that by these words, which are PROBET SEIPSUM HOMO, etc. [let a man improve himself, etc.], that St. Paul did command us to receive under both kinds. For the sense of the words are that he who will eat of this bread and drink of this cup, let him first examine himself, not commanding any man; and I say that it was the use of the church to receive under both kinds and also myself have seen the laity receive under both kinds.

Fulke. You hold that Christ is bodily in the sacrament. Ergo, he is not then bodily in heaven because it is contrary to the nature of the verity of his body, and heaven doth hold him as St. Augustine saith.

Campion. I answer that heaven doth hold him; that is, heaven is his palace, his dwelling place, not a Tower; and there he must be until the day of judgment; and yet it followeth not that he is not in the sacrament.

Four errors granted by Fulke. The first, that David when he committed adultery was not at that instant the slave of sin. To the which Campion answered, QUI FACIT PECCATUM SERVUS EST PECCATI [whoever sins is the slave of sin]. Which they answered thus, that he who committed sin of malice was a slave of sin, which David did not but of frailty. Which answer Campion disproving was interrupted. The second, that infants if they died immediately after baptism, for ought that they knew, go to hell. The third, that only notion to sin is a sin. The fourth, that those that be Catholics cannot become heretics, and that Fulke would have proved in this manner, that none is born of the spirit but is predestinate to eternal life, which exposition Campion denying, Fulke did not go any further.

[Fourth Debate]

A disputation had between Mr. Campion, Jesuit, and Dr. Walker and Mr. Charke, Ministers, the 27 of September in the hall of Sir Owen Hopton within the Tower.

Campion. I confess that the Lutherans have cut off from the body of the Testament certain books which are canonical scripture, and therein they have erred and committed blasphemy, which Walker and Charke deny not and say they cannot tell whether they have done so or no.

Question. Whether Tobias and the rest be in SINCERA CANONE [the true canon].

Walker. St. Augustine forbiddeth to read the apocrypha. Ergo, apocrypha be not canonical. And all this Mr. Campion granteth to make nothing against his position. Walker allegeth St. Jerome that the book of Tobias and the rest are not in the canon.

Campion. I answer not in the canon of the Hebrews but of the Christians.

Charke. I prove the Machabees not to be canonical scripture thus: The writer asketh pardon for his style. Ergo, it is not decreed by the Holy Ghost.

Campion. I answer that the writer asketh pardon for his style, not the Holy Ghost for the effect.

Charke. The second book of the Machabees was written by a profane spirit because he doth ask pardon either for the matter or style. Ergo, not by the Spirit of God.

Campion. I answer that to acknowledge his style, not to please his auditors, cometh of the Holy Ghost.

Charke. Whatsoever is in the word of God is full, sound, and perfect and needeth no pardon. But this needeth pardon. Ergo, it is not the word of God.

Campion. I answer that in respect of itself it needeth no pardon, but in respect of dainty hearers it may ask pardon of style.

Charke. Whatsoever is in the scriptures is of the Holy Ghost both for matter, style and circumstance. Ergo.

Campion. I answer that the asking of pardon is of the Holy Ghost because it proceeded of humility.

Charke. Judith doth pray that Holofernes might be taken with the snare of her beauty. Ergo, she doth not well, and by consequence the book is not canonical.

Campion. I answer that seeing it hath pleased God to give Holofernes over to the lust of the flesh, she prayeth that he would turn this sin of his to the benefit of his people. So they turned to the text to prove it to be fraud and therefore unlawful.

Campion. I answer that it was material fraud but not formal, that is, in truth such as when Abraham offered his son Isaac, it was material killing but not formal.

Charke. Allegeth a place of St. Cyprian upon the creed.

Campion. I answer that particular councils allege such books as were called in question in those parts where they lived.

Charke. The apostles did teach all things. Ergo, they wrote all things. I prove it thus: What care they had of the churches present, the same care they had of the churches to come.

Campion. I answer that they had the same care which was expedient, and yet it was not expedient they should write every syllable, and yet they have opened all things either in special or general writings and that out of three places of scripture: OBEDITE PRAEPOSITIS; AUDITE ECCLESIAM; ECCLESIA EST COLUMNA [obey your prelates; hear the church; the church is the pillar of support].

Charke. Either the apostles could not or they would not, but it is blasphemy to say they could not and to put a blot in their foreheads to say they would not. Ergo, they did.

Campion. I answer to have a door to traditions which may be delivered by the Holy Ghost to the true church is a manifest matter and secure without blot or blasphemy. To a place which they allege out of Ignatius, being St. John's scholar, an eyewitness of many things which St. John did write, thought good because he was going to his martyrdom to leave in writing such things as he both heard and saw and was not written before.

Thus broke up the disputation in the forenoon.

* * *

[Afternoon Session]

In the afternoon they argued whether faith did only justify.

Campion. When God doth justify, he giveth three things unto us as causes of our justification: faith, hope and charity.

Walker. What is the etymology of faith?

Campion. I answer according to the grammarians. It is A FIENDO QUIA FIT QUOD DICTUM EST [from FIENDO because what is said happens].

Walker. Faith is the ground. Ergo, it is before all other things that come after.

Campion. QUODAMMODO [in a certain way].

Walker. Ergo, before hope and charity.

Campion. In nature, but it doth not justify before they do come.

Walker. Faith is set before. Ergo, it is more worthy.

Campion. If it be set before in dignity but not in order, and I say that faith is a cause antecedent but not efficient. Faith is the foundation and an argument of things that we hope for. And therein they all agree.

Walker. What is the SUBJECTUM FIDEI [subject of faith]?

Campion. SUBJECTUM FIDEI is man to whom God hath given this faith and thereof man is denominated faithful.

Walker. Whether standeth man of one part or more?

Campion. Man consisteth of body and soul.

Walker. Do we receive faith into the body or into the soul?

Campion. Into the soul by the instrument of the body.

Walker. Whether do we receive that PER MEMORIAM, INTELLECTUM, or VOLUNTATEM [by memory, understanding, or will]?

Campion. PER INTELLECTUM which is illuminated by faith.

Walker. What is the OBJECTUM FIDEI [object of faith]?

Campion. OBJECTUM FIDEI is truth inspired by God.

Walker. AETERNA VERITAS EST DEUS. ERGO, DEUS EST OBJECTUM FIDEI [God is eternal truth. Therefore, God is the object of faith].

Campion. I answer that God to be known is the object of faith. As he is to be beloved, he is the object of charity.

Walker. Whether to apprehend these things effectually be sufficient?

Campion. To apprehend these things effectually is sufficient. That is, not only to grant it to be true, but also to apply by his passion these things to be benefit of our salvation.

Walker. CREDIDIT ABRAHAM DEO [Abraham believed in God].

Campion. I answer that that made the faith of Abraham meritorious.

Walker. What is SUBJECTUM SPEI [the subject of hope]?

Campion. I answer that it hath some SUBJECTUM and is in the same soul of man but more properly in VOLUNTATE [in the will].

Walker. What is the OBJECTUM SPEI [object of hope]?

Campion. The good of the life to come.

Walker. What is the object of the faith of Abraham?

Campion. The same that is of all other Christian men.

Walker. What is promised us in Christ?

Campion. Salvation, and the man that is enlightened hath a desire also.

Walker. What is the OBJECTUM of charity?

Campion. God, QUATENUS APPETITUR PROPTER SE [insofar as he is desired in himself].

Charke. It is the pure sense of the word of God that faith only doth justify. Ergo, etc.

Campion. I answer with this proposition: Faith only doth justify is not in all the word of God.

Charke. If anything be to be proved out of the scripture, this is by eleven places which be negative unto works. Rom. 11.

Campion. Where there is nothing more urged in all the scripture than justification by faith, it is meant that faith without the works of the law doth justify against the Jews, and that is one general cause. And another general cause is this: for that the wise men of the Gentiles did allege their moralities as a cause of their election which St. Paul meant to refute in the Epistle to the Romans. Generally these be the answers, but incidentally others may be given.

[Marginal note in a different hand:] (The works of the Jews by the law and works of the Gentiles without law excluded from justifying by his own confession. Ergo, all works.)

Charke. St. Paul doth not exclude the profane works of the Gentiles but moral works.

Campion. The general scope of the apostle is to exclude all works both of Jews and Gentiles that go before faith, but in the way of discourse, incidentally another answer may be given.

Charke. Abraham had nothing to glory in. Ergo, he is justified by faith only.

Campion. I answer that the meaning of the apostle is to declare that Abraham was justified by works done in grace and excludeth works void of Christ.

Charke. Abraham's works which Paul excludeth were not without Christ. Ergo, your answer standeth not.

Campion. I answer that no works of Abraham are excluded, and that Abraham cannot glory because his works were founded in Christ. And I add that Abraham before he did this thing was just.

Charke. Whosoever is justified is justified EX FORMULA FOEDERIS [by the form of the covenant]. Ergo, by the first or by the second; not by the first; ergo, by faith only.

Campion. I grant all to be true in this sense by faith only, not as faith is distinct from charity, but as it is distinct from the old law.

Charke. The first covenant is: do this and thou shalt live; the second, that the righteous liveth by faith.

Campion. I answer that the form of the second covenant is all the religion of Christ.

Charke. It is against the word of the apostle. The law is not of faith.

Campion. The law, as it is a naked commandment, is a burden and so it is not faith; that is, it doth not give the justice we have by faith.

Charke. If your interpretation be true, the covenant of the law is mingled with the gospel; but that cannot be.

Campion. I answer that the covenant of the law, as it is of the old law, is not mingled with the gospel; but as it is the covenant of the eternal law, so it is mingled with the gospel.

Charke. It is absurd to make a substantial distinction of the law in regard to the minister or the time. But all these be but words. It is written in the 6 of Deut.: NON IBITIS POST DEOS ALIENOS [ye shall not go after other gods]; and in the 4 of Mat. Christ expoundeth after this manner: ET ILLI SOLI SERVIES [and him only shalt thou serve]. And therefore in like sort when he saith that faith doth justify without works, I may conclude by faith only.

Campion. I answer that this word ADORABIS [you shall adore] doth signify so much because there is but one God. But this word *justify* doth not import so much, and therefore your allusion is not good.

Walker. We are justified by that means that Abraham was, but Abraham was justified by faith. Ergo, etc.

Campion. I answer to the major that like as Abraham a just man was made more just by a living faith, even so the children of Abraham increased their righteousness by a living faith.

Walker. Whether we be justified by the same means that Abraham was or no?

Campion. We are.

Walker. But Abraham was justified [by] only faith. Ergo, we.

Campion denieth it.

Walker. Faith only did give credit to the promise of God. Ergo, etc.

Campion. I answer that to give credit to the promise of God is the proper part of faith, but effectually is the office of faith and charity. For the apostle speaketh of Abraham, justified [BLOT] by charity, and therefore it must needs be so understood.

Charke. Faith as it is a work doth not justify but as it apprehendeth. Ergo.

Campion. There is a habit which is called FIDES [faith]; and it hath two acts: one interior, and that is CREDERE [to believe]; and another exterior, and that is PROFITERI FIDEM [to profess faith openly] consonant to the apostle. With the heart I believe, and with the mouth I confess. Now I believe that faith is a good work.

Charke. Whatsoever is of sanctification is not of justification, but the blessing of the Holy Ghost to love is of sanctification. Ergo.

Campion. I answer that it is of both.

Charke. Christ died by imputation only. Ergo, by imputation only we are justified.

Campion. I answer that Christ had our sins by imputation only because he was not capable of sins inherent. But we be capable of justice inherent which Christ doth give us. And therefore, we are [sharers in] the justice of Christ both by imputation and also inherent by him, and therefore it is called the justice of Christ.

Charke. Our sins were sufficient by imputation only to put Christ to death. Ergo, his righteousness was sufficient to justify us only by imputation.

Campion. We do not reason how Christ might have justified us, but we dispute how he hath justified us.

Much more was spoken which I could not remember.

Appendix B [Campion's "Challenge"[1]] To the Right Honourable Lords of Her Majestie's Privy Council

Right Honourable,

Whereas I have come out of Germanie and Boemeland, being sent by my Superiours, and adventured myself into this noble Realm, my deare Countrie, for the glorie of God and benefit of souls, I thought it like enough that, in this busie, watchful, and suspicious worlde, I should either sooner or later be intercepted and stopped of my course. Wherefore, providing for all events, and uncertaine what may become of me, when God shall haply deliver my body into durance, I supposed it needful to put this writing in a readiness, desiringe your good Lordships to give it the reading, for to know my cause. This doing, I trust I shall ease you of some labour. For that which otherwise you must have sought for by practice of wit, I do now lay into your hands by plaine confession. And to the intent that the whole matter may be conceived in order, and so the better both understood and remembered, I make thereof these ix points or articles, directly, truly and resolutely opening my full enterprise and purpose.

1. I confesse that I am (albeit unworthie) a priest of the Catholike Church, and through the great mercie of God, vowed now these viii years into the Religion of the Societie of Jhesus. Hereby I have taken upon me a special kind of warfare under the banner of obedience, and eke resigned all my interest or possibilitie of wealth, honour, pleasure, and other worldlie felicitie.

[1] For a brief historical and critical commentary on Campion's "Challenge," see Southern, *Elizabethan Recusant Prose*, pp. 148–56. I have adopted J. H. Pollen's text of the "Challenge" which Southern reprints (pp. 153–55) with the caution that not all the principal copies of it have been collated (p. 153).

2. At the voice of our General Provost, which is to me a warrant from heaven and Oracle of Christ, I tooke my voyage from Prage to Rome (where our said General Father is always resident) and from Rome to England, as I might and would have done joyously into any part of Christendome or Heathenesse, had I been thereto assigned.

3. My charge is, of free cost to preach the Gospel, to minister the Sacraments, to instruct the simple, to reforme sinners, to confute errors—in brief, to crie alarme spiritual against foul vice and proud ignorance wherewith many my dear Countrymen are abused.

4. I never had mind, and am strictly forbidden by our Father that sent me, to deal in any respect with matter of State or Policy of this realm, as things which appertain not to my vocation, and from which I do gladly restrain and sequester my thoughts.

5. I do ask, to the glory of God, with all humility, and under your correction, iii sortes of indifferent and quiet audiences: *the first* before your Honours, wherein I will discourse of religion, so far as it toucheth the common weale and your nobilities; *the second*, whereof I make more account, before the Doctors and Masters and chosen men of both Universities; wherein I undertake to avow the faith of our Catholike Church by proofs innumerable, Scriptures, Councils, Fathers, History, natural and moral reasons; *the third* before the lawyers, spiritual and temporal, wherein I will justify the said faith by the common wisdom of the laws standing yet in force and practice.

6. I would be loth to speak anything that might sound of any insolent brag or challenge, especially being now as a dead man to this world and willing to put my head under every man's foot, and to kiss the ground they tread upon. Yet have I such a courage in avouching the Majesty of Jhesus my King, and such affiance in His gracious favour, and such assurance in my quarrel, and my evidence so impregnable, and because I know perfectly that no one Protestant, nor all the Protestants living, nor any sect of our adversaries (howsoever they face men down in pulpits and overrule us in their kingdom of grammarians and unlearned ears), can maintain their doctrine in disputation. I am to sue most humbly and instantly for the combat with all and every of them, and the most principal that may be found: protesting that in this trial the better furnished they come, the better welcome they shall be.

7. And because it hath pleased God to enrich the Queen my Sovereigne Ladye with noble gifts of nature, learning and princely edu-

cation, I do verily trust that—if her Highness would vouchsafe her royal person and good attention to such a conference as, in the ii part of my fifth article I have mentioned, or to a few sermons, which in her or your hearing I am to utter,—such manifest and fair light by good method and plain dealing may be cast upon those controversies, that possibly her zeal of truth and love of her people shall incline her noble Grace to disfavour some proceedings hurtful to the Realm, and procure towards us oppressed more equitie.

8. Moreover I doubt not but you her Highness' Council, being of such wisdom and discreet in cases most important, when you shall have heard these questions of religion opened faithfully, which many times by our adversaries are huddled up and confounded, will see upon what substantial grounds our Catholike Faith is builded, how feeble that side is which by sway of the time prevaileth against us, and so at last for your own souls, and for many thousand souls that depend upon your government, will discountenance error when it is bewrayed, and hearken to those who would spend the best blood in their bodies for your salvation. Many innocent hands are lifted up to heaven for you daily by those English students, whose posteritie shall never die, which beyond seas, gathering virtue and sufficient knowledge for the purpose, are determined never to give you over, but either to win you heaven, or to die upon your pikes. And touching our Societie, be it known to you that we have made a league—all the Jesuits in the world, whose succession and multitude must overreach all the practices of England—cheerfully to carry the cross you shall lay upon us, and never to despair your recovery, while we have a man left to enjoy your Tyburn, or to be racked with your torments, or consumed with your prisons. The expense is reckoned, the enterprise is begun; it is of God, it cannot be withstood. So the faith was planted, so it must be restored.

9. If these my offers be refused, and my endeavours can take no place, and I, having run thousands of miles to do you good, shall be rewarded with rigour, I have no more to say but to recommend your case and mine to Almighty God, the Searcher of Hearts, who send us of His grace, and set us at accord before the day of payment, to the end we may at last be friends in heaven, when all injuries shall be forgotten.

Appendix C
Account of First Debate by Bombino[1]

[FIRST DEBATE]
CHAPTER 46

Nowell inveighs against Campion. Campion makes answer. Luther is falsely defended by the heretics.

So soon as the martyrs were once seated and the murmur of the multitude allayed, Nowell, who was chief in this disputation, composing his countenance to gravity and seeking to beget a great expectation in all the auditors, begins with a long preamble in his mother tongue, a quaint oration, much before pre-meditated and artificially trimmed. First he gives them to understand that there was no other cause of this their present meeting than to try out the truth in matter of religion. Moreover, he added that this truth was now long since well known to himself and those of the godlier sort of his countrymen. Wherefore no need was there that they should now, as it were anew, with so great preparation seek it out, as if it

[1] Paolo Bombino, born at Cosenza in southern Italy about 1575, entered the Society of Jesus in 1592 and taught sacred scripture in Rome. He later left the Society to join the Clerks Regular of Somascha in which he took vows in 1629. He died in 1648. His biography of Campion, *Vita et martyrium Edmundi Campiani*, was first published at Antwerp in 1618 and reprinted soon after. Bombino repudiated these printings in the Mantuan edition of 1620 because, he claimed, they contained corrections by others.

For the English translation of Bombino's Latin life of Campion, I have used a previously unpublished, seventeenth-century manuscript (Tanner 329) at the Bodleian Library. The translator is unknown, and the translation itself is incomplete. Nor is it known how the manuscript came into the possession of the antiquarian Archbishop Sancroft. The translator captures the spirit of Bombino's inflated prose style and contributes some of his own.

were a thing wherewith they were unacquainted, save only that it conduced to the good of the weal public openly to convince the pertinency and pull down the pride of a few contumacious persons.

Thus having said, on the sudden he passionately fell upon Campion with hot speeches and contumelious terms.

"For Campion," said he, "to speak to thee in milder terms than thou deservest, what a boldness was it, what an uncomparable pride for thee, like another Golias, to challenge all the English divines to public combat? Be thou what thou wilt be, thou art but one man; and yet all of them thou hast thus vaingloriously provoked to the field. I verily believe, thou never thoughtest that challenge would have proceeded further than to a proud ostentatious bravado, a vain vaporing of words, that thy lurking places, as they gave thee liberty to bark, so they promised thee impunity. But Almighty God, the due revenger of all such intolerable insolency, hath brought thee now at last into the light and upon the public stage, though thou soughtest never so much to avail it, where, whether thou wilt or no, thou must give proof of what thou hast so vauntingly promised. Thou hast here now prepared for the combat, not all the English divines, whose very aspect, thou, most vainglorious soldier, wouldst never be able to endure. But from amongst them all, but one or two. And yet I verily suppose enow for thee. Never look to escape the battle at this gap, that thou art called unto it unprovided. For although since the time that thou hast published thy flaunting book, whereby thou darest all our men to dispute with thee of religion, giving as it were the sign of the battle, to charge upon thee at their pleasure, thou hast given unto them with all public liberty to dispute with thee when they will. Yet my part it is, lest the truth which I hold undertaken to defend should suffer detriment, to stop by all such gaps. Wherefore this day's disputation shall be only of those questions, which thou with so great preparation didst vomit out in that goodly book of thine, to the defending of which thou oughtest no less to be provided, being their author, than a lawful father to acknowledge and defend his own children. And yet, in very deed, no humanity at all hast thou deserved at our hands, having with so impudent a lie so inhumanely torn our fame in pieces. For what outrageous jury was that which compelled thee to accuse us of cruelty against the men of thy religion? Now wouldst thou call to mind that evermore in times past, either absent before the eyes of thy mind or present before thy corporal eyes, there were for one Catholic, which perhaps was hardly handled by Protestants, whole hundreds of Protestants burnt by Catholics, whom thou callest the mildest of men. Moreover, it was no other than that untowardly spirit of lying which persuaded thee to write that Luther did not only condemn the Epistle of James the Apostle, but also with most notorious and virulent railing shamefully defame it. For, to my remembrance, these be thy words."

And herewith on the sudden as if the man had been mad, he rehearsed these words out of Campion's book: "What caused Luther, that wicked apostate to call the Epistle of James contentious, swelling, dry, strawy, and to esteem it unworthy an apostolical Spirit?" Having thus recited these words, he suddenly stopped, peradventure that he might make the fury of these words more eminent; or that he choked with anger; or that artificially he paused and meditated to the end he might begin, as it were, a new course of railing; or else, for that unawares, he cut off his speech.

Whereupon Campion, thinking assuredly that Nowell had ended his oration, turned towards him with a pleasing countenance and plausible voice, is said to have answered much after this manner.

"Learned sir, that the fault, which in the first place you object against me, hath so easy and apparent a defense, I attribute to the felicity of the cause which I undertook to defend. Moreover that you so vehemently expostulate with me, for that I provoked all the English divines into the lists of disputation, as if I had no evident cause, but no less than ten most just causes of this my confidence, which I see you have in your hands, right in this present place, and sufficiently declare, neither you nor any of yours to be ignorant of. These if they wash not away from me that crime of impudency, wherewith you were pleased to charge me in the beginning of this disputation, no speech of mine, no silence will ever be able to do it. But lest if I should give no answer at all to this crime wherewith at first you tax me, it might be imputed to pride, or arrogancy, thus I reply. Evermore, Nowell, it hath been my opinion that truth of her own nature is confident, and the mother of modest and fearless liberty; let lying hide itself and lurk in holes and corners; in them it lives; by them it is suckled and nourished; and no sooner comes to light, but it vanisheth. To fly the light, Nowell, to shun the sight and conversation of men is a token of fraud or vileness, vileness evermore the confirmed source of verity hateth; plain and sincere dealing detests all fraud and juggling. What marvel then, if in defense of verity I provoke all Englishmen to the field? In very deed, in doing this, in provoking to this combat, to this theater I was well assured, not to oppose myself against all your divines, but my faith and religion, my Catholic faith, which is to be found everywhere all over the Christian world, against yours, which divorced from it, is but called a private sect. Nor was it then mine own strength that I had before the eyes of my consideration, but the strength of my cause, when I so confidently challenged the field to enter the lists, to endure the dust and scorching sunshine against your men. Nor will I here be ashamed to own those words as mine, which heretofore I wrote and published. 'As for myself,' for to my best remembrance, these were my very words to the academicians of Oxford, 'if it were either out of confidence of my wit, learning, art, memory, that I thus provoked such expert adversaries, I should think myself most vain and insolent, who neither considered myself nor them I were to deal with; but if, weighing duly the cause that moves me, I thought myself able to prove this sun to shine at noontide, you must give me leave to show the fervor which the honor of Jesus Christ, my King, and truth invincible have commanded me.' This I suppose a sufficient answer to that impudence wherewith you charge me.

"Now I come to that of fear, for that you say you are afraid lest that combat which heretofore so voluntarily I offered in absence, now present, I should seek to eschew; which fear of yours to be in vain, that end will show. For although I am not so dull, but I easily prescribe upon how unequal conditions you offer it. Yet I will never give you occasion to think I find more incommodity in mine own weakness than strength, and safeguard in the firmness of my cause. Do you take heed, lest whilst you would be thought to discourse so publicly of the inequality of conditions, whereat we find ourselves so much aggrieved, you bethought to discourse less truly. For feign you would persuade us that for so much as you have only taken for questions to dispute of the points of religion, which myself have set down and published, you cannot be deemed to wage war against me unprovided. But I contrariwise affirm; this is no otherwise than if a man who is challenged to fight a duel in a certain place should not refuse the place, but subtract all weapons from his adversary. Know, Nowell, those points of religion, which I have set down, are but the places wherein to try the combat; the weapons, books and study; whereas therefore you vauntingly challenge me, naked and unadorned as I am, to dispute of those points, you accept indeed of the place I have appointed for the combat, but withdrawing the weapons. For otherwise, why should not I have the use of books as well as you, either before this time appointed or at leastwise even now, when I see those that are brought hither, not so much as to be touched, or looked upon, by any of us, without your leave? And in very deed I, spent though I am and almost exhausted with pain and miseries, could hardly erewhile forebear laughter to hear you go about to persuade how equal my conditions were with yours, unless you think I might as well be prepared for a learned disputation by being three times racked, as you by turning books. But I, say you, in sending letters to the council gave free liberty that all might come, that come would against me; this I can disprove for by this I thought to try the council's pleasure only, not to provoke any. But say I had provoked them, would I, think you, dispute of religion with my body torn with torments, all disjointed, and destitute of books? I have much ado, Nowell, to keep life, to retain any spirit: my very soul, through torments, is even almost on my lips. Is it so easy a matter, amidst all this, to have my wits about me? But this preamble I am willing to make, rather to testify the truth than any way to hinder our prepared combat. Christ my captain, he it is that affords me strength and courage. Nor do I fear that, since sundry times it hath been in his power to raise the dead to life, he will be as able this day to excite and strengthen me, half dead, to the combat. Thus much of the condition of our disputation.

"Now I will examine briefly what you have touched concerning the cruelty of our men. In very deed, Nowell, I plainly perceive, you thought yourself to have given sufficient answer to the cruelty of your men against us by way of recrimination; for, to show yourselves to be falsely accused by me of cruelty, you argue that we Catholics are crueler. But this is not so; for in complaining of your cruelty, I never went about to compare it with any other. And if you doubt, then seek to be resolved of this. There be yet alive some of those, who in the reign of Catholics, kindled the fires, brandished the sword, against those of yours. You were best go ask this question, treat this business with them. How be it if you will have me (who have so lately felt your torments) speak my opinion, I verily think your hellish torments of the rack were never wont to be exercised against any of yours with such violence, with such cruelty, as it is now by your men against us, which torment I esteem more cruel than any one single death."

Scarcely had he uttered these last words, when Hopton, looking upon him, counterfeiting laughter in his countenance and voice, said: "Verily, Campion, you are one of these nice, these delicate Jesuits, who, being but favorably stretched, call this gentle straining, this small extension wherewith you were examined, a formidable torment."

Thus unseasonably did this sporting companion seek to stir up laughter upon so doleful a subject; but merry only as he was in cruelty and mischief, his mirth at that time succeeded accordingly; and Campion's ensuing speech moved all there present to pity him.

"Very well, sir," said he, "yet when the question is of the extremity of the rack, much better may his testimony be taken who hung upon it than his that looked on. But I would have you know, I complain not so much of my own particular torments, in declaring the torment of the rack to be more terrible than death, as of the common misery of Catholics which I deplore, seeing them daily racked and torn, examined like thieves and murderers."

Upon which words, one of the noblemen, seeing the whole assembly much moved, asked, "And Campion, shall we suffer thee thus to delude so great a multitude as this, as if, forsooth, thou seemest to suffer all these punishments for thy religion, whereas indeed thou didst it for thy most grievous offenses? Dost think that though thou obstinantly didst suppress them, when thou wast examined, they are not manifest enough to the whole state and those that were thy judges? Be thy religion, Campion, whatsoere it will be, it was thy wicked conspiracies against thy country that hailed thee to these torments."

This man's loud and desperate lie proved profitable to the cause of Campion and his companions. For forthwith for the love he hath to truth, he summoned all the forces he had remaining in his poor afflicted body, and with that mighty fervor of his invincible mind, which sparkled even through his very eyes rose up, and said: "If anyone, setting my religion aside, dare charge me with any crime whatsoever, I ask no favor; make me an example to the whole kingdom; discharge on me all the cruelties you can."

This when he had said, with a countenance all inflamed, the deep silence which ensued, even amongst the Lords themselves and the whole assembly, gave a most evident testimony to the truth. Wherefore after this no one ever contradicted him, so that he proceeded to declare that he was not for any other cause so terribly tortured, but for that he persisted still to conceal in whose house he had been entertained, by whom relieved, to whom according to the rites of the Catholic Church he had communicated the sacraments, and with whom he had had commerce in matters of religion. And of such force was this verity, so fresh and recent in men's memory, that amongst so many enemies of his, that lay in wait to overleave him with lies, no one was thenceforth found who could refell [deny] these words of Campion.

After this manner was the prelude of the future disputation. And Nowell ended this debate by beginning his former complaint, how foully Luther had been defamed, prosecuting it so vehemently, and with such shameful railing, that he snatched up that book of Luther's, which was most suspected, opened it, and with a solemn oath affirmed that there was no such reproach against the sacred Epistle of Saint James in that whole book, and that Campion falsely belied him, nor was able to show any copy of the work now extant at London that did not witness against him to be a most impudent liar. This when with many big words he had ambitiously exaggerated, with a loud voice he concluded thus in Latin, ERGO IMPUDENTISSIME MENTIRIS, CAMPIANE [therefore, Campion, thou liest most shamefully].

This contumely, cast forth with such prepared pomp of words, moved all the audience more than him against whom they were cast. For he said no more but that what he had written he had read in Luther's own book, and that other writers of great account (whereas some of them he cited by name) had sharply, before him, reprehended Luther for the same fault. And as touching the copies now extant in London, he knew that Luther's disciples, jealous of their master's reputation, had rased [erased] many things privily and some openly out of these his books. Yet if they would give him leave, he could erelong without any great difficulty send for out of Germany into England one of those very copies of Luther's first edition to testify that truth. Here in very deed, as if Campion, despairing of his cause, sought to find as far as thence to Germany for a book to patronize it, the ministers, bursting forth into laughter, saucily interrupted him, as he was speaking, with scoffs and taunts began to exercise their wit upon him, exprobated [reproached] unto him his fetching a book as far as Germany, his flying to Bavaria for the patrons, to the Emperor for succor of his cause. For whereas Campion chanced to promise by the help of the Emperor and the Duke of Bavaria to get Luther's entire books transported, this they scoffed at, as if it had been but a vain bravado.

But Campion, for so much as he perceived, if he went away with this calumny upon him, he should thenceforth render his authority more weakened and suspected in that assembly; turning to the priests, his companions and fellow-soldiers, he asked them openly whether they had not in Catholic writers, of most grave credit and authority if not elsewhere, read those sacrilegious speeches of Luther. And all of them, in the open hearing of the whole multitude, answered that they had sundry times read them. Nevertheless Campion's adversaries, thinking themselves to have convinced him of a notorious lie, persisted still by insulting over the supposed conquered person, to make their conquest the more remarkable, and offered to show him the very same books of Luther which he had cited in the margin of his little book, when he reproved Luther's impiety. The one of them was that wherein his preface upon Saint James his Epistle, and the other the Captivity of Babylon was contained.

After this they grew earnest with great clamors, pressed him, so precise as he was, to calumniate others, and pick holes in their coats, to show what reproachful words, cast out by Luther against Saint James, he could even carp at. Campion accepts their offers, and supposing some footsteps, at least, might remain of this sacrilege, which they had sought to wash away, he began to read both books alternately. And it fell out just as he conjectured, many things forthwith he noted, and produced apparently tending to that sentence which was expunged; amongst which were these very words: AFFIRMANT NONNULLI EPISTOLAM JACOBI, APOSTOLICO SPIRITU INDIGNAM [some affirm the Epistle of St. James to be unworthy of an apostolical spirit]. Through which and other words Campion gathered by sharp and witty reasons, which were too long to set down in this place, that Luther differed not from some of those wicked censurers; nor in fine could Nowell deny it, only brought the ancient writers for excuse, amongst which many doubted of the authority of Saint James his Epistle. And hereupon they began curiously to search into antiquity, what their sense was of Saint James his Epistle; and by the most clear testimony of all the ancients, the authority of so worthy an epistle was vindicated; and most plainly it was demonstrated that of all that number which the adversaries had alleged, to overthrow the authority of that sacred epistle, beside Cajetan only of this later age, no one had descended from all antiquity. These things when the heretical ministers had seen our men explain by most grave arguments, they turned as their usual manner is to railing, and so concluded the whole matter with reproaches and foul language.

Four whole hours were spent in this first disputation, which space of time was set down for that and the rest of their meetings and punctually observed. Wherefore Nowell, to dismiss in fine this assembly, began briefly to repeat what in that whole disputation had been said or alleged against Catholics. And craftily, as the man was and eloquent, he used much fraud, repeating only his own arguments and adding what strength or weight he could unto them, sprinkling here and there quips and nipping taunts; and what he saw weak and invalid, that he suppressed, and finally framed all to the pomp and, as far forth as he could, to the triumph of heresy.

After he had ended his speech, our men in most humble manner entreated that they likewise might have leave succinctly to recollect, and briefly represent unto them, what they had answered or affirmed for themselves; but presently they were rebuked and cried down by the ministers and the queen's servants silenced them. This was the order and end of the forenoon's controversy; and so much the more joyfully did the heretics seem to part from it, for that, in their opinions, they thought they had exempted Luther from calumny; howbeit that joy of theirs proved but vain and of no long continuance, for soon after our men, bending all their endeavors to search out a thing which so nearly concerned them, looked into certain of Luther's books, which were uncorrupted, and found those very words which Campion had excerpted against in that APOSTATA [apostate]. And for so much as the thing was apparent, and the very heretical ministers themselves, amongst which Whitaker was one, openly confessed that those marked speeches of Luther were found in his old original copies; and so, much against their wills, were forced, themselves, with their own hands, to pull off the visard and unmask that lie through which they were ready, even then, to have triumphed over us.

Chapter 47

The self same day they dispute again with the heretics of religion.

It was the law of history that constrained me to set down more at large the first encounter of Campion with his enemy; seeing that containing as it doth and defending many acts of his lately and many formerly past, it was not fit it should be obscured with too much brevity of style. For I hold it not my part, recounting as I do not the battles of famous captains, or the governments of cities, but the acts of martyrs, to set down over precisely every little thing or word. Yet were it not I intend to set forth in a treatise by themselves Campion's disputations word for word, as I have rendered them by help of a friend out of English into Latin, I would not suffer so much as one word of those disputations to be wanting here in this present history. Now in my ensuing discourse, I will only rehearse what shall seem to appertain to the actions of modesty, fortitude, or Christian liberty. The place of the disputation, the authors and maintainers I will declare, what also was acted in that meeting, of what thing disputed, with what assent of the audience, with what judgment of the wiser sort transacted. Nor will I conceal, if anything happened in that disputation, either extremely dull and absurd, or contrariwise notably sharp and witty. By which means I suppose I shall not cloy my reader, but feed him evermore and delight him with fresh supply and variety of words and deeds on both sides. For surely it seems somewhat strange that so often as these disputations were reiterated they had nothing common each with other, save only the time of the conflict which lasted full four hours.

The place therefore for the afternoon's disputation was all one, the concourse much greater. The heretical cause, Nowell giving way thereto, Day defended; for so they had agreed betwixt them to take their turns. And he also began to make his flourish before the battle impertinently cavilling at some little word or other in the decretals of Leo IV, reciting the letters out of Gratian's decree whereby the authority of holy scripture is orderly defined and set down, an ominous cavil to their future disputation which was directly determined to be of the justifying by faith only, out of Campion's own words which depending wholly upon his rebuking Luther for his censure of St. James his epistle.

Day recited out of his *Ten Reasons* in this manner: HOC ENIM SCRIPTO CONFOSSUS MISER ET DISRUPTUS EST, CUM IN SOLA FIDE JUSTITIAM INSTITUERET [for by this epistle the wretch, having placed justice in faith only, was wounded and confounded]. Whilest, therefore, the heretic defended this opinion of Luther, he vouched, I know not upon what occasion, the Greek text and withal offered the book to Campion who for so much as he knew the Greek text to be wickedly corrupted by heretics answered, "I thank you, sir." And without opening the book [he] laid it aside.

Heretics persuade themselves that Catholics have either little knowledge or none at all of these ancient tongues. Wherefore amongst their ignorant brethren they curiously hunt after this glory of hidden wisdom, spicing one while with Greek, another with Hebrew words whatsoever they speak or write; and by this means they think they speak mysteriously and in the clouds if they can but with big supercilious looks mutter out three strange words of things vulgar and not strange. And there be no kind of men that they more suspect to be ignorant of foreign language than those that are religious. For so much as for the most part, they see many of them most intentive to the deep contemplation of divine and human things and negligent of words; whereupon they conclude them to be altogether rude and barbarous both in pen and tongue, void of all politeness and elegancy, and this suspicion the ancient writers in plainer ages have increased, being as they are grave in sentences, gross and rude in words; amongst which some are found to have said GRAECUM EST, NON LEGITUR [it is Greek, it cannot be read]. And our adversaries usually pronounce this as a proverb, supposing they point thereby at our ignorance, nor is there anything, so oft as they can lay hold of it, that they more laugh at. Wherefore imagining this refusal of the Greek book to be by reason of his unskillfulness in the Greek language, a wonder it is with what laughter, with what base jests, what hissing, they both often inculcated that old saying, and heaped upon it many quips and biting taunts.

Meanwhile Campion tolerated this so great disgrace with marvelous patience and with so much the more for that he was able at his pleasure to render his enemy more ridiculous as being himself singular in the Greek. But, as a good religious man, he made his benefit of it and most earnestly took this occasion of suppressing and overcoming his shame and absolutely resolved with silence to swallow down this ignominy.

When the enemies were once weary of laughing and hissing, they returned sportingly, as it were, to their determinate disputation of justifying faith and scornfully said they saw no reason why Luther should be so afraid of St. James' Epistle, seeing the ancient fathers, who professed the same cause, and were of the same opinion with Luther, were so well acquainted with that epistle and stood in no fear of it at all. For although that word *only* so frequent with our men be not found in holy scriptures, when they speak of justifying faith, yet the fathers who interpret scriptures do many times use it. To testify which thing they chiefly vouched two out of antiquity, to wit, Hilarius out of the Latin, and Basil out of the Greek; and to the end they might fall again to make themselves merry with jesting and hissing Campion, they pitched more willingly upon the Greek. Wherefore with their eyes and whole aspects swimming, as a man may say, and soused in saucy laughter, they ran many of them by heaps to thrust Basil upon Campion. Now began the whole multitude of people that were present to murmur and raise up themselves, as it were, upon tiptoes, ready to clap their hands by way of derision.

When Campion, without any trouble or show of distemper at all, takes up the book and with a serene and settled countenance, as if he had minded nothing less than them that watched to disgrace him, began to read the place designed; whereby he first repressed those eyes of theirs that were so boldly cast upon him, then restrained their laughter wherewith they were brim full, and even ready to have burst forth. But when soon after they saw him with the selfsame confidence and constancy read the whole place in Greek and render it word for word in English so, not only properly but even elegantly, that he seemed as well to all his enemies as friends equally master of both languages. His enemies began to wax pale, to hang their heads and never afterward could so much as well endure to behold him, or the multitude about him. Meanwhile Campion with a resolute countenance closed the book and redelivered it with these words: "You henceforth, I suppose, will bear me witness I somewhat understand Greek."

At which speech the whole audience were even ready to have given their applause, but suddenly turned it into a kind of festival and soothing murmur, admiring no less his modesty than learning; and as the common sort are for the most part on either side immoderately changeable, they exceeded no less in too much favoring and applauding him than they did before in disgracing and hissing at him.

Thus the boldness of the enemy being broken, our men plainly showed what appertained to the purpose, to wit, that it was [the] sense and meaning of the fathers that if the precept of the old Mosaical law were compared to the faith of Christ, no justice were ever to be acquired by that law or any work thereof, but by the only faith of Christ. Although what need was then to urge the fathers since Luther's faith is no faith but a certain vain confidence of an arrogant mind which confidence in very deed, according to the fathers who follow the faith of St. Paul which worketh by charity, is directly none at all. For what is surer than that Luther's faith subsisteth only by a vain and frivolous faith whereby men certainly persuade themselves that howbeit they be covered with all the most heinous sins of the world, yet God will pardon them through the merits of Christ their redeemer? Which persuasion of mind, what communion or conformity hath it with that faith through which "the saints overcame kingdoms, obtained the promises, stopped the mouths of lions, extinguished the force of fire, prevailed over infirmity?" This when Campion had said to conclude, as it were, the whole matter compendiously by St. Paul's testimony whereby he advertiseth the Galatians in his cap. 1. that neither circumcision nor PRAEPUTIUM [foreskin] avail any thing, but faith which worketh by charity; he after the manner of logicians briefly darted against them this argument. If faith only justify, it justifies without charity; but without charity, if we believe St. Paul, it justifies not; therefore, faith only justifies not.

This so terrible a weapon galled much the adversaries, and after a long while, clamoring confusedly, trembling for fear what to hold, what to deny, or how to frame their words, they answered only at the length, many of them foolishly laughing, that this was a false and captious argument, as consisting of four TERMINI [terms], with their subtle skill in logic, although Campion with his pleasant wit might well have played upon, yet far as he was from all intemperance of his tongue, he only earnestly at that time contended that they should prove that argument to be false as they pretended by the rules of logic. Moreover those others of ours instantly requested this, but could not prevail any more, but still they cried out it was so, take their words for it. After this the martyrs sharply urged how vain a thing Luther's faith was, and how unknown altogether to former ages, the heretical ministers giving little or no answer unto it. Sherwin showed himself most courageous herein whom, pressing stoutly as he did and eagerly, and the adversary shrinking and giving ground, they silenced by authority, since by reason they could not. And one of the ministers bade him reserve his speech till that day which should be freely allowed him to oppose; when nevertheless, few were there but knew the heretics had given him leave to speak as well as Campion. And Sherwin himself stuck not to tell them so, adding moreover that it was no new thing for him to be thus checked for his free speaking of religion, that it had cost him something in his days, and yet he was ready at any price to profess his faith wheresoever or in whatsoever audience. Hereat, in very deed the heretics grew extreme angry; and as he began now out of his former argument boldly to frame another, they all with one loud voice commanded him silence, bidding him again and again in plain English, "Hold thy tongue." But he resolutely answered, "I will hold my tongue. I will hold also my faith."

At last Campion, being asked his opinion of the whole and sole cause of justification, fell to expound the sense and meaning of the Catholic Church with so great approbation of all the audience that Nowell, seeing men's minds inclined so much to favor our cause and fearing the overthrow of theirs, interrupted him craftily in his speech and took occasion to divert him as if he had digressed from the intended question, and so at unawares broke off the disputation and dissolved the company. Thus ended the first day's disputation with great commendation on our side, as even the enemies themselves confessed. Howbeit extreme spiteful as they were against Campion, they attributed all the praise of the day's success to Sherwin, who as he most duly deserved praise of all, so did he nothing obscure the glory of Campion.

Account of First Debate by Bartoli[2]
[First Debate]

They call Father Edmund, who has recently been tortured, to argue under most iniquitous conditions with two Protestant theologians. His modesty and learning, their arrogance and confusion. The part played by Ralph Sherwin, whose imprisonment, tortures, and generosity are pointed out. New tricks of the enemy to trouble the Catholics and make them dispise Father Edmund.

Third Chapter

The Chancellor and Hopton ordered that the torture of Father Edmund be kept as hidden from the Catholics as possible. There were several reasons for that, inappropriate to mention here, but among others was that of protecting the reputation of the sect. Because they having already decided to bring him to argue, it would seem very bad to the public, even the Protestants, if it were known that they had first given him over to the torturers to be broken on the rack, and only later had delivered him to their theologians to be fought with arguments. Indeed it had from early times been the custom of the fiercest persecutors of our faith first to allow doctors of the Catholic Church to argue with their gentile or heretical ministers and then, not having been able to overcome them with arguments, to try to overcome them with torture. For that reason too

[2] Daniello Bartoli (1608–85), noted Jesuit historian and author, was born in Ferrara, studied philosophy and theology at Parma, and was ordained in 1636 at Bologna. He requested missionary work but was retained in Italy where he won praise as an orator in many Italian cities. Concerned about the harmful effect of popular romances on young readers, Bartoli wrote *L'uomo di littere* (Rome, 1645), which in its first year went through nine editions and was translated into English, German, and French. At the request of his superior, he wrote a history of the Society of Jesus in Italian. The history, arranged by geographical divisions, appeared in five volumes, *Dell' istoria della compagnia di Gesu* (Rome, 1653–73). The following account of the first debate, translated by Professor M. Bonner Mitchell for this edition, is taken from *Libro Terzo*, pp. 165–72. Bartoli also wrote biographies of several Jesuit saints, books on literature, and treatises on asceticism, natural science, and philology. The most nearly complete collection of his works appears in thirty-eight volumes, *Opera del Padre Daniello Bartoli* (Turin, 1825–56). See also *The learned man defended* . . . , Englished by Thomas Saulsbury (London, 1660).

they did not stretch Father Edmund on the rack these first two times with cords attached to his fingers, but with ropes on his wrists, with the result that he was able to have his right hand still strong enough to sign, as is the custom for examined people to do. The ministers used this signature to deceive the people, and the Queen herself, as we shall see in the proper place. Despite all their diligence, a rumor spread through London that Campion had been tortured two times, and it came from the Catholic prisoners in the Tower, who made a point of learning day by day what happened to the confessors of Christ and their companions, partly in order to be ready in need to exchange prayers for each other. The ministers then persisted in denying it with oaths, their consciences not suffering from this perjury so long as it turned to the advantage of their sect. We shall see from here on that that was a constant practice, with great harm to the truth and to the reputation of the Catholics, especially the priests killed for confession of the faith. Nor should my readers find too heavy the brief examples that I shall point out from time to time to uncover these frauds, since there has been no lack of historians unpracticed in English affairs who, if no one took the pen from their hands, were willing to write in their ecclesiastical annals, about English Catholics, that which is found in the books of the heretical chroniclers of that country, or in that other so clearly lying and slanderous book entitled *The Justice of Britain*.[3] The result of this was to take away from those killed only for their Catholic faith that crown which, according to every just reason of merit, was owed to them—as (justifying in everything the judgment of the mother and teacher of the truth, the Holy See of Rome) has been justly proved by Father Francisco Suarez, whom we shall mention again in a more appropriate place.[4]

Father Edmund was thus still broken and hurting from the harshness of the rack that he had twice undergone, so that, as they wrote from there, he seemed to be half dead, when, quite unexpectedly, having been taken out of prison and led to the parish church right there in the Tower, or Castle, of London, he found himself awaited

---

[3] *The Justice of Britain* refers to Burghley's *The Execution of Justice in England* (1583).

[4] Francisco Suarez (1548–1617), a distinguished Spanish Jesuit theologian, held a number of teaching appointments in Spain and Italy before being granted a chair as Professor of Theology at the University of Coimbra (Portugal), which he held from 1599 to 1615. He published his elaborate *Defensio fidei catholicae* in 1613.

by a full theater of hearers and spectators who had assembled to see him and to hear him defend in debate what he had written in the book of the *Ten Reasons*. The motivation for this procedure arose mainly from the ill-founded opinion of himself held by the Dean of Saint Paul's of London, who considered himself to be the most learned, as he was the fiercest, theologian. He imagined that everybody had eyes fixed on him and was saying to him that to live up to his reputation as a man he could not fail to stop up and silence the mouths of all Jesuits in the person of this one, which they had sent there to speak and to write with the learning of all. By doing so, he would win the glory of knowing by himself as much as both the universities of Cambridge and Oxford, which Campion, in order to magnify himself by making himself equal to such great enemies, had challenged. Therefore he arranged that the proceeding be a solemn thing, open to everyone to attend; otherwise if the victory were private, his glory would also be private. But despite his great confidence in himself, and great expectation from his knowledge, he was not so eager to fight Father Edmund as to allow the conditions to be equal. He thus prepared himself in advance very carefully with arguments and with authorities and texts to cite. He conferred about all his arguments with Doctor Day, Provost at Eton College, whom he made his second in the field. Father Edmund, apart from not being given even a single book, was not even told what subject in particular, or in general, was to be argued. He was strictly forbidden to do anything except stay on his guard, defending himself, not attacking, that is, shielding himself from the blows of arguments, never giving any such blows himself by proposing either authorities or arguments that might impugn their religion, or rebutting, as one sometimes does in passing, or even questioning. And as though he were still to be feared, after they had tied his hands so tightly with so many coils, they gave him over just before the disputation to be tormented on the rack to take away from him that vigor of spirit that the mind normally loses when the soul is afflicted in great pains of the body. Nor was it to give him help, but to take away from him honor (to add to their own) that they joined to him as a partner in speaking that Ralph Sherwin whom we have already seen travelling with Father Edmund from Rome to Rheims.

This man, Sherwin, as a result of having waited in vain there in Rheims for the Bishop of Saint Asaph to get well and accompany him, was the last of the priests to enter England and, as it pleased God, the first to be captured in London. With him was taken Roscarrock, the gentleman who was sheltering him, to the great harm of that English Church, which was thus so quickly deprived of the apostolic spirit,[5] through which Sherwin alone would have been able to minister to many men. His working hard to help others was thus changed into suffering much to increase his own merit. Held first in the prison called Marshalsea, where he was in chains and bore very hard treatment for a month, he was then at the beginning of December taken to the prisons of the Tower. There twice in four days he was tortured on the rack in order to find out from him the whereabouts of Persons and Campion, which he never told them. And meanwhile, as the torturers were pulling apart his joints and his bones, Roscarrock, who had sheltered him, was taken to a place nearby where he saw him and heard his moans with which nature confesses the bitterness of an intolerable pain. Finally, put into a cell to languish in such great misery, the saintly young man had already endured it for nine months with so much resignation and strength of spirit that he had added to his misery, as though it were not enough, by inflicting himself with continual penitences.

In the church, which had been made into the field and theater of this novel joust, the people were arrayed, and places were divided in good order. In the most honorable place were two seats, and in them the Dean Alexander Nowell and Day. In front of them was a table, and on it a great provision of books, authors whose texts were prepared for using against Campion. Below them was a long array of other men: doctors, preachers, Calvinist theologians, each one having in his hand Father Edmund's book. On the opposite side there was another table, and there were sitting Doctors William Whitaker and Charke, charged with writing down the proposals of their people and the answers of ours, with the faithfulness that they later showed. Nor should one have expected anything better from such a pair of men, who were not only our enemies pledged to the opposing religion, in which they were experts, but also motivated by self interest, since Whitaker had already committed his pen and his reputation to

[5] Nicholas Roscarrock was Ralph Sherwin's host and former fellow student at Oxford. See A. L. Rowse, *Tudor Cornwall* (London: Jonathan Cape, 1941) pp. 368–69.

writing against the *Ten Reasons* of Father Edmund the book which he later gave to the printer.[6] Camden, who was just a historian and not at all a theologian, thought it proper to celebrate the book with the title of *Solid Answer* just because it was by someone in his party. The book would not have been written if the author had first seen the rebuttal of Father John Dury, a Scot, which showed how light and vain a work was the book of Whitaker, which had nothing solid except the hard head of the author, and nothing weighty except the grave and outrageous insults thrown by his style of iron.[7] After these two notaries, in the prominent seats, came Lieutenant Hopton and a fine array of other lords, titled persons and nobles of every kind. And then, all around, were crowded as many ordinary people as could get in. There were even some women, with little respect for nobility, and we shall hear from one of them in a more appropriate place. For Father Edmund, Sherwin, and the others, many of them gentlemen who were prisoners in the same Tower, there had been prepared simple benches where they could sit facing the Dean and Day. The length of time fixed for the contest was six hours a day: three in the morning from eight to eleven, according to the clock used there; and three in the afternoon, from two to five. Translated into our Italian way of telling time, for that day of August 31, the two periods correspond to from thirteen to sixteen hours, and from nineteen to twenty-two hours.[8] Father Edmund thus came onto the field at eight o'clock, and the eyes of that whole great multitude turned upon him, both because of the figure he was and out of expectation for what was coming.

Now I am going to write about the things that happened during the course of the six [*sic*] disputes which is how many there were.[9] I

---

[6] Whitaker's reply to *Rationes Decem* is entitled *Ad Rationes Decem Edmundi Campiani Iesuitae, quibus fretus certamen Anglicanae ecclesiae ministris obtulit in causa fidei Responsio Guilielmi Whitakeri Theologiae in Academia Cantabrigiensi professoris Regii*. 1581 (STC 25358). See Milward, *Religious Controversies of the Elizabethan Age*, p. 58.

[7] Dury's book is entitled *Confutatio responsionis Gulielmi Whitakeri in Academia Cantabrigiensi Professoris Regii ad Rationes Decem, quibus fretus Edm. Campianus, Anglus, Societatis Iesu theologus, certamen Anglicanae Ecclesiae ministri obtulit in causa fidei. Authore Joanne Duraeo Scoto, Soc. Iesu presbytero*, 1582. See Milward, *Religious Controversies of the Elizabethan Age*, p. 58.

[8] In Italy the numbering of the hours began at sunset.

[9] Bartoli's comments on the number of debates is confusing. Here he says that there were six debates and later that there were four after the first. He may have been counting the debaters rather than the debates, for Campion does indeed face a total of six different opponents, four of them after the first debate.

shall draw in part from actual proceedings that I have, written by hand steadily and without interruption, compiled with great fidelity by the very people who took part in it; and in part from the account printed shortly thereafter, which was also taken from the writings of those who saw the actions with their own eyes and heard the words with their own ears.

Nowell began by pronouncing a pompous preamble, a studied, carefully prepared thing, to the effect that in this theological experiment one wished to seek nothing but the plain truth. Or rather, to speak more correctly, not to seek it, since England, thanks be to God and to Queen Elizabeth, who was for that reason worthy of eternal memory, had finally found it, but in order to prove it to those senseless Papists, and above all to their leaders. The latter were blind, not because they really were, but because they voluntarily made themselves so, closing their eyes in the face of the sun and screaming that what they did not see was not there. After that speech he turned an evil face, an evil eye and, worse than either of those, his tongue, onto Father Edmund, reproaching him for his shameless daring, his mad presumption and immodesty in asking, as though he were a giant instead of just half a man, for a battle with all the squadrons of the god of armies drawn up together, all the theologians of those two teachers of the world, the Academies of Cambridge and Oxford. In this it was easy to recognize the arrogant spirit of the Papists. But, said Nowell, Campion had not understood that it is one thing to make oneself invisible, hiding God knows where, in some underground den and to be brave there with one's pen, defying everybody to battle with four pages of an unfortunate little book, but another thing to test oneself by deeds, coming out of the den into the open field to use one's own tongue in a confrontation before entire universities, any one of whose members, whoever he is, will be, to Campion's shame, more than he can handle. And having said these things and opened the book of the *Ten Reasons* of the father, he recited that part on which they had prepared to argue. Nowell could not have rendered Father Edmund more illustrious if he had raised him up with as many praises as were the injuries with which he put him under his feet, since the father's virginal modesty, the tranquility of his soul, words, face, and manners seemed all the more beautiful for being put next the absolute opposite of these things that Nowell had shown himself to be. To the accusation of temerity and presumption, he needed to give no answer beyond the words that everyone had before his eyes, printed in the letter with which he sent his book to those learned academies:

> If by relying on my ability, learning, art, reading and memory I have provoked the most skillful adversary, I have been most vain and proud and have looked into neither myself nor others; but if, the cause being considered, I have judged myself to be sufficiently strong that I may say the sun shines at noon, you ought to concede to me the fervor which the honor of Jesus Christ, my King, and the invincible truth have commanded.[10]

Then Nowell having bitterly complained because the Catholics, he said, had painted the ministers of the Queen to other nations as completely inhuman barbarians by printing accounts of the torture given them, tortures in part not true and in part exaggerated far beyond the truth, Father Edmund, both to exonerate the Catholics and to repress the excessive animosity of Nowell by bringing out that which the latter thought to be hidden, said that as for himself he could affirm by all the joints of his life that Catholics about to dispute concerning religion were given the rack one and [even] two times. Here Hopton, hearing made public that which he had so much perjured himself in denying, was very much ashamed, both for himself and for the reputation of his men, and having no hope of being believed if he denied what Campion said, made a big mocking face and said: "Oh! So much resentment for a little tickling, or for our getting rid of your cramps once or twice, because your rack was scarcely so painful as that, or no more so." To which Father Edmund replied humorously: "I can talk about it better and more truly than you because I know about it from experience and you merely commanded that it be done." Then Hopton became animated and talked in another tone, on hearing himself denounced, saying that whatever were the tortures given to Campion and the other Catholics, these were not a subject of merit, much less the honor they gave themselves, because the men were under accusation on matters of state, not religion. "Bring him out," said Campion, "if there is anyone who can bring a shadow or a breath against me in political affairs, and I will give myself over to you for the most terrible rending

[10] The source is *Rationes Decem*.

of a human body that is possible." And taking up again all the questions that had been made to him on the rack, he showed that they all had to do with religion and none with matters of state. Nor did he go any further in that subject, because Hopton not having anything to reply, everyone was silent before Campion.

The article on which Nowell chose to argue was drawn from the first of the *Ten Reasons* of Father Edmund. The heretics, it says, reject the traditions of the church; they do not go by the decrees and canons of the ecumenical councils; they scorn the common sentiment and doctrine of the fathers; they adhere only to the text of Holy Scripture. And since there are entire books or passages that clearly convict them of being in error, their first concern has been to reject as apochryphal that which is contrary to them. Having thus recalled, after the Manichaean heretics, the heretic Ebion, who in the New Testament rejected the fourteen letters of Saint Paul almost in toto just because they forbid circumcision, and that heretic wanted to add it to baptism, the article continues as follows, put into our language: "And Luther, the cursed apostate, what else was it besides desperation that led him to say that the Epistle of James—he means Saint James the Apostle—is quarrelsome, haughty, arid and pure straw, and unworthy of the apostolic spirit. The wretched man saw that that letter is the one that strangles him and destroys him [Luther] in his having justification reside in faith alone." So he said. Now at this point Nowell started to pretend desperation over the intolerable calumny that statement was, and he asked whether Campion could be trusted in what remained if he had begun his book with such a shameless lie. "Because, here it is, thanks be to God, in the works of Luther (which he had in front of him and now opened). Here is the place where it is, the place where it is affirmed that the alleged words are found (he was quoting the preface to the Epistle of Saint James). Let one read them, and reread them; there isn't a syllable of that, not on your life! Ergo," he yelled, standing straight up on his feet, "you are lying shamelessly, Campion!"

I am telling at length how this incident happened, because there followed from it a great triumph for the adversaries, and then just as great a shame. Father Campion had copied those words very faithfully from the works of Luther, from the old edition of Jena in Thuringen of Saxony, a city quite devoted to that heretic, as having been among the first to receive the evil seed of his errors. Now you should know that the Lutherans, many together in synods or colloquia, or one or another of them alone, have in their books denounced to the world the unfaithfulness of the Zwinglians, pure Calvinists, and Calvin himself as falsifiers of the works of Martin Luther, which they have reprinted sometimes deformed, sometimes mutilated, in order to draw from them, or twist them around as they pleased to a contrary meaning. The edition in the possession of the Calvinist Nowell was one of those re-editions denounced by the Lutherans as unfaithful and lying. In this edition, since his people had taken away those words, it was useless to search for them. Nor for this reason, when Campion asserted that he had seen the words with his own eyes and read them in that very preface of Luther, and had copied them faithfully, was any credence given to him. Instead, when upon being asked where and in what books, he answered that it was in Germany, in a book printed in Jena. Nowell laughed scornfully and said that it was a good stratagem to defend oneself against a lie demonstrated in England by calling for a witness that was in Germany. And with this they dispatched him as an obvious and convicted falsifier. And Nowell was so pleased that less than two weeks later he gave an account of that great victory of his to the press, and after him Whitaker also committed himself in print. But the virgin text of the Jena edition having been found not long afterward right in London, and they having been shown and allowed to read in it the words reported by Father Edmund, without a syllable missing, the unfortunate men were obliged in spite of themselves to put on a good countenance by cancelling this error in the account that they wrote for their books. But they did not cancel the shame for themselves, so that the great triumph of the Protestants was given over to the Catholics, whose diligence had resulted in finding in London that book which the enemies had scornfully urged them to send someone to look for in Saxony. The rest of those first three morning hours they continued talking about the validity of that same Epistle of Saint James, which Father Edmund showed had been accepted by the Catholic Church, and always held by the fathers to be canonical scripture, all through the past centuries up to the present.

Two hours after noon both sides returned to the field. Everything was as before except that their advocate was changed, Nowell being replaced by Day. The latter began to discuss the subject of justification, giving all power and worth of it to faith and none to works. In the thick of arguing he brought up a passage of the divine scripture which was just right for his purpose in that it was falsified. Father Campion therefore denied that such words had ever come out of the mouth of God, or from the pen of any canonical writer. Thus the contest focused on whether this was true or not. It was something easy to clear up right away on the spot, Day having the Bible on the table, in a Greek text without Latin translation. He thus took it and, having found the place, handed it to Father Edmund. He, instead of reading the passage proposed to him, turned his eyes on the title page of the book and found it to be just what he had imagined, one of the Bibles ruined by the Calvinists. (For every sect of heretics has corrupted it and made it speak in their way—to leave aside for the moment Father Edmund, who by the way talks about this in the beginning of the first of his *Ten Reasons*—and among the heretics themselves one sect justly reproaches the other for such corruption of the Bible. Luther for this reason calls the Zwinglians half-witted and asinine and anti-Christs, tricksters and men with the understanding of beasts, and the Calvinists call him similarly impious, sacrilegious, a corrupter of the word of God—and they are all telling the truth.) Having thus discovered that that Bible was falsified, and a false witness, Father Edmund, without saying anything else, closed it and continued demonstrating with other contrary references that what was proposed to him could not be the word of the Holy Spirit. On seeing this, Day, Nowell and the whole college of preachers and theologians, sitting in a circle, considered that Campion had confessed not knowing Greek, which, with them and almost all modern heretics, is the same as saying that one cannot be a theologian, even if one were a second Saint Augustine, who, he too, knew very little of the language. And to bring into discredit Pope Saint Gregory the Great, so much hated by them and so much revered by the Greeks, they looked up and down in the *Annals* of Cardinal Baronio seeking the evidence of conjectures that he did not know Greek.[11] And so looking at each other, laughing scournfully and singing aloud the GRAECUM EST, NON LEGITUR [it is Greek, it cannot be read],

[11] Caesare Baronio (1538–1607) was an Italian ecclesiastical historian, student of Philip Neri's, and librarian at the Vatican Library. He wrote *Annales ecclesiastici a Christo nato ad annum 1198* (1588–1607).

they got the whole audience to join them in a triumph deriding Campion. He noticed it and without becoming moved or showing that he perceived that those sarcasms were falling on him, continued talking on the subject of the dispute. And if those valiant men had been content with celebrating no more than one time, they would perhaps have won that day, with the humility of Father Edmund, who, dissimulating and keeping quiet, had shrugged off that undeserved scorn by virtue of patience. But the audacious Day, because the dishonor of the enemy was his honor, tried to double the celebration. After having talked for a while more, and having accepted the point, or rather having let it drop, he returned to the game of referring to the authority of a Greek father. It was Saint Basil the Great, whose works he had there in front of him. It little mattered to him whether the new reference was relevant to the subject under discussion, his main intention being to send the text to Father Edmund, as he immediately did, telling him in a loud voice: "It is Greek; read it if you know how." Nor did he and the others wait for the father to confess himself ignorant of it; but while the book was being carried to him, those grave men of the circle, and with them the people of the audience, were already cutting capers worse than those of children, and were getting ready to cut a lot more. Now the thing came out as much as possible to the honor of Father Edmund, and to the consolation of the Catholics, of whom there were many present and, not knowing what was going to happen, in anxiety. The honor that turned to Father Edmund was not for his knowing Greek, because in England it is something that every boy studies, and there is more shame in not knowing it than glory in knowing it. The honor came rather from his modesty, his mastery of himself and his tranquil spirit. Because without answering anything to Day, much less reproaching him, or casting his eye around with the air of getting back at his scorners, he took the book and read aloud without hesitation the passage referred to by Day, and then repeated it, translated into the English tongue (for they were arguing in English to make themselves better understood to everyone) and glossed it, pointing out what there was in the Greek to apply to the subject. Then he closed the book and said graciously to those sitting in a circle. "You will be witnesses that I can read Greek." These men turned their faces to the floor and people around them applauded. He took no more notice of that than of the mockery shortly before; and Day, with a little more consideration than heretofore, proceeded with reasoning about the subject.

In this dispute it happened that Ralph Sherwin, who, as we said, was also taking part, rebutted the evidence of his adversary with such fire through religious zeal and through the strength of having the truth on his side—and he was defending that truth excellently—that the Protestants would not suffer that liberty on his part, falsely interpreting it as lacking in the respect they thought was owed them. Their protests not sufficing to make him be quiet, they raised their voices higher in an imperious manner used there, saying, "Keep your tongue to yourself." To this he replied: "I shall keep my tongue to myself, and my faith too." After that they wouldn't have him at any of the other four [*sic*] disputations that were held somewhat later, because, they said, he was too irascible. Thus they falsely imputed the fervor of his zeal to the fire of anger. However, these malicious people, once the disputations were over, did not shrink from contradicting themselves when giving an account of the proceedings to people who had not been present, by saying the better speaker had been Sherwin. This was not to exalt him but to debase Campion by giving it to be understood that anyone who had been inferior to Sherwin could not have been superior to themselves. Moved by this same "honesty," Nowell and Day, in the publication they immediately made of the proceedings of those two contests, when reporting the propositions and the answers, made the former so vigorous and the latter so weak—both things being far from the truth—that they seemed to be the winners. But they did not succeed in persuading even their own partisans, the Protestant historians who wrote about it, some nearer the event and some later. And I shall show in the proper place how things went quite differently from how the clumsy efforts of the interested parties tried to make one believe.

Nowell and Day had intended to cross swords with Father Edmund for four days, but they had enough—not to say too much—with a single day, and they abandoned the field to anyone who might have more courage than they. And in fact the disputes would not have proceeded further if one had not been overcome by requests from persons of such authority that it was not possible to refuse them.

Appendix D
Campion's Trial

In dealing with Campion, Elizabeth and her advisers seem to have considered two available legal options. According to the first, Campion could have been tried under recently enacted laws of 1581, which made an attempt to convert an English subject to Catholicism an act of treason. In fact, such an indictment was drawn up (Lansd. MSS. 33, art. 64), but the authorities, apparently fearing that the charge would expose the government to the countercharge of religious persecution, rewrote the indictment and exercised the second option (Lansd. MSS. 33, art. 65). Under a statute against treason enacted during the reign of Edward III in 1352, Campion would be indicted not for the practice of his religion but as a traitor to his country. The indictment charged Campion and his fellow Catholic prisoners with plotting the death of the queen, the overthrow of religion, the subversion of the state, and with stirring up foreigners to invade England. The document must have been prepared hastily for it cites journeys by the prisoners that would have tested the stamina of the hardiest travelers. Campion, Allen, Persons, and others, it states, were together in Rome on March 31, in Rheims on April 30, back in Rome on May 20, and back in Rheims on May 31. Then Campion and Persons supposedly left Rheims the following day for England.[1] The anomalies and false charges of the indictment aside, the date of the trial was set.

On November 14, 1581, Campion, Sherwin, Kirby, Bosgrave, Cottam, Johnson, Orton, and Rishton were arraigned at Westminster Hall before a grand jury.[2] When the indictment of treason was read, Campion insisted that he was not guilty of any treason whatsoever and stated that he and many of his fellow prisoners had never met or

[1] Simpson, *Life of Edmund Campion*, p. 396.
[2] See Harl. 6265, ff. 14–23^{v}.

known one another "before our bringing to this bar." Sir Christopher Wray, the Chief Justice, assured them that they would have an opportunity to defend themselves at their trial and ordered them by a show of hands to plead guilty or not guilty to the charges.[3] When Campion was unable to raise his arm because of his recent racking, one of his companions raised it for him to signify not guilty. The next day, November 15, the other Catholic prisoners were similarly arraigned.

Campion and his fellow defendants reassembled at Westminster Hall on Monday, November 20, and were found guilty at a trial that Hallam describes "as unfairly conducted, and supported by as slender evidence, as any, perhaps, that can be found in our books."[4] But the fairness of the trial was not what the authorities had in mind. They desired only that it have the formal appearance of justice and, more important, that it result in a conviction. To ensure the desired outcome, the government engaged some of the leading legal minds in England. In addition to Chief Justice Wray, who reportedly was a Catholic sympathizer and later had serious misgivings about the trial, Edmund Anderson, John Popham, and Thomas Egerton conducted the prosecution.

Edmund Anderson (1530–1605), one of the most highly regarded lawyers in England, had risen by his own ability as well as by his loyalty to Elizabeth. In addition to the Campion trial, he was also involved in such famous state trials as those of Essex, Raleigh, Babington, Mary Stuart, the Earl of Arundel, Sir John Perrot, and John

---

[3] Christopher Wray (1524–92) studied at Cambridge and Lincoln's Inn, where he was also a Reader. He served in Parliament from 1553 to 1567, was employed at the trial of the northern rebels (1569–70) and became Speaker in the House of Commons in 1571. He was appointed Justice in 1572 and named Chief Justice of the Queen's Bench in 1574. Other notable trials that he presided over include those of John Stubbs, William Perry, Lord Vaux, William Davison, the Earl of Arundel, and Sir John Perrot.

[4] Henry Hallam comments on the injustice of Campion's condemnation in his *The Constitutional History of England from the Accession of Henry VII to the Death of George II*, 2 vols. (London, 1827), 1:156–57.

For an account of the trial of Campion, Sherwin, Kirby, and others, see Howell, *State Trials*, vol. I, cols. 1049–84.

The unfairness of Campion's trial was not unique in sixteenth-century England. See, for example, Lacey Baldwin Smith, "English Treason Trials in the 16th Century," *Journal of the History of Ideas* 15 (1954): 471–98.

Udall. Reports of his work in civil cases between 1578 and 1603 were published in 1664 in a book that lawyers valued as an authority.[5] John Popham (1531?–1607), Attorney General, eventually became Chief Justice of the Queen's Bench in 1592, and Thomas Egerton (1540?–1617), Solicitor General, was later raised to the peerage as Lord Ellesmere in 1596.

After the clerk had read the charges and instructed the jury, Campion immediately requested that he and his companions be granted individual indictments and separate trials to avoid confusing the jurors and to ensure that one of them "is not to be tainted with the crime of the other." Although Wray admitted that he "would have wished also" for separate trials, time would not allow. The government strategy of a group trial instead of a series of individual ones obviously worked against the Catholics. First, it suggested visually that these men were involved in a conspiracy against Elizabeth and England—that is, they had acted not as individuals but collectively as part of a pre-invasion force sent by the pope. Second, by including Campion with the group, the government avoided the potential legal embarrassment he might have caused if he had been allowed to defend himself. The disputations at the Tower had already demonstrated how effective he was as a speaker. Third, the condemnation of a group would be easier for both the prosecution and the jury. The prosecution need present only generalized evidence of a circumstantial nature, together with a few witnesses, and the jury could take at least psychological comfort in making the assumption that in such a large group someone must be guilty of something. Lengthy individual trials would have forced the prosecution to present specific evidence against each individual and would have required the public repetition of evidence that, at best, was flimsily circumstantial and, at worst, obviously suborned.

The weakness of the state's case against Campion and his companions must have been apparent even to the non-legalists who packed Westminster Hall. Anderson's lengthy opening speech

[5] Edmund Anderson, *Les reports du treserudite Edmund Anderson des mults principals cases argues adjuges en le temps del jardis roign Elizabeth cibien en la* (London, 1664). These reports consist of a collection of his notes on trials between 1574 and 1603. A manuscript copy in French is at the British Library (Addit. MS. 25193). Anderson also wrote expositions of statutes enacted in Elizabeth's reign which remain in manuscript at the British Library (Lands. MS. 37, f. 6, 21, 38).

charged the Catholics with conspiring with the pope, England's archenemy, against the queen and England. Among their other illegal activities, he claimed that the prisoners had commended the Rebellion of the North, praised the constancy of Story, counseled about the papal bull that excommunicated Elizabeth, and supported Sanders's foreign invasion of Ireland. They were all traitors, he insisted, and must be treated as such. Campion, speaking for the prisoners, replied that the laws of England did not admit conjectural surmises in trials of life and death. The law required proof of the crime by evidence and supported by reliable witnesses. Anderson, Campion continued, had simply charged the prisoners with treason. But what was his proof? Rather than presenting proof, Anderson had based all his charges on circumstances and conjectures. Anderson himself then stated that all seminarians had taken a traitorous oath to fulfill all "matters" in Bristow's *Motives*, an oath contrary to English law.[6] Campion answered that the charge did not apply to them, for they had not sworn such an oath.

The prisoners then objected that they had been indicted and were being tried for treason on the basis of religion. Campion asserted that they had received an offer containing the provision that if they would agree to attend church and to hear sermons, they would be freed. Having refused the offer, they were now being tried as traitors, which proved that they were being tried for their religion.

Anderson next argued that because the prisoners had received

[6] Richard Bristow (1538–1581), a brilliant student at Oxford, was chosen with Campion to debate before Elizabeth on the occasion of her visit there in 1566. After leaving Oxford, Bristow joined Allen at the English College at Douai. He was ordained a priest in 1573 and lectured on the Bible. With Allen he revised and corrected Gregory Martin's translation of the New Testament and wrote defenses of the Roman Catholic positions. His best-known work was termed "Bristow's *Motives*" in England, and passages from it, together with passages from the writings of Nicholas Sanders and William Allen, were excerpted by John Hammond and used by Protestant interrogators to trap Catholics into making treasonous statements about the Rebellion of 1569, the bull of excommunication, and similar matters. For a fuller account of Bristow's *Motives*, see Milward, *Religious Controversies of the Elizabethan Age*, pp. 39–45; and Southern, *Elizabethan Recusant Prose*, pp. 390–94.

When asked to respond to the writings of Bristow, Allen, and Sanders, Campion replied that they should answer for themselves. And when asked to acknowledge Queen Elizabeth to be true and not just queen *de facto*, Campion answered that he could not judge. Similar "confessions" followed by Sherwin, Briant, Kirby, etc., and were witnessed by Hammond, Hopton, Beale, and Norton. See *A Particular Declaration. . . .* London, Imprinted by Christopher Barker, 1582 [a 32-page pamphlet].

money from the pope, their journey to England proved that their intent was to advance his treacheries. Campion answered that it was not treason to accept money from the pope and that they had accepted the money in order to preach the gospel, not to carry out treacheries.

J. Caddy (or Cradocke), the first state witness, testified that he had heard English priests vow before the pope in Rome to restore religion in England. Two hundred priests were to be sent, and Ralph Shelley, an English knight, had been asked to lead an army into England to destroy the heretics. Campion and his fellow prisoners were identified as members of this papal invasion force. Campion answered that the charge lacked proof. The state must prove, he insisted, that a vow had been taken by two hundred priests and also that he and his fellow prisoners had been included among the two hundred: "All the treason rehearsed is imputed to Sir Ralph Shelley; not one syllable thereof was referred to the priests."[7] And even Shelley had rejected the proposal. The testimony of the witness, Campion claimed, was actually proof of their innocence rather than of the government's charge of treason.

The prosecution then cited particular evidence against each prisoner. They turned first to Campion. Anderson charged him with having had a conference ten years earlier with the cardinal of Sicily in which they had discussed the bull of Pius V. Since this bull contained treason, Campion's discussion of it made him a traitor. In his answer Campion admitted having met with the cardinal, who had offered him a special place of service which he had declined. When the cardinal had asked him for his opinion of the papal bull, Campion had answered that it would cause much severity in England against the Catholics. The cardinal had stated that in his view the bull would be mitigated in such a way that the English Catholics would be permitted to acknowledge Elizabeth as their queen. There had been nothing treasonable about their conference. Anderson replied that since the bull had been mitigated only against the Catholics, the principal force of it, excommunication, remained in effect. Therefore, Campion's "privity thereto" made him a traitor. Campion responded that his knowledge of the bull did not constitute his approval of it. On the contrary, his statement that it would cause

[7] Howell, *State Trials*, col. 1056.

severity indicated his disapproval. Actually, since the bull had been well advertised, everyone knew about it.

Anderson then charged Campion with having had communication with the bishop of Ross, a known enemy of England. To what end could there have been communication between Campion and Ross except for the practice of treason? Campion replied that the bishop of Ross had nothing to do with him. He denied having had a conference with Ross and demanded that Anderson prove his charge.

The clerk then read a letter from Allen to Sanders that dealt with the causes of the failure of the insurrection in the North. Anderson claimed that Campion, having been called from Prague to Rome and sent by the pope to England, must have known that the pope, the king of Spain, and the duke of Florence had planned to gather an army and place Mary, queen of Scots, on the throne of England. Also, on his way from Rome to England, Campion had had a conference with Allen about preparing English Catholics to receive foreign powers. Campion answered that he had traveled from Prague to Rome and from Rome to England because he had been so ordered by his superior and that he had been assigned to minister the sacraments, not to conspire as a traitor. In response to Anderson's second point, Campion admitted that he had met with Allen in Rheims and had walked with him in the garden, talking about old friends and former days. There had been no discussion about the crown or the state of England. Yet even if there had been, Campion pointed out that, since Allen was not his superior, he owed him no obedience. He further denied knowing anything about Allen's letter to Sanders in Ireland. Anderson replied that they might believe Campion's words if his actions had not argued otherwise. Why had Campion changed his name? Why had he worn disguises? Why had he hidden in secret places? All Campion's actions had indicated mischievous intent. Campion justified himself by pointing out that St. Paul had done exactly the same. Were such actions proper for St. Paul but improper for him? Did clothes make one a traitor? Campion argued that there was no charge in the indictment about his apparel.

The clerk next read a letter from Campion to Pounde in which Campion stated that he had confessed the names of some gentlemen and friends in whose houses he had been entertained but that he had not disclosed the secrets they imparted to him. Anderson argued that Campion must have been concealing matters of treason. Campion explained that the secret information that he would not disclose was not treason. He had been simply hearing the private confessions of Catholics, and his priestly vow prohibited the disclosure of private confessions.

The clerk continued. He read papers containing oaths for renouncing obedience to the queen and swearing allegiance to the pope as supreme head and governor. These papers had been found in the homes Campion had visited. When Anderson charged Campion with treason for administering these oaths, Campion answered that administering such oaths was repugnant to his vocation; nor had he the authority to administer them. But even if he were authorized, the oaths had not been in his hand; nor had they been derived from him. That they had been found where he had been proved not that he had brought them or administered them. Surely other Catholics, he pointed out, visited these houses.

Anderson then charged Campion with refusing to swear the oath of supremacy and with stating that the oath was a form of legal entrapment. Commissioners Norton and Hammond testified that Campion had given evasive answers. Campion replied that he had recently given his answer directly to Elizabeth herself when she had asked if "I did acknowledge her to be my Queen or no."[8] He admitted that he had acknowledged her queen and "Lawful governess." In answer to her further question about whether the pope might lawfully excommunicate her, he had disqualified himself as a judge, for on this controversial problem not even the best theologians were in agreement. He admitted Elizabeth his sovereign *de facto et jure* and confessed his obedience to her as queen and temporal head. When asked whether, if it were decided that the pope had power to excommunicate, he would see himself discharged of his allegiance to her or not, Campion replied that the question was dangerous and that his examiners were demanding his blood. Since he did not admit the possibility, the question should not be put to him. When he did not answer what he could not answer, his examiners charged him with evasions. Campion insisted that these questions about unresolved spiritual matters were not part of his indictment and were unfit to be discussed at the King's Bench. They were not matters of fact; they had no part in his trial; and laymen of the jury were not qualified to deal with them.

[8] Ibid., col. 1062.

Two additional witnesses, George Eliot and Anthony Munday, presented testimony against Campion before the prosecutors began questioning the other prisoners. Eliot stated that he had heard Campion preach a sermon which "sheweth many vices and enormities . . . in England" and that Campion looked forward to "a day of change comfortable to the catholics . . . and terrible to the heretics."[9] Anderson interpreted "a day of change" to mean a papal invasion of England. Campion answered that vices and enormities existed in every country in the world and that he had used the expression "a day of change," as Protestant preachers did, to mean Judgment Day. Munday deposed that he had heard Allen and others conspire against England and that Campion later "had conference with Dr. Allen." Campion dismissed the testimony as "nothing against me" and added that he had already commented on his conference with Allen.

Evidence was next presented against the other prisoners. Sherwin was charged with persuading "the people to the catholic religion" and plotting the invasion of England. He answered the first charge by pointing out that the apostles had done the same, and he denied the second. Bosgrave was then charged with treason for not revealing plots against England that he had heard reported on the Continent. "What?" Bosgrave asked. "Am I a traitor because I heard it spoken?"[10] Campion, seeing that Bosgrave was "daunted with the matter," intervened on his behalf by reminding the jury that since rumors were totally unreliable, Bosgrave's discretion in not repeating a false rumor was more deserving of praise than blame. Anderson next turned to Cottam. Because Cottam had returned to England at about the same time as the other priests, he must have been a fellow conspirator. When Cottam answered that he had been ordered to return by his superior because he was ill, Anderson asked him to explain his possession of a seditious Catholic book, *Tractatus conscientiae* by D. Espigneta. Cottam denied that the book was his and was thus at a loss to explain how it had come to be among his possessions. Noting Cottam's inability to respond to questioning, Campion again interceded, explaining that often either by our own negligence or by the duplicity of others we acquire things. But these acquisitions were private errors, not public offenses. Even granting that

---

[9] Ibid., col. 1063.
[10] Ibid., col. 1064.

Cottam had owned it, did the possession of a book dealing with spiritual matters constitute treason?

Johnson was next singled out. Eliot testified that Johnson had been a member of a group of Catholic conspirators who had plotted the assassinations of Elizabeth, Burghley, Leicester, Walsingham, and others. Johnson flatly denied the charge. Bristow [Rishton], the next one questioned, stated that he had returned to England to care for his mother, but Munday testified that Bristow, an expert in "fire works," had intended to "burn her majesty when she were on the Thames in her barge."[11] Bristow denied the charge. Sleidon (Sledd?) next deposed that Kirby had informed him about papal plots against the queen and had also been present at a seditious sermon by Allen. Kirby denied the allegations. Munday next testified that Orton had told him in Lyon, France, that Elizabeth "was not lawful queen of England." Orton denied having ever spoken with Munday. Orton and the other prisoners accused Munday of false testimony and charged that another witness was a confessed murderer. Campion summarized all the "evidence" in an eloquent but futile appeal to the jury.

> What charge this day you sustain, and what accompt you are to render at the dreadful Day of Judgment, whereof I would wish this also were a mirrour, I trust there is not one of you but knoweth. I doubt not but in like manner you forecast how dear the innocent is to God, and at what price he holdeth man's blood. Here we are accused and impleaded to the death; here you do receive our lives into your custody; here must be your choice, either to restore them or condemn them. We have no whither to appeal, but to your consciences; we have no friends to make there but your heads and discretions. Take heed, I beseech you, let no colours nor inducements deceive you; let your ground be substantial, for your building is weighty. All this you may do sufficiently, we doubt not if you will mark intentively what things have been treated, in three distinct and several points. The speech and discourse of this whole day consisteth, first, in Presumptions and Probabilities; secondly, in matters of Religion; lastly, in Oaths and Testimonies of Witnesses. The weak and forceless Proof that proceedeth from conjectures are neither worthy to carry the Verdict of so many, nor sufficient evidence for trial of man's life. The constitutions

[11] Reynolds points out that Bristow should read "Rishton" (*Campion and Parsons*, pp. 189, 198*n*28).

of the realm exact a necessity, and will that no man should totter upon the hazard of likelihoods; and albeit the strongest reasons of our accusers have been but in bare and naked Probabilities, yet are they no matters for you to rely upon who ought only to regard what is apparent. Set circumstances aside, set presumptions apart, set that reason for your rule which is warranted by certainty. But Probabilities were not the only matters which impertinently have been discussed, they were also points of doctrine and religion, as excommunications, books, and pamphlets, wherein a great part of the day hath been as unfitly consumed. Insomuch as this very day, you have heard not only us, but also the pope, the king of Spain, the duke of Florence, Allen, Sanders, Bristow, Espigneta, and many more arraigned. What force excommunications be of, what authority is due to the bishop of Rome, how men's consciences must be instructed, are not matter of fact, nor triable by Jurors, but points yet disputed and not resolved in Schools, how then can be determined by you, though wise, yet lay, though otherwise experienced, yet herein ignorant. But were it so that for your knowledge and skill in divinity yet might seem approved censurers of so high a controversy, yet are they no part of all our Indictment, and therefore not to be respected by the Jury. You perchance would ask of me, if these prove nought against us, what then should we enquire of, for these, set aside the rest, is almost nothing? Pardon me, I pray you, our innocency is such that if all were cut off, that hath been objected either weakly or untruly against us, there would indeed rest nothing that might prove us guilty, but I answer unto you, that what remaineth be Oaths, and those not to rest as proofs unto you but to be duly examined and fully considered, whether they be true and their deposers of credit. In common matters we often see witnesses impealed, and if any time, their credit be little, it ought then to be least when they swear against life. Call I pray you to your remembrance how faintly some have deposed, how coldly others, how untruly the rest; especially two who have testified most. What truth may you expect from their mouths, the one hath confessed himself a murderer, the other well known a detestable Atheist, a profane heathen, a destroyer of two men already. On your consciences would you believe them? They that have betrayed both God and man, they that have left nothing to swear by, either religion nor honesty. Though you would believe them, can you? I know your wisdom is greater, your consciences uprighter; esteem of them as they be, examine the other two, you shall find two of them precisely to affirm that we or any of us have practised ought that might be prejudicial to this state or dangerous to this commonwealth. God give you grace to weight our causes aright, and have respect to your own consciences, and so I will keep the Jury no longer. I commit the rest to God, and our convictions to your good discretions.[12]

After an hour of deliberation, the jury returned with the predicable verdict of guilty. Justice Wray asked the prisoners if they wished to make a statement about why they should not die. Campion answered for them: "It was not our death that ever we feared. We knew that we were not lords of our own lives, and therefore for want of answer would not be guilty of our own deaths. The only thing that we have now to say is, that if our Religion do make us Traitors we are worthy to be condemned; but otherwise are and have been as true subjects as ever the Queen had any."[13] With Sherwin and Briant, Campion was hanged, drawn, and quartered at Tyburn on December 1, 1581.[14] On the scaffold before he died, he repeated that he was innocent of all treason, and he prayed as a loyal Catholic subject that his queen, Queen Elizabeth, would have "a long quiet raigne, with all prosperity."

By hindsight at least, we recognize that Campion's death marked the climax of the first concerted Catholic efforts either to win back England to the old faith or to achieve for English Catholics some form of religious toleration in their native land. In the years following Campion's death, many more priests would be sent to the English mission. Many of these young men would be captured and executed as traitors, but none of them would be accorded the profound respect that English Catholics and Protestants alike reserved for Campion. Nor would any of them in the future send political shock waves to the highest levels of government. If a man of Campion's stature, entirely honest, sincerely religious, and intellectually gifted, could not persuade the authorities and his fellow countrymen that one could, at the same time, be a true Catholic and a loyal subject of the

[12] Howell, *State Trials*, cols. 1070–71.

[13] Ibid., cols. 1071–72.

[14] William Cardinal Allen, *A Brief History of the Glorious Martrydom of xii Reverend Priests* . . . (Rheims, 1582), reprinted and edited by J. H. Pollen, S.J. (London, 1908). See also Milward, *Religious Controversies of the Elizabethan Age*, pp. 64–65; and Dom Bede Camm, O.S.B., ed., *Lives of the English Martyrs Declared Blessed by Pope Leo XIII in 1886 and 1895* [1st series], 2 vols. (London: Burns & Oates, 1904–1905), in which see Vol. 2, pp. 266–357 for Campion; pp. 358–96 for Sherwin; pp. 397–423 for Briant; and pp. 500–22 for Kirby.

queen, then no one else was likely to succeed. After his day, Elizabeth treated her Catholic subjects more brutally, and Rome retaliated with political intrigues against her. Campion's execution became Elizabeth's answer to the bull of Pope Pius V, and his death lost for both queen and pope a measure of their honor and dignity.

Appendix E
Texts of the Debates

As one might expect, the various contemporaneous accounts of Campion's debates at the Tower of London in 1581 are reported with either a pro-Protestant or a pro-Catholic bias. According to the published Protestant account, for example, Campion lost. According to unpublished Catholic manuscript accounts, however, he won. A brief survey of these published and unpublished accounts may provide a helpful context for a fuller understanding of the debates.

The only complete published account of Campion's four disputations appeared in 1583 [O.S.] with the lengthy title: *A true report of the Disputation or rather private Conference had in the Tower of London, with Ed. Campion Iesuite, the last of August, 1581. Set downe by the Reverend learned men them selves that dealt therein. Whereunto is ioyned also a true report of the other three dayes conferences had there with the same Iesuite. Which nowe are thought meete to be published in print by authoritie* (London: Christopher Barker, 1583–84) [STC 18744]. This authorized account was apparently prepared at Burghley's urging and with Elizabeth's approval. Before 1583, Catholic accounts of some of the debates had been privately circulated. And the two Protestant participants, Nowell and Day, had distributed their account of the first day, which included excerpts from the Catholic versions.

From the available evidence it seems clear that the Catholic accounts had caused enough public turmoil that the government felt compelled to direct the publication of a complete official account. To that end, John Field, an ardent Puritan who had served as a notary at three of the debates, was charged with preparing an authorized edition.[1] This he did by attaching revised notary versions of the

[1] John Field (Feilde) attended Oxford during the time that Campion was there. With Thomas Wilcox he wrote the Presbyterian manifesto "An Admonition to the Parliament" (1572) for which he was sentenced to a year in prison for breach of the Uniformity Act. After his release from prison, he preached at St. Mary Aldermary

last three days to the Nowell-Day version of the first day, and by adding a separate title page and a brief introduction. (See above, p. xi, note 1.) As he tells us in his introduction, he ensured the correctness of his texts by having each of the Protestant debaters review the recorded account for accuracy. Field's editorial procedure, of course, not only provided the Protestant debaters with an opportunity to include many scholarly references but also, one may assume, gave them a chance to revise what they themselves had or might have said. Field admits that he himself took responsibility for reporting what Campion had said. He states his editorial practice: "If Campion's answers be thought shorter than they were, thou must know that he had much waste speech, which being impertinent, is now omitted: although I protest, nothing is cut off from the weight and substance of the matter: for of that I made conscience, and had special regard" (*A true report*, G4).

Although one may regret that Field did not allow his readers to decide for themselves whether or not Campion's "waste speech" was "impertinent," an official edition ordered by the government, intended to refute private Catholic accounts, prepared by Campion's opponents, and edited by a religious activist is not the sort of document to invite full trust. Field's conscience is one matter; his editorial judgment is quite another. In spite of its shortcomings, however, the 1583 authorized edition, *A true report*, has remained the only complete account of the disputations ever published, and it is now a rare book (STC 18744). Moreover, even though Campion's complete answers have admittedly been cut, the 1583 edition remains useful for the purpose of comparison with the Catholic versions. I have noted a number of the major differences between the two versions in my introduction and notes.

Unlike the published Protestant edition, *A true report*, the Catho-

---

for four years until Bishop Aylmer inhibited him. When barred from the pulpit, Field wrote a number of Puritan tracts, translated religious material (including a number of Calvin's sermons), and edited Campion's disputations for the government. After being reinstated briefly as a reward for his work, he was again suspended in 1584 and died in 1588.

For additional information on this religious controversialist, see Patrick Collinson, "John Field and Elizabethan Puritanism," *Elizabethan Government and Society* (London: Athlone Press, 1961), pp. 127–62; J. C. Hill, "Puritans and the Dark Corners of the Land," in *Transactions of the Royal Historical Society*, Series Five, vol. 13, pp. 77–102; and Rosenberg, *Leicester, Patron of Letters*, pp. 243–56.

lic versions of the debates survive only in manuscript form. Not long after Campion's death in 1581, both William Allen and Paolo Bombino had promised to publish a full Catholic account of the disputations, but neither did. As a result no complete Catholic version of them has been published; nor has a single, complete manuscript account of them survived. This present Catholic edition, therefore, had to be assembled and arranged from various extant, partially complete manuscripts.

The gathering and editing of these various accounts has proved to be no easy task, for the manuscripts exist in a number of versions in different hands, and they are located at different places. At the British Library, for example, among the Harley papers are two manuscript accounts of the second debate (Harl. 433. No. 7 and No. 310), one of the third (Harl. 422. No. 31), and one of the fourth (Harl. 422. No. 8). Also at the British Library among the Scudamore papers (Add. 11055) is an account of the afternoon session of the second debate and of both the morning and afternoon sessions of the fourth debate. In addition, at the Bodleian Library at Oxford the Rawlinson collection contains a partially damaged manuscript account of the second, third, and fourth debates (Rawl. D. 353). But the Harley, Scudamore, and Rawlinson MSS do not contain the first debate. For this we must turn to the Tresham papers, which contain the first debate but not the other three. Thus, this edition of the Catholic versions represents a combination of four different sets of partially complete accounts.

I have brought these different accounts together as follows: I have used the Tresham manuscript for the first debate because it is the only surviving account of that debate. For the second, third, and fourth debates I have collated the Harley and Rawlinson manuscripts because they are the most complete accounts. And as a supplement to the Harley and Rawlinson MSS, I have placed the brief, incomplete, and slightly different Scudamore version of the second and fourth debates in Appendix A.

In addition to the various manuscript accounts of the four debates, two once-prominent Catholic writers, Paolo Bombino and Daniello Bartoli, also provide summaries of the debates prepared from sources no longer available. Because Bombino and Bartoli include information not found elsewhere, and also because they reveal how the debates had been reported and received on the Continent,

I have placed translations of their Latin and Italian accounts of the first debate in Appendix C as a supplement to the brief Tresham account of that day.

These various Catholic manuscripts may be listed as follows:

1. First Debate: The Tresham MS is supplemented in Appendix C by translations of the Bombino (Latin) and the Bartoli (Italian) accounts.

2. Second Debate: The four manuscript sources are: Harl. 442, No. 7, and No. 31; Rawl. D. 353; and Scudamore Add. 11055 (afternoon session).

3. Third Debate: The two manuscript sources are: Harl. 422, No. 31, and Rawl. D. 353.

4. Fourth Debate: The three manuscript sources are: Harl. 422, No. 8, Rawl. D. 353, and Scudamore Add. 11055.

Because of the diversity and the number of manuscripts for the four debates, and because no published survey of them exists, it may be appropriate to furnish the reader with a brief historical and textual commentary on each.

First Debate: Tresham Account (August 31, 1598)

The author of the Tresham account of the first disputation is unknown. The account itself was first discovered among the papers of Sir Thomas Tresham (1543?–1605) in 1828 at Rushton Hall, Northamptonshire, when a partition was removed in the Great Hall and revealed a secret closet. In the closet, wrapped in a large sheet, were bundles of papers covering the period from 1575 to November 28, 1605. Because the end date of these secreted papers coincides with the Gunpowder Plot, in which Francis Tresham, Sir Thomas's son, was implicated, it may be assumed that the closet was walled in at that time. The papers contain Sir Thomas's correspondence, recusant history, building plans, and steward accounts.

It is not surprising that this manuscript of the first debate should have been among the Tresham papers, for Sir Thomas, a well-known sixteenth-century English recusant, had been arrested together with Lord Vaux and William Catesby for having harbored Campion. He was tried, imprisoned, and heavily fined.

Why Thomas Tresham possessed a manuscript copy of only the first debate but not the other three is unknown. One may speculate that he was anxious to see if Campion had revealed him as a host. Perhaps accounts in the same hand of the subsequent three debates may eventually emerge; or it may be that the author of the Tresham account did not attend the other debates. In any event, because the Tresham MS is so brief, I thought it fitting to enlarge its context by including secondary, published accounts of the first debate by Bombino and by Bartoli in Appendix C. Both these accounts, written by Roman Catholic priests, were intended originally for a Catholic audience on the Continent. Because translations of the writings of neither man have been published in English, and because both accounts are now rare books, I have supplied English translations. For Bombino's Latin account I have used a seventeenth-century manuscript translation that I found at the Bodleian Library (Tanner 329), and Professor M. Bonner Mitchell has provided me with a modern translation of Bartoli's Italian account. Both these accounts of the first debate are, of course, biased in Campion's favor, but in that regard they serve to balance John Field's biases in the authorized Protestant edition, *A true report*.

Of all the Catholic manuscripts, only the brief Tresham account has appeared in print. It was calendered by Mrs. Lomas and published by the Historical Manuscripts Commission in *Various Collections*, 3 (1904): 8–16.

Second, Third, and Fourth Debates (September 18, 23, and 27, 1581)

Accounts of the second, third, and fourth debates present a difficult set of editorial problems. Unlike the first debate, none has ever been published, and multiple versions of each are extant. The most complete accounts of them are contained in the Harleian and Rawlinson manuscript collections. The accounts of all three debates in both collections are virtually identical, undoubtedly copies composed from a single source. I have reviewed carefully all versions of each debate, but, because the textual variants are trivial rather than substantive, I have included in the notes only examples of typical differences. Additional background information on the collections may be helpful.

Harleian MS 422

Robert Harley (1661–1724), first Earl of Oxford, began collecting manuscripts in 1705, obtaining them from John Foxe, the martyrologist; John Stow, the chronicler; and Simon D'Ewes, the antiquarian; and many others. His son, Edward (1689–1741), second Earl of Oxford, enlarged the collection. After Edward's death, his wife, Henrietta, sold all the Harleian manuscripts to the nation for the sum of £10,000 so that the collection would not be dispersed. The entire Harleian collection, including manuscripts and books, now located at the British Library, consists of 7,639 volumes.

The Harleian manuscript accounts of the Campion debates, catalogued as Harley 422, contain two copies of the second debate (Harl. 422. No. 7, ff. 148–160, and Harl. 422, No. 31, ff. 161–167), one copy of the third debate (Harl. 422, No. 31, ff. 168–173^{v}), and one of the fourth debate (Harl. 422, No. 8, ff. 136–147). Humphrey Walney, Robert Harley's librarian, purchased these and additional manuscripts in 1709 for forty guineas from John Strype, the ecclesiastical historian. Strype had obtained the manuscripts from John Foxe, who had obtained them from Richard Topcliffe, the notorious rack-master, after Topcliffe had seized them at the house of William Carter, a recusant printer.[2]

Except for a few interpolations in No. 31, the two Harleian manuscripts of the second debate (Harl. 422, No. 31 and No. 7) are virtually identical. With regard to the interpolations, we find written across the top of No. 31, f. 161 the notation: "Confessed by Carter

[2] John Foxe (1516–1587), author of the popular *Acts and Monuments* (1563), commonly called *The Book of Martyrs*, wrote a Protestant martyrology. His work was placed with the Bible in all cathedral churches and was read by many.

Richard Topcliffe (1532–1604) was a persecutor and torturer of Catholics. He studied at Cambridge and Gray's Inn, and served in Parliament. Although involved in a number of legal suits over acquisition of land, he was regularly employed by Burghley and was vaguely identified as one of her Majesty's "servants," though his capacity was not formally or generally specified. For twenty-five years he hunted and tortured Catholics, especially priests. He was granted authority to torture his victims in his own home where, he boasted, his racking device made the common rack in the Tower seem mere child's play. His torture of Southwell was incredibly cruel. Complaints about his severity, even by Protestants, twice led to his being briefly imprisoned. In short, Topcliffe is one of the most repulsive men associated with Elizabeth's court.

For Carter, a printer and publisher, see *Concertatio ecclesiae*, pp. 127–33; and Southern, *Elizabethan Recusant Prose*, pp. 350–53, 389, 489, and 452–53.

to be in Vallenger's hand."[3] Also written in a different hand on the top left margin of f. 161 appears: "Taken in Carter's house, a printer, in the presence of Mr. Payne, Mr. Norris, the persevant, etc." Beneath this entry is the signature "Rich. Topcliffe," and below the signature is written, "I had this of Whyting. William Carter." These interpolations reveal how the manuscripts originally came into the hands of the authorities, and that Vallenger had apparently copied them so that Carter or another recusant printer might publish them. No. 31, written in the beautiful small hand of Vallenger, lists by number in the margin the arguments advanced at the second debate. Whether or not Vallenger, the copyist, was actually present at the debates, as Reynolds claims, is uncertain, but the finished state of this manuscript indicates that it had been copied from another document.[4]

The other Harleian manuscript of the second debate, Harl. 422, No. 7, ff. 148–160, is also in Vallenger's hand, although he is not identified as the copyist, but the writing is less crowded than that of No. 31. Other differences between No. 31 and No. 7 worth noting are that in No. 7 the arguments are not numbered, and the speaker's name, placed in the margin, is separated from the text. Also, No. 7 contains a larger number of corrections, cancellations, and insertions than No. 31 does. (See, for example, No. 7, f. 150^{v}.) Other differences between the two manuscripts are simply minor rewordings or inversions by the copyist which do not change the meaning of any passages. For my copy text I have followed No. 31 because it is a cleaner text, and I have noted typical differences between the two manuscripts. Because No. 7 contains no interpolations stating how it was acquired, as No. 31 does, one may assume that No. 31 had been placed at the top of a packet of manuscripts of the debates when they were seized at Carter's house.

---

[3] See Anthony Petti, "Stephen Vallenger (1541–1591)," *Recusant History*, 6 (1961–1962), 248–64. Vallenger was born in Norfolk and educated at Cambridge. When his home was raided by government authorities in 1582, a manuscript copy in his hand of *A true reporte of the death and martyrdome of M. Campion* . . . was found. See Milward, *Religious Controversies of the Elizabethan Age*, pp. 62–63. Although he admitted that the manuscript was in his handwriting, Vallenger denied authorship of it. He was tried in the Star Chamber, May 16, 1582, fined £100, lost both ears, and was imprisoned in the Fleet where he died November 29, 1591. See also Strype, *Annals*, III.ii.600, and Southern, *Elizabethan Recusant Prose*, pp. 279–82 and 378–79.

[4] Reynolds, *Campion and Persons*, p. 139.

The Harleian manuscript of the third debate (Harl. 422, No. 31, ff. 168–173^{v}) is, like the No. 31 version of the second debate, in the crowded hand of Vallenger. The speakers' names are not set off in the margin, as they are in the No. 7 version of the second debate, and there are few insertions and corrections in the text itself.

The Harleian manuscript of the fourth debate (Harl. 422, No. 8, ff. 136–147), like the Harleian No. 31 account of the second debate, contains a notation in the upper left margin (f. 136): "Taken in Carter's house, a printer, in the presence of Mr. Payne, Mr. Norris, etc. Rich. Topcliffe." Below Topcliffe's signature appears: "I had this of Whiting of Lancashire William Carter." The notation suggests that this manuscript had been placed at the top of a second packet, and indicates that Carter had eventually obtained it from Whiting. This partially damaged manuscript is not in Vallenger's hand. There are some corrections and cancellations, and the names of the speakers are separated from the text and placed in the margin.

These various Harleian manuscripts, one may speculate, reveal the process of preparing a manuscript for publication. The account of the fourth debate (Harl. 422, No. 8, ff. 136–147), for example, appears to be a first draft, probably composed from rough notes taken by some Catholic at the debate. This draft would probably then be recopied by an expert, like Vallenger, as in Harl. 422, No. 31, ff. 161–167, before a final draft was prepared for publication, as in Harl. 422, No. 7, ff. 148–160. Unless otherwise stated, I have used Harl. 422 as my copy text.

Rawlinson MS D. 353

An additional manuscript account of the second, third, and fourth debates appears in a folio volume containing miscellaneous theological and historical papers in the Rawlinson collection at the Bodleian Library at Oxford. The catalogue listing states that this manuscript is generally shorter than the authorized printed report (that is, *A true report*, 1583), and varies considerably from it.

Thomas Rawlinson (1681–1725), like Robert Harley a bibliophile, collected books, manuscripts, and antiquities throughout his life and had assembled a large collection[5] before it was sold in sixteen parts

[5] Rawlinson studied at Eton, Oxford (St. John's College), and the Middle Tem-

from 1722 to 1734. At the final sale Rawlinson's manuscripts (1,020) were sold. The fourth debate is catalogued as Rawl. MS D. 353, ff. 1–13; the second debate follows it at ff. 14–16^{v}; and the third, at ff. 26^{v}–35.

As mentioned above, Rawlinson's manuscripts, written in a large neat secretary hand, are so similar to the Harleian 422 versions that both must have been transcribed from the same source. Unfortunately, however, parts of the Rawlinson manuscripts are so stained and torn, especially along the margins, that many passages are illegible. Nevertheless, the Rawlinson manuscripts are occasionally useful in clarifying certain unclear or smeared passages in Harleian 422. It should also be noted that the Rawlinson manuscripts contain no interpolations, that the names of the speakers are separated from the text and placed in the margin, as in Harl. 422, No. 7, that there are very few insertions or cancellations, and that only in the account of the second debate are the arguments numbered. The author and copyist are unknown.

Scudamore MS Add. 11055

Additional MS 11055 (ff. 188–192^{v}), part of the Scudamore papers (nineteen volumes) acquired by the British Library in 1837, is bound with sixteenth- and seventeenth-century letters of bishops and with miscellaneous ecclesiastical and theological papers and tracts (Volume XV Folio). Except for two brief interpolations, apparently made by a Protestant reader, the manuscript of the debates is in the same secretary hand, but it is stained by a few blots and imperfections. The first interpolation (f. 188) states in a headnote that the manuscript is: "A true copy of some disputations in the Tower as it was gathered and given out by some papists, but most falsely and untruly." The second interpolation rejects one of Campion's arguments. Only accounts of the afternoon session of the second day and of the morning and afternoon sessions of the fourth day are included in it. Whether or not the anonymous writer also wrote accounts of the other debates is unknown. Because Add. 11055 differs from

ple. For an account of the Rawlinson manuscripts at the Bodleian, see R. W. Hunt, "The Cataloguing of the Rawlinson MSS., 1771–1844," *Bodleian Library Record* (1947), 190–95.

other Catholic and Protestant accounts in its brevity and objectivity, it serves as an interesting complement to them. The author, for example, shows a distinct preference to record the issues debated rather than to prove that Campion or his opponents had won. He concludes his summary with the observation: "Much more was spoken which I could not remember." The statement suggests that the accounts may have been composed soon after the debates from a set of hastily written notes, probably taken at the debates.

Textual Conclusions

Precisely how the Catholic writers actually gathered and composed these accounts of the debates is uncertain. A few assumptions, however, may be made. First, because the Catholic versions are considerably shorter and usually less detailed than the authorized published account (*A true report*), it seems evident that a few Catholics, who were actually present at the debates, took hurried notes and later expanded them for copyists like Vallenger. Apparently, the primary intent of the notetakers seems to have been to include only the major points of the principal arguments and to portray Campion favorably. Thus, the Catholic accounts differ markedly from the more detailed authorized version that was prepared from the verbatim notes of official notaries present at each debate and revised by the Protestant debaters themselves before John Field edited them for publication. Second, because of the differences in reporting the debates by Catholic writers (for example, authors of the Tresham and the Scudamore accounts are quite different in approach, format, and detail from the Harley and Rawlinson versions), one may reasonably assume that more than one Catholic observer must have taken notes at the various debates. The Tresham and Scudamore versions appear to be copies from two different sources; the Harley and Rawlinson versions are copies from a single source. Because Harleian MS 422 is the most complete and least damaged account of the second, third, and fourth debates, I have chosen it as my copy text. I have confirmed the accuracy of my transcription of the Harleian MS 422 by consulting J. H. Pollen's unpublished transcription of it, which was made available to me by Rev. Francis Edwards, S.J.

BIBLIOGRAPHY

Acts of the Privy Council.

Allen, William. *A Brief History of the Glorious Martrydom of xii Reverend Priests. . . .* Ed. J. H. Pollen, S.J. London, 1908.

Allen, William. *The Execution of Justice in England, by William Cecil, and A True, Sincere, and Modest Defence of English Catholics.* Ed. Robert M. Kingdon. Ithaca, N.Y.: Cornell University Press/Folger Shakespeare Library, 1965.

Allison, A. F., and D. M. Rogers, eds. *A Catalogue of Catholic Books in English Printed Abroad or Secretly in England, 1558–1640.* Bognor Regis: The Arundel Press, 1956.

———. *The Contemporary Printed Literature of the English Counter-Reformation Between 1558 and 1640: An Annotated Catalogue.* 2 vols. Aldershot, Hant., and Brookfield, Vt.: Scolar Press, 1989, 1994.

Anstruther, Godfrey, O.P. *The Seminary Priests: A Dictionary of the Secular Clergy of England and Wales, 1558–1850.* 4 vols. Great Wakening: Mayhew-McCrimmon, 1975–77.

———. *Vaux of Harrowden.* Newport, Mon.: R. H. Johns, 1953.

An answere to a seditious pamphlet lately cast abroade by a Iesuite, with a discoverie of that blasphemous sect. By William Charke. 1580. (STC 5005).

Aristotle. *Categories.* In *The Complete Works of Aristotle* I. Trans. J. L. Ackrill. Princeton, N.J.: Princeton University Press, 1985. Pp. 3–24.

Aveling, J. C. H. *Catholic Recusancy in the City of York, 1558–1791.* St. Albans, Hertfordshire: Catholic Record Society, 1970.

———. *The Handle and the Axe: The Catholic Recusants in England from Reformation to Emancipation.* London: Blond and Briggs, 1976.

Bagwell, Richard. *Ireland Under the Tudors.* 2 vols. London: 1885–90.

Balbino, Bohuslao. *Miscellanea, Historica regni Bohemiae decadisti.* Prague, 1682. Book IV.

Bangert, William V., S.J. *A History of the Society of Jesus.* St. Louis: Institute of Jesuit Sources, 1972.

Barnad, Miguel A., S.J. "The 'Treatise on Imitation' of Blessed Edmund Campion." *Folia* 6 (1952): 100–14; 7 (1953): 20–29.

Basset, Bernard, S.J. *The English Jesuits, From Campion to Martindale*. London: Burns & Oates, 1967.

Beales, A. C. F. *Education Under Penalty: English Catholic Education from the Reformation to the Fall of James II, 1547–1689*. London: Athlone Press, 1963.

Bindoff, Stanley T. *Tudor England*. (1950). Baltimore: Penguin, 1964.

Birt, Henry N. *The Elizabethan Religious Settlement*. London: G. Bell, 1907.

Black, John B. *The Reign of Elizabeth, 1558–1603*. (1936). Oxford: Oxford University Press, 1959.

Bombino, Paolo. *Vita et martyrium Edmundi Campiani*. Antwerp, 1618.

Bossy, John. *The English Catholic Community, 1570–1850*. New York: Oxford University Press, 1976.

Brooks, Eric St. John. *Sir Christopher Hatton: Queen Elizabeth's Favorite*. London: Jonathan Cape, 1947.

Byrne, M. St. Clare. *Elizabethan Life in Town and Country*. New York: Barnes & Noble, 1961.

Calendar of State Papers, Domestic, Elizabeth, 1581–1590.

Camden, William. *The Historie of the Most Renowned and Victorious Princesse Elizabeth*. London: Benjamin Fisher, 1630.

Camm, Dom Bede, O.S.B. *Lives of the English Martyrs Declared Blessed by Pope Leo XIII in 1886 and 1895*. First Series. 2 vols. London: Burns & Oates, 1904–1905.

Campion, Leslie. *The Family of Edmund Campion*. London: The Research Publishing Co., 1975.

Caraman, P., and J. Walsh. *The Catholic Martyrs of England and Wales, 1535–1680: A Chronological List*. London: Catholic Truth Society, 1979.

Caraman, Philip. *The Other Face: Catholic Life under Elizabeth I*. London: Longmans, 1960.

Clancy, Thomas H., S.J. *Papist Pamphleteers: The Allen-Persons Party and the Political Thought of the Counter-Reformation in England, 1572–1615*. Chicago: Loyola University Press, 1964.

Clapham, John H. *A Concise Economic History of Britain from the Earliest Times to 1750*. Cambridge: Cambridge University Press, 1949.

Collinson, Patrick. *The Elizabethan Puritan Movement*. London: Jonathan Cape, 1967.

———. "John Field and Elizabethan Puritanism." *Elizabethan Government and Society*. London: Athlone Press, 1961. Pp. 127–62.

Concertatio ecclesiae Catholicae in Anglia adversus Calvinopapistas et Puritanos. (1588). Westmead, England: Gregg International Publishers, 1970.

Curtis, Mark H. *Oxford and Cambridge in Transition, 1558–1642*. Oxford, Clarendon Press, 1959.

Dibelius, Martin. *A Commentary on the Epistle of James*. Rev. Henrich Greeven. Trans. Michael A. Williams. Philadelphia: Fortress Press, 1976.

Dickens, A. G. *The Counter Reformation*. Norwich: Jarrold and Sons, 1969.

———. *The English Reformation*. London: B. T. Batsford, 1965.

Dugmore, C. W. *The Mass and the English Reformers*. London: Macmillan; New York: St. Martin's Press, 1958.

Elton, Geoffrey R. *England Under the Tudors*. (1955). London: Cox & Wyman, 1974.

England and Wales, Court of Common Pleas. *Les reports du treserudite Edmund Anderson des mults principals cases argues adjuges en le temps del jardis roign Elizabeth cibien en la Common-Bank come devant touts les juges de cest roialme*. London, 1664.

Erickson, Carolly. *Bloody Mary*. Garden City, N.Y.: Doubleday, 1978.

———. *The First Elizabeth*. New York: Summit, 1983.

Eusebius of Caesarea. *The History of the Church from Christ to Constantine*. Trans. G. A. Williamson. New York: New York University Press, 1966.

Every, George. *The Mass*. London: Gill and Macmillan, 1978.

Falls, Cyril. *Elizabeth's Irish Wars*. London: Methuen, 1950.

Fathers of the Congregation of the London Oratory. *The First and Second Diaries of the English College, Douay, and an Appendix of Unpublished Documents*. London, 1878.

———. *The Letters and Memorials of William Cardinal Allen*. London, 1882.

Field, John. *A true report of the Disputation or rather private Conference had in the Tower of London, with Ed. Campion Iesuite, the last of August, 1581. Set downe by the Reverend learned men them selves that dealt therein. Whereunto is ioyned also a true report of the other three dayes conferences had there with the same Iesuite. Which nowe are thought meete to be published in print by authoritie*. 1583 [O.S.]. [STC 18744]. *The three last dayes conferences had in the Tower with Edmund Campion Iesuite, the 18: 23: and 27. of September, 1581, collected and faithfully set downe by M. Iohn Feilde student in Divinitie. Nowe perused by the learned men them-selves, and thought meete to be published*. 1583 [O.S.]. [STC 18744].

Foley, H., S.J. *Records of the English Province of the Society of Jesus*, 7 vols. London: Burns & Oates, 1877–83.

Fraser, Antonia. *Mary Queen of Scots*. (1969). New York: Dell, 1972.

Frere, W. H. *The English Church in the Reigns of Elizabeth and James I, 1558–1625*. London: Macmillan, 1904.

Gerard, John. *The Autobiography of an Elizabethan*. Trans. Philip Caraman. London: Longmans, Green, 1951.

Gillow, Joseph. *Bibliographical Dictionary of the English Catholics*, 5 vols. London, 1885.

Gottfried, Rudolf B., ed. *A History of Ireland (1571) by Edmund Campion*. New York: Scholars' Facsimiles and Reprints, 1940.

Green, V. H. H. *Religion at Oxford and Cambridge*. London: SCM Press, 1964.

Grene, C., S.J. *Collectanea P*, vol I. In *Letters and Notices* 11 (1877): 219–42, 308–39; and 12 (1879): 1–68.

Haigh, Christopher. "The Continuity of Catholicism in the English Reformation." *Past and Present* 93 (1981): 37–69.

———. *Reformation and Resistance in Tudor Lancashire*. Cambridge: Cambridge University Press, 1976.

Haile, Martin. *An Elizabethan Cardinal: William Allen*. London and New York: Pitman, 1914.

Hallam, Henry. *The Constitutional History of England from the Accession of Henry VII to the Death of George II*. 2 vols. London, 1827.

Hammer, Carl I. "Robert Campion: Edmund Campion's Brother?" *Recusant History* 6 (1980): 153.

Henderson, T. F. *Mary Queen of Scots*. London: Scribner's, 1905.

Hill, J. C. "Puritans and the Dark Corners of the Land." In *Transactions of the Royal Historical Society*, Series Five, vol. 13, pp. 77–102.

Hodgetts, Michael. "Elizabethan Priest-Holes," *Recusant History* 1 (1972): 279–98; 2 (1973): 99–119; 3 (1974): 171–97; 4 (1975): 18–55; and 5 (1976): 254–79.

Howell, Roger. *Sir Philip Sidney: The Shepherd Knight*. London: Hutchinson, 1968.

Howell, T. B., comp. *A Complete Collection of State Trials and Proceedings for High Treason and Other Crimes and Misdemeanors from the Earliest*

Period to the Year 1783, with Notes and Other Illustrations. 21 vols. London, 1816–1828.

Hughes, Paul L., and James F. Larkin., C.S.V., eds. *Tudor Royal Proclamations*. 3 vols. New Haven, Conn.: Yale University Press, 1969.

Hughes, Philip. *The Reformation in England*. 5th ed. 3 vols. in 1. (1950). New York: Macmillan, 1963.

Humphrey, Laurence. *Iesuitismi pars prima: sive de Praxi Romanae Curiae contra respublicas et principes, et de nova legatione Iesuitarum in Angliam . . .* , 1582.

———. *Iesuitismi Pars Secunda: Puritanopapismi, seu doctrinae Iesuiticae aliquot Rationibus ab Ed. Campiano comprehensae . . .* , 1584.

Hunt, R. W. "The Cataloguing of the Rawlinson MSS., 1771–1844." *Bodleian Library Record* (1947): 190–95.

Hurstfield, Joel. *Elizabeth I and the Unity of England*. (1960). New York: Harper & Row, 1969.

Hutton, William Holden. *St. John Baptist College*. London: F. E. Robinson, 1898.

Knappen, M. M. *Tudor Puritanism*. (1939). Chicago: The University of Chicago Press, 1970.

Lake, Peter. "The Significance of the Elizabethan Identification of the Pope as Antichrist." *Journal of Ecclesiastical History* 31 (1980): 161–78.

LaRocca, John J., S.J. "Popery and Pounds: The Effect of the Jesuit Mission on Penal Legislation." *The Reconed Expense: Edmund Campion and the Early English Jesuits*. Ed. Thomas M. McCoog, S.J. Woodbridge, Suffolk: Boydell Press, 1996. Pp. 249–63.

Lennon, Colm. *Richard Stanihurst, the Dubliner, 1547–1618: A Biography, with a Stanihurst Text, On Ireland's Past*. Blackrock, County Dublin: Irish Academic Press, 1981.

Leys, M. D. R. *Catholics in England, 1559–1829: A Social History*. London: Longmans, 1961.

"Life and Martyrdom of Thomas Alfield," *Rambler*, N.S., 7 (1857): 420–31.

"Lord Burghley's Map of Lancashire, 1590," *C.R.S., Miscellanea*, 4:162–222.

MacLure, Millard. *The Paul's Cross Sermons, 1534–1642*. Toronto: University of Toronto Press, 1958.

Manning, R. B. *Religion and Society in Elizabethan Sussex*. Leicester: Leicester University Press, 1969.

Mathew, David. *Catholicism in England: The Portrait of a Minority—Its Culture and Tradition*. (1936). London: Eyre & Spottiswoode, 1955.

Mattingly, Garrett. *The Armada*. Boston: Houghton Mifflin, 1959.

McConica, James. "The Catholic Experience in Tudor Oxford." In *The Reconed Expense: Edmund Campion and the Early English Jesuits*. Ed. Thomas M. McCoog, S.J. Woodbridge, Suffolk: Boydell Press, 1996. Pp. 39–63.

McCoog, Thomas M., S.J. " 'Playing the Champion': The Role of Disputation in the Jesuit Mission." In *The Reconed Expense: Edmund Campion and the Early English Jesuits*. Ed. Thomas M. McCoog, S.J. Woodbridge, Suffolk: Boydell Press, 1996. Pp. 119–39.

———. *The Reconed Expense: Edmund Campion and the Early English Jesuits*. Woodbridge, Suffolk: Boydell Press, 1996.

McGrath, Patrick. *Papists and Puritans Under Elizabeth I*. London: Blandford Press; New York: Walker, 1967.

Meyer, Arnold Oskar. *England and the Catholic Church Under Queen Elizabeth*. Trans. J. R. McKee. (1916). London: Routledge & Kegan Paul; New York: Barnes & Noble, 1967.

Milward, Peter. *Religious Controversies of the Elizabethan Age: A Survey of Printed Sources*. Lincoln: University of Nebraska Press, 1977.

Moody, T. W., F. X. Martin, and F. J. Byrne, eds. *A New History of Ireland.* III: *Early Modern Ireland, 1534–1691*. Oxford: Clarendon Press, 1976.

Morey, Adrian. *The Catholic Subjects of Elizabeth I*. London: George Allen & Urwin; Totowa, N.J.: Rowman and Littlefield, 1978.

Morris, John, S.J. "Blessed Edmund Campion at Douay." London, 1887.

———. *The Troubles of Our Catholic Forefathers Related by Themselves*, 3 vols. London: Burns & Oates, 1872–1877.

Neale, J. E. *The Age of Catherine de Medici*. (1913). New York and Evanston, Ill.: Harper & Row, 1962.

———. *Elizabeth I and Her Parliaments, 1559–1601*. 2 vols. (1953). London: Jonathan Cape, 1957.

———. *Queen Elizabeth*. London: Jonathan Cape, 1934.

Nichols, John Gough, ed. *The Chronicle of Queen Jane and of Two Years of Queen Mary*. N.p.: Camden Society, 1850.

O'Donovan, John, ed. *Annals of the Kingdom of Ireland by the Four Masters* V. (1854). New York: AMS Press, Inc., 1966.

Osborn, James M. *Young Philip Sidney, 1572–1577*. New Haven, Conn.: Yale University Press, 1972.

Pamphlet lately cast abroade by a Iesuite, with a discoverie of that blasphemous sect, By William Charke. 1580 [STC 5005]; and *The great bragge and challenge of M. Champion a Iesuite, commonlye called Edmunde Campion, latelye arrived in Englande, contayninge nyne articles here severallye laide downe, directed by him to the Lordes of the Counsail, confuted & answered by Meredith Hanmer, M of Art, and Student in Divinitie*. 1581. [STC 12745].

Parmiter, Geoffrey de C. *Elizabethan Popish Recusancy in the Inns of Court*, Bulletin of the Institute of Historical Research, Special Supplement No. 11, November 1976.

Parr, Robert. "Yoxford Yesterday." Typescript.

Pastor, Ludwig. *The History of the Popes*. Ed. Ralph Francis Kerr. 35 vols. London: Kegan Paul, 1930.

Pendry, E. D. *Elizabethan Prisons and Prison Scenes*. 2 vols. Salzburg: Institut für Englische Sprache und Literatur, Universität Salzburg, 1974.

Persons, Robert. *Of the Life and Martrydom of Edmund Campion*. Archives of Stonyhurst College, England.

Petti, Anthony. "Stephen Vallenger (1541–1591)." *Recusant History* 6 (1961–62): 248–64.

Plowden, Alison. *Danger to Elizabeth: The Catholics Under Elizabeth I*. New York: Stein and Day, 1973.

Plummer, Charles. *Elizabethan Oxford*. Oxford, 1887.

Pollard, Albert F. *The History of England from the Accession of Edward VI to the Death of Elizabeth, 1547–1603*. London: Longmans, 1910.

Pollen, J. H., S.J. "Blessed Edmund Campion's 'Challenge.'" *The Month* 115 (1910): 50–65.

———. *The Journey of Bd. Edmund Campion from Rome to England, March–June, 1580, with an Unpublished Letter of St. Charles Borromeo and of Bd. Ralph Sherwin*. Roehampton, S.W.: Manresa Press, n.d.

Prescott, H. F. M. *Spanish Tudor*. (1940). Rev. ed. *Mary Tudor*. New York: Macmillan, 1953.

Pritchard, Arnold. *Catholic Loyalism in Elizabethan England*. Chapel Hill: University of North Carolina Press, 1979.

Read, Conyers. *Lord Burghley and Queen Elizabeth*. London: Jonathan Cape, 1960.

———. *Mr. Secretary Cecil and Queen Elizabeth*. London: Jonathan Cape, 1955.

———. *Mr. Secretary Walsingham and the Policy of Queen Elizabeth*. 3 vols. Oxford: Clarendon Press, 1925.

Reynolds, E. E. *Campion and Persons: The Jesuit Mission*. London: Sheed and Ward, 1980.

———. *The Roman Catholic Church in England and Wales*. Wheathampstead, Hertfordshire: Anthony Clarke, 1973.

Rickaby, Joseph, trans. *Campion's Ten Reasons*. London: Manresa Press, 1914.

Rose, Elliot. *Cases of Conscience*. Cambridge: Cambridge University Press, 1975.

Rosenberg, Eleanor. *Leicester, Patron of Letters*. New York: Columbia University Press, 1955.

Ross, W. David. *Aristotle*. (1923). London: Methuen; New York: Barnes & Noble, 1964.

Rowse, A. L. *The England of Elizabeth: The Structure of Society*. New York: Macmillan, 1957.

———. *Tudor Cornwall*. London: Jonathan Cape, 1941.

Rudolf B. Gottfried, ed. *A History of Ireland (1571) by Edmund Campion*. New York: Scholars' Facsimiles and Reprints, 1940.

Sacred Congregation of Rites. *ARCHDIOCESE OF WESTMINSTER. Cause of the Canonization of Blessed Martyrs John Houghton, Robert Lawrence, Augustine Webster, Richard Reynolds, John Stone, Cuthbert Mayne, John Paine, Edmund Campion, Alexander Briant, Ralph Sherwin and Luke Kirby, Put to Death in England in Defence of the Catholic Faith (1533–1582)*. Vatican City: Vatican Polyglot Press, 1968. Pp. 107–76.

Schmidl, Joannes. *Historiae Societatis Jesu Provinciae Bohemiae*. Prague 1747–59.

Silvester, P. *Edmundi Campiani, Angli e Soc. Iesu, Decem Rationes propositae in causae fidei, et opuscula eius selecta*. Antwerp: Balthasar Moretus, 1631.

Simons, Joseph, ed. and trans. *Ambrosia: A Neo-Latin Drama by Edmund Campion, S.J.* Assen, The Netherlands: Van Gorcum, 1970.

Simpson, Richard. *Life of Edmund Campion*. (1866). London: John Hodges, 1896.

Smith, Lacey Baldwin. "English Treason Trials in the 16th Century," *Journal of the History of Ideas* 15 (1954): 471–98.

Southern, A. C. *Elizabethan Recusant Prose, 1559–1582*. London: Sands & Co., 1950.

Stevenson, W. H., and H. E. Salter. *The Early History of St. John's College, Oxford*. Oxford: Oxford Historical Society, 1939.

Stonor, Robert Julian. *Stonor: A Catholic Sanctuary in the Chilterns from the Fifth Century Till To-day*. 2nd ed. Newport, Mon.: R. H. Johns, 1952.

Strype, John. *Annals of the Reformation under Elizabeth*. 4 vols. in 7. Oxford, 1824.

———. *Historical Collections of the Life and Acts of John Aylmer*. Oxford, 1821.

———. *The Life and Acts of John Whitgift*. 3 vols. Oxford, 1822.

———. *The Life and Acts of Matthew Parker*. 3 vols. Oxford, 1821.

Tawney, R. H. *Religion and the Rise of Capitalism*. (1926). New York: Harcourt, 1952.

Taylor, J. *A Calendar of Papers of the Tresham Family*. London, 1811.

Trimble, William Raleigh. *The English Laity in Elizabethan England*. Cambridge, Mass.: Harvard University Press, 1964.

Veech, Thomas McNevin. *Dr. Nicolas Sanders and the English Reformation, 1530–1581*. Louvain: Bureaux du Recueil, Bibliothèque de l'Université, 1935.

Vossen, A. F. *Two Bokes of the Histories of Ireland*. Assen, The Netherlands: Van Gorcum, 1963.

Waugh, Evelyn. *Edmund Campion, Jesuit and Martyr*. (1935). London: Longmans, 1961.

Webb, Sidney, and Beatrice Webb. *English Prisons Under Local Government*. London: Longmans, Green, 1922.

Whitaker, William. *Ad Rationes Decem Edmundi Campiani Iesuitae, quibus fretus certamen Anglicanae ecclesiae ministris obtulit in causa fidei Responsio Guilielmi Whitakeri Theologiae in Academia Cantabrigiensi professoris regii*. 1581.

Wicks, Jared, S.J. *Cajetan Responds: A Reader in Reformation Controversy*. Washington, D.C.: Catholic University of America Press, 1978.

Williams, Michael. *The Venerable English College, Rome: A History*. London: Associated Catholic Publications, 1979.

Williamson, James A. *The Age of Drake*. Cleveland: World, 1965.

Wilson, Derek. *Sweet Robin: A Biography of Robert Dudley, Earl of Leicester, 1533–1588*. London: Hamish Hamilton, 1981.

Works, K. R. *Elizabethan Recusancy in Cheshire and Manchester*. N.p.: Chetham Society, 1971.

Wormald, Jenny. *Court, Kirk, and Community: Scotland, 1470–1625*. London: Edward Arnold, 1981.

Wright, Thomas, ed. *Queen Elizabeth and Her Times*. 2 vols. London: Henry Colburn, 1838.

Youngs, Frederick A. *The Proclamations of Tudor Queens*. Cambridge: Cambridge University Press, 1976.

Ziegler, Donald J., ed. *Great Debates of the Reformation*. New York: Random House, 1969.

INDEX